FROM
WARDSHIP TO
RIGHTS

Landmark Cases in Canadian Law

Since Confederation, Canada's highest court – first the Judicial Committee of the Privy Council in England and then the Supreme Court of Canada – has issued a series of often contentious decisions that have fundamentally shaped the nation. Both cheered and jeered, these judgments have impacted every aspect of Canadian society, setting legal precedents and provoking social change. The issues in the judgments range from Aboriginal title, gender equality, and freedom of expression to Quebec secession and intellectual property. This series offers comprehensive, book-length examinations of high court cases that have had a major impact on Canadian law, politics, and society.

Other books in the series are:

Flawed Precedent: The St. Catherine's *Case and Aboriginal Title* by Kent McNeil

Privacy in Peril: Hunter v Southam *and the Drift from Reasonable Search Protections* by Richard Jochelson and David Ireland

The Tenth Justice: Judicial Appointments, Marc Nadon, and the Supreme Court Act *Reference* by Carissima Mathen and Michael Plaxton

For a list of other titles,
see www.ubcpress.ca/landmark-cases-in-canadian-law.

**LANDMARK CASES
IN CANADIAN LAW**

FROM WARDSHIP TO RIGHTS

The *Guerin* Case and Aboriginal Law

Jim Reynolds

UBCPress · Vancouver · Toronto

29 28 27 26 25 24 23 22 21 20   5 4 3 2 1

Printed in Canada on FSC-certified ancient-forest-free paper (100% post-consumer recycled) that is processed chlorine- and acid-free.

Library and Archives Canada Cataloguing in Publication

Title: From wardship to rights: the Guerin case and Aboriginal law /
   Jim Reynolds.
Other titles: Guerin case and Aboriginal law
Names: Reynolds, James I., author.
Series: Landmark cases in Canadian law.
Description: Series statement: Landmark cases in Canadian law, 2562-5241 |
   Includes bibliographical references and index.
Identifiers: Canadiana (print) 20200184377 | Canadiana (ebook) 20200184415 |
   ISBN 9780774864565 (hardcover) | ISBN 9780774864572 (softcover) |
   ISBN 9780774864589 (PDF) | ISBN 9780774864596 (EPUB) |
   ISBN 9780774864602 (Kindle)
Subjects: LCSH: Coast Salish Indians – Legal status, laws, etc. – British
   Columbia – Vancouver. | LCSH: Coast Salish Indians – Land tenure –
   British Columbia – Vancouver. | LCSH: Coast Salish Indians – Canada –
   Government relations. | LCSH: Canada. Supreme Court. | LCSH:
   Musqueam First Nation.
Classification: LCC KE7709 .R496 2020 | LCC KF8205 .R496 2020 kfmod |
   DDC 342.7108/72 – dc23

Canadä

UBC Press gratefully acknowledges the financial support for our publishing program of the Government of Canada (through the Canada Book Fund), the Canada Council for the Arts, and the British Columbia Arts Council.

This book has been published with the help of a grant from the Canadian Federation for the Humanities and Social Sciences, through the Awards to Scholarly Publications Program, using funds provided by the Social Sciences and Humanities Research Council of Canada.

UBC Press
The University of British Columbia
2029 West Mall
Vancouver, BC V6T 1Z2
www.ubcpress.ca

For Delbert Guerin and his family

The house post of *Qiyəplenəxʷ*, carved by Musqueam artist Brent Sparrow Jr., is located adjacent to the Peter A. Allard School of Law at the University of British Columbia. A detail of this house post appears on the cover of this book. *With the permission of the artist*

Contents

Illustrations

Preface

THIS BOOK IS PART of the UBC Press Landmark Cases in Canadian Law series. The series is an avenue for publishing comprehensive book-length examinations of high court cases that have had a major and permanent impact on Canadian law, politics, and society and that have grappled with issues of public discussion and debate in Canada. The books investigate and explain the events that gave rise to the case, the working of the case through the courts, and the final decision and its after-effects. They are also written in a manner that appeals to both scholars and the interested public. My purpose in writing this book on the *Guerin* case is to satisfy these requirements. It is for the reader to say if I have succeeded. There is no doubt in my mind, however, that the case fully deserves to be included in the series as one that has had a major and permanent impact on Canadian law, politics, and society.

This book is dedicated to Delbert Guerin and his family. As discussed in Chapter 4, the *Guerin* case and the changes it introduced into the law could not have happened without Delbert's determination to obtain justice for his people. Others certainly participated in the litigation – both from the Musqueam community and non-Musqueam individuals such as lawyers and expert witnesses. Without Delbert, however, there would have been no case or, perhaps, the fundamental changes in the law to which it led. For years, he persisted in trying to find out the true terms of the lease with the Shaughnessy Golf and Country Club – the key document in the case – seeking legal advice and a law firm that was willing to take the case to trial. Unfortunately, and as he predicted, Delbert did not live to see the year 2033, when the Shaughnessy lease ends, so that he could tell the Shaughnessy directors, "Get the heck off my land,"[1] but he achieved a great deal for his people and all Indigenous peoples. Throughout the litigation process, he was a constant source of ideas and encouragement and an important witness at the trial. His wife, Fran, was also a key member of the litigation support team.

Delbert was a great teacher, freely sharing his knowledge and experience, especially of the struggles of Indigenous people to improve their conditions and protect their rights – passing on the knowledge and experience that he had himself gained from Andrew Paull of the Squamish Nation as a youth. He was also a good man. John Ralston Saul described Delbert as "one of the great figures of contemporary Canada. By formally reintroducing ethics into the core of public administration, he changed the way we must think of ourselves. We owe him a great deal."[2] I agree.

I was honoured to have known Delbert and to regard him as a friend and teacher. I was especially honoured to be asked to be a witness at

Delbert Guerin, 5 January 2013.
Courtesy of Don Bain, Union of BC Indian Chiefs, IMG 4327

the traditional Musqueam memorial ceremonies for him held recently at the longhouse on the reserve. It is a large wood building. Around the central earthen floor are benches for the different First Nations present. Two large fires are located in the central area and the smoke rises to escape from openings in the roof. It is dark and smoky even at midday, and the wise will wear suitable clothing and bring cushions to sit on on the hard benches during the lengthy ceremonies. Painted and masked dancers in traditional dress circulate around the floor to the accompaniment of drumming and singing. It was in such buildings that, over centuries, gatherings were held to mark important occasions such as namings or anniversaries of deaths, as well as to apply Indigenous laws to resolve disputes – a setting so different from the European grandeur of the Supreme Court of Canada building in which the dispute over the Shaughnessy lease was resolved. Witnessing the ceremonies, it was impossible not to reflect on the depth of culture and an ancient way of life that continues to exist only a short distance from supermarkets and the University of British Columbia campus.

I have also been honoured to have known Fran and other members of Delbert's family. I dedicate this book to them with deep gratitude.

Acknowledgments

THIS BOOK TELLS A VERY small part of the long history of the Musqueam people. I was the general counsel for the Musqueam Band for a number of years until my retirement. This book is purely a personal account, however, and does not necessarily reflect the views of the band or its members. The following members of the band reviewed an earlier version of Chapter 2 dealing with that history: Andrew Charles; Delbert, Fran, and Victor Guerin; and Leona Sparrow. It was also reviewed by anthropologist Dr. Michael Kew, long associated with the band both as a scholar and through marriage. I would like to thank them for their comments. To all the Musqueam people, I express my best wishes and thanks, "hay chxw q'a."

I am very grateful for the comments received from anonymous reviewers as part of the peer review process. Their willingness to give their time, knowledge, and expertise without receiving any credit is very commendable and in the best traditions of scholarship.

Thanks are also owed to the following, who guided me during the process of preparing this book and turned my messy drafts into a book that makes me look better than I deserve: Randy Schmidt, Senior Editor; Holly Keller, Manager of Production and Editorial Services; Frank Chow, copy editor, and Judith Earnshaw, proofreader; Judy Dunlop, indexer; Eric Leinberger, cartographer; Will Brown, cover designer; and Brent Sparrow Jr., artist (who carved the house post that appears on the cover and on page vi of this book).

Special words of recognition are owed to the other members of the legal team who worked on the *Guerin* case: Marvin Storrow, lead counsel and Graham Allen, Bob Banno, Lew Harvey, Doug Sanders, and Steve Schachter. Our success was due in large part to our ability to work as a team.

As always, I owe a debt of gratitude to my wife, Pui-ah, and our sons, Christopher and Alistair.

FROM WARDSHIP TO RIGHTS

INTRODUCTION

THIS BOOK TELLS THE story of the determined search by the Musqueam people to find justice. In 1958, the Canadian government leased over one-third of their small reserve in Vancouver – the highest and the best land – to an exclusive golf club at less than market value and on terms to which they did not agree. They were repeatedly advised to drop the case but their tenacity led to the 1984 decision of the Supreme Court of Canada in *Guerin v The Queen*.[1] That decision recognized for the first time that legally enforceable fiduciary obligations are owed to the Indigenous peoples of Canada and that, in some situations, there is a duty on governments to consult with Indigenous groups concerning their land. In a subsequent decision involving the Musqueam, the court applied the *Guerin* decision to give substance to the then-recent constitutional recognition of existing Aboriginal and treaty rights.[2] The application and development of the fiduciary duty (to act in the best interests of another person) by the Supreme Court of Canada and other courts was a major factor in the dramatic changes in the laws affecting Indigenous peoples over the years since *Guerin*. The case also had a discussion of the legal nature of Aboriginal title and was a stepping stone in the development of the law that led to its full recognition. It upheld Aboriginal title as a legal right that pre-existed British sovereignty and was not dependent on a grant of rights by the Crown. Taken together, these legal developments had a major and permanent impact on Canadian law, politics, and society.

The importance of *Guerin* has been widely acknowledged by writers on the law and I will examine their views in Chapter 6. Justice Ian

Binnie of the Supreme Court of Canada, who had been one of the lawyers in the case, described it as a "seismic blast."[3] It may be noted here that the importance of the case has also been recognized by non-lawyer writers on Indigenous matters. In his account of land issues in *The Inconvenient Indian,* Thomas King includes the case as one of six stories that frame those issues.[4] John Ralston Saul describes it as "one of those Aboriginal victories at the highest court that have shaped Canada over the last forty years" and "one of the most important court cases of the twentieth century."[5] It may also be noted that its influence has not been limited to Canada. It was heavily relied upon by a majority of the Supreme Court of New Zealand in a 2017 case that found that the government owed fiduciary obligations to the Maori.[6]

For five years, I had the good fortune to be part of the legal team that represented the Musqueam people in their groundbreaking legal struggle. In writing this record of the case, I have drawn upon the recollections of Delbert Guerin and other members of the Musqueam people and my own recollections and those of other members of the Musqueam legal team. I have also drawn upon the trial record, the reported decisions, and contemporary newspaper reports, as well as background research on the legal issues involved, the history of the Musqueam, some of the key individuals involved in the case, and the history, theory, and practice of colonialism in the British Empire generally and in Canada in particular. The details of the Musqueam story provide a compelling context for investigating and explaining that history, theory, and practice as well as the legal principles arising from the *Guerin* case.

My involvement with the case began four years after the Musqueam had commenced it in the Federal Court of Canada. In 1979, I had joined what was then Davis & Company, the largest law firm in Vancouver, to complete the process of requalifying as a Canadian lawyer. I had qualified in England as a barrister in 1974, and, after teaching law at the London School of Economics, immigrated to Toronto to work in a bank with plans of a career in international banking. Having decided to make our home in Canada but defeated by the Toronto climate, my wife and I headed west by train to settle in Vancouver. I was hired to work on banking files, but shortly after my arrival at the firm, I received a message asking me to meet one of the partners, Marvin Storrow. He explained that the firm was handling a file for a First Nation that required expertise in trust law. He said that, since I was an English barrister, he assumed that I knew all about trusts. Not wishing to contradict a partner, I mumbled words to the effect that I knew something about them. Marvin took my reply as a form of modesty and set me to work. Thus began my involvement in the *Guerin* case and in Aboriginal law, which has lasted for over forty years.

I was one of the counsel in *Guerin* but this book is intended to be more than a lawyer's "war story." In his account of *Mabo*, a landmark decision in the Aboriginal law of Australia, one of the counsel involved in that case commented that "lawyers' 'war stories' about their favourite cases are generally of little interest to anyone, save the author. But the account which follows contains, I hope, some inherent justification and intrinsic interest."[7] I hope that this is equally true of this book. I have included some anecdotes based on my personal experience but have tried to be as objective and fair as possible in this account.

The *Guerin* case shows that, with determination, Indigenous people can overcome some of the historical disadvantages under which they have struggled for too long and achieve some, although incomplete, measure of justice. In the process of seeking justice for themselves, the Musqueam brought about fundamental improvements in the way the Canadian legal system deals with the rights of all Indigenous peoples. In rejecting the argument that the Musqueam could not enforce the government's obligations to them in the courts (the "political trust" argument), the Supreme Court of Canada strengthened the legal protection provided to all Canadians against the wrongdoings of governments. In that way, *Guerin* provided an example of how the law as enforced in the courts can "move us incrementally towards a just society."[8] I think that is a story worth telling.

The story is told in the following way. Part 1 investigates and explains the events that gave rise to the case. Chapter 1 discusses colonial theory, policy, and administration in the British Empire and, in the case of Canada, "Indian policy" until the 1950s, when the events in *Guerin* took place. Chapter 2 gives background material on the Musqueam and those events, including the creation of the reserve at issue in the case; the role of the Department of Indian Affairs and, in particular, Earl Anfield, the Indian agent most involved in negotiating the lease to the Shaughnessy Heights Golf Club (now the Shaughnessy Golf and Country Club); the influence and history of the club; the clash of cultures and power between the band and the club; and the experiences of Chief Guerin. Chapter 3 gives the historical, political, and legal context of the fiduciary relationship recognized in *Guerin* and examines the relationship between the governments and Indigenous peoples in the British Empire and Canada. The fundamentals of fiduciary law are summarized, as are the relevant legal cases prior to *Guerin*, including the political trust cases.

Part 2 explains the working of the case through the courts, including the decision of the Supreme Court of Canada. Chapter 4 explains how the case got to trial, including the discovery of the lease by Chief Guerin and his difficulties in obtaining legal representation. It also provides some of the background of the participants and describes how the trial unfolded. The trial decision is summarized and critiqued (especially on the limited remedy provided), as is the decision of the Federal Court of Appeal, the disappointment it created, and the serious questions it raised for the rule of law in a liberal democratic society by upholding the defence of political trust. Chapter 5 examines the process to get leave to appeal to the Supreme Court of Canada and the legal arguments presented by the parties, and gives a sense of what took place during the hearing. It summarizes and analyzes the three judgments given by the Supreme Court justices.

Part 3 investigates and explains the after-effects of the case and how it had a major and permanent impact on Canadian law, politics, and society. Chapter 6 provides an overall review of legal developments flowing from *Guerin*. The Conclusion gives my views on the impact of the case on Canadian law, politics, and society. It also considers some of the criticisms of the case and resulting developments, such as the charge of paternalism and even colonialism.

I have told some of this story before as part of a comprehensive study of the fiduciary obligations owed by governments to Aboriginal peoples in Canada.[9] The objective of this book is less ambitious – it is to tell the story of the *Guerin* case and its impact on Canadian law, politics, and society. It borrows from my earlier book and updates it to cover developments over the last fifteen or so years, but it is not an account of the substantive law, although I hope it will help readers gain a better understanding of that law by explaining its origins. In terms of technical legal doctrine, Professor Leonard Rotman has commented that the judgments in *Guerin* "do not delve into any substantial discussion of Crown-Aboriginal fiduciary relations generally."[10] This is an accurate observation. The contribution of *Guerin* was broader and more profound than technical legal doctrine. This book takes an equally broad approach to doctrinal issues. In line with the requirements of the Landmark Cases in Canadian Law series, I have tried to keep the general reader in mind and avoid an overly technical account.

Readers who would like a detailed account of fiduciary law in Canada should obtain Professor Rotman's *Fiduciary Law*.[11] It and his earlier book, *Parallel Paths,* contain a detailed discussion of the substantive law relating to fiduciary obligations and Indigenous peoples, as does *The Honour of the Crown and Its Fiduciary Duties to Aboriginal Peoples* by J. Timothy McCabe.[12] Readers who are interested in an introduction to Aboriginal law in Canada may wish to read my book *Aboriginal Peoples and the Law: A Critical Introduction,* published by UBC Press/ Purich in 2018.

This book is as much about history as law. It seeks to investigate and explain the forces that led to two key events: (1) the signing of the Shaughnessy Heights Golf Club lease in January 1958 and (2) the decision of the Supreme Court of Canada in November 1984. The former event was a direct result of the history of the British Empire, not just in Canada but around the world. As will be seen, the imperial legacy was still very evident on that fateful day when the lease was signed. Reflecting the wardship nature of the relationship, it was signed by the government but not by the band, and the government refused to provide a copy to the band for several years. That legacy was still the driving force behind the administration in Canada of "Indian" affairs, including reserve lands. Although the British had made important changes and created a more professional "modern" colonial policy and administration designed to prepare Indigenous peoples for independence, they had not been emulated by their Canadian heirs and independence was not (and is not) an option.

The decision in 1984 also reflected social and political forces that had developed in Canada by then. Indigenous groups had pushed back against the colonial mentality that saw them as a "problem" that had to be solved by loss of their separate legal status through assimilation. They obtained rights under the Constitution, although vague in nature. These constitutional rights, like the *Guerin* decision, demonstrated that, although the law had been primarily a tool for the forces of the colonial society, it could still be used to mitigate the impact of those forces. *Guerin* was key to the history of the Canadian Aboriginal rights movement. Indeed, one writer has compared it to *Brown v Board of Education*, the landmark decision in the US civil rights movement.[13]

Taken together, these two events make *Guerin* an instructive case study to show (1) the continuing impact of colonial thinking on Indigenous peoples, which viewed them as wards whose lives and property had to be managed by colonial administrators until they could be assimilated into Canadian society, and (2) the modern and developing law on Aboriginal rights that commenced in the 1970s and of which the decision in *Guerin* was an important part.

Guerin is about more than technical legal doctrine. It represented a major development in the political character of the relationship between non-Indigenous people as represented by their governments (the "Crown") and Indigenous peoples. That relationship was first based on treating Indigenous peoples as warriors and necessary allies. It changed in the early nineteenth century when conflicts with other countries ended and British authorities had acquired effective control. The former allies were then reduced to child-like "wards of the state" without enforceable rights. Wardship and similar terms, such as guardianship and tutelage, were used in a general sense to denote the incapacity and dependency of Indigenous peoples rather than in a technical legal sense. However, it may be noted that the origins of wardship go back to medieval England and the right of a feudal lord to control the lands and take the rent of an orphan heir and to sell that right. It had more to do with profit than protection.[14] *Guerin* was an important step in again recasting the relationship between Indigenous peoples and the Crown from one of wardship to one of rights by rejecting the long-held view that any obligations owed by the Crown were political in nature and could not be legally enforced. This was a major and permanent change in Canadian law, politics, and society.

PART 1

THE CONTEXT

1

The Colonial Context

OR THE BRITISH, THE declaration of Vancouver Island in 1849 and then British Columbia in 1858 as colonies meant only two more colonies added to an expanding empire centred on India and the East rather than the western edge of North America.[1] They had potential as sources of raw materials and as settlement destinations for British emigrants but, in the scheme of things, they were insignificant. Viewed in the historical and global context of migrations of populations around the world, the colonies represented just another displacement of hunter-gatherers by farmers.[2] In contrast, colonialization turned the world upside down for the Musqueam and other Indigenous peoples in the region. As part of the Dominion of Canada from 1871, the unified province of British Columbia remained a colony of Britain until the Balfour formula, proposed at the Imperial Conference of 1926 and implemented in the *Statute of Westminster* in 1931, transformed the Dominion into an autonomous nation within the British Empire.

As we shall see, the colonial legacy persisted beyond 1931 and into the 1950s, when the key events in the *Guerin* case took place. It was the essential backdrop to those events. As observed by anthropologist Michael Kew in 1970, in words that are as true today as they were in the 1950s, "the Musqueam have not been assimilated into Canadian society but reside physically and socially apart like the members of some tiny colonial territory."[3] The process of encapsulation or incorporation into the Canadian state, society, and economy is still a work in progress.[4]

COLONIAL THEORY AND PRACTICE

In the early days of the fur trade, the British had no great need for land beyond the immediate area of their trading posts. They made use of the hunting and fishing way of life of the Indigenous population, which was largely left undisturbed (except by diseases). With colonialization came an economic system based on agriculture and industry.[5] These required land and labour. The major contribution of the Indigenous people would be land and resources, and getting them would be the overriding colonial policy. Indigenous peoples were initially used as a source of labour but the preferred workers were immigrants. The Catalogue of Exhibits from Vancouver Island at the London International Exhibition of 1862 noted: "As the colony is at present too poor to pay the passages of labourers from home (a thing it would gladly do if able), the natives will occupy their place in a measure."[6]

As with all settler colonies, land was the prize to be gained and it could be obtained only if it was acquired one way or another from the existing owners. Pre-emption, or the granting of land to settlers who would occupy and use it in accordance with European notions of land use and improvement, was the predominant method used in British Columbia.[7] In much of what became Canada, especially on the Prairies, treaties were signed with Indigenous groups under which, according to the written English version of the treaties, they gave up their interest in most of the land to enable settlement. With the exception of small areas of Vancouver Island, no such treaties were signed in the two new colonies. No consent was sought from the Indigenous peoples, and their laws and customs regarding land ownership and use were ignored despite fundamental legal principles recognizing them.[8] Proclamations allowed the land to be surveyed and granted unless it was the site of an existing Indian settlement. Rough sketches or surveys were made, fences erected, and Indigenous peoples, such as the Musqueam, dispossessed.

Settlers from the British Isles were attracted by the opportunities to be found in the new colonies, glowingly described in various publications. For example:

In the far West, bordering the great Pacific, facing the once famed "Cathay" of our fathers, to which the hardy mariners of old considered this the way, and forming a key through British America to regions hitherto almost unknown, there is a golden land just brought under official notice, and now attracting public attention. It is a land where the wild Indian is as yet almost in his savage state! it is a land where nature reigns in wonderful majesty! it is a land where a sudden transformation is about to take place! and it is a land whither thousands of the civilized inhabitants of the globe are rushing in hot haste to gather of the new found spoil! [9]

These new colonies had special attraction to the occupants of those overcrowded islands: "In a latitude the same as that in which we now live, and with a climate in many respects better than our own, there needs but little to call it a second England."[10] The historian-geographer Cole Harris commented on the special factors that had enabled British settlement: "British Columbians, particularly males of British background, were extraordinarily lucky to encounter a bounteous, depopulated land just when railway, telegraph and post had brought it within relatively easy reach of the outside world."[11]

Probably most of the new settlers were too interested in "the new found spoil" and the "sudden transformation [that was] about to take place" to give much thought to the situation of "the wild Indian." If they had, they would almost certainly have agreed with the predominant justification of overseas settlement going back to at least 1516, when Thomas More explained in *Utopia* that the Utopians were entitled to colonize another country if land in that country was not being sufficiently used.[12] The theory of the inferior claim of hunters and gatherers was widely used in Canada to justify the dispossession of the Indigenous peoples. This can be seen from a contemporary account from colonial Vancouver Island of a conversation between a settler and a Chief who said that his people did not want the white man "who steals what we have." The settler replied that "the high chief of King George men [the English], seeing that you do not work your land, orders that you shall sell it. It is of no use to you." Theory went only so far, however. Recognizing that "we had taken forcible possession of the district," he said the practical answer to the question of "the right of any people to intrude upon another and to dispossess them of their country" is "given by the determination of intruders under any circumstances to keep what has been obtained; and this, without discussion, we, on the west coast of Vancouver Island, were all prepared to do."[13] In the final analysis, the dispossession was explained by "the loaded canon pointed towards the [Tseshaht] village." The Supreme Court of Canada has confirmed that the Indigenous peoples were never conquered.[14] However, duress and the threat of force if they failed to comply with the colonial authorities were always present.[15]

If further justification was required, then the civilizing role of Empire would provide it. This role provided the raison d'être for colonial administration – an administration that was central to the *Guerin* decision. That arch-imperialist Winston Churchill described the imperial ideal:

> What enterprise that an enlightened community may attempt is more noble and more profitable than the reclamation from barbarism of fertile regions and large populations? To give peace to warring tribes, to administer justice when all was violence, to strike the chains off the slave, to draw the richness from the soil, to plant the earliest seeds of commerce and learning, to increase in whole peoples their capacities for pleasures and diminish their chances of pain – what more beautiful ideal or more valuable reward can inspire human effort?[16]

Rudyard Kipling, the high priest of the imperial religion, summarized the nobility of the cause in his poem *The White Man's Burden,* urging the United States to follow the British example and take up the burden of unselfishly and tirelessly serving the interests of the "new-caught sullen peoples" of the Philippines by spreading the benefits of civilization. Many religious people thought that "primitive" peoples were being punished by God for having fallen from a previous state of grace and needed religious instruction to be civilized.[17] The scientific basis for those of European ancestry to assist the civilizing process for Indigenous peoples was developed in the latter half of the nineteenth century by the new discipline of anthropology. In England, Edward Tylor set out his thesis that "the savage state in some measure represents an early condition of mankind out of which the higher culture has gradually been developed or evolved."[18] Many saw it as their Christian duty to help move Indigenous peoples along in this "progressive development." It was certainly a convenient cover for dispossessing them and disrupting the culture and forms of government they enjoyed.

Churchill was not blind to the fact that colonization had "sinister features." It brought "the figures of the greedy trader, the inopportune missionary, the ambitious soldier, and the lying speculator, who disquiet the minds of the conquered and excite the sordid appetites of the conquerors."[19] He might well have added the land-hungry settler, who will play a large role in this account. Commencing in the last quarter of the eighteenth century, it was recognized in colonial theory and administration that Indigenous peoples needed protection as well as "civilization."[20] Of special interest to us are the views of Herman Merivale, who became the senior official in the British Colonial Office. He delivered a series of lectures at Oxford University on colonization and colonies from 1839 to 1841. He concluded that "the duties of the colonial government towards the natives comprised within the limits of the colony, then seem to arrange themselves under two heads — protection and civilization ... For the protection of aborigines the first step necessary is, the appointment in every new colony of a department of the civil service for that especial purpose."[21]

This protection required an exception to the liberal view of individual freedom that the only purpose for which power could be rightfully exercised over someone against his will was to prevent harm to others. As the philosopher J.S. Mill wrote in his classic work *On Liberty*, "Despotism is a legitimate mode of government in dealing with barbarians, provided the end be their improvement, and the means justified by actually effecting that end."[22] Humanitarianism was conveniently linked to missionary zeal and commerce. Civilization and imposed government would lead both to the saving of souls and to trade.[23]

A key issue in colonial policy was whether the responsibility and power to deal with Indigenous peoples should rest with the central or local government. Merivale was clear:

> It is a recommendation of the Committee on Aborigines (1837) that their protection should in all cases be withdrawn altogether from the colonial legislature, and entrusted to the central executive. And in this, I think, even the most jealous friends of colonial freedom must acquiesce.[24]

The committee had said that the protection of Aboriginal peoples was "not a trust which could conveniently be confided to the local legislatures" on the grounds of the obvious conflict between the interests of settlers and their representatives and those of the Indigenous peoples.[25] Merivale saw as one of the most useful functions of a distant central authority – counterbalancing to a certain extent its disadvantages – its ability to arbitrate dispassionately between groups having so many mutual subjects of irritation.[26]

In practice, as we will see repeatedly in this book, the will and power of the central government to protect Indigenous groups was very limited. In 1861, just as colonialism was getting under way in British Columbia, Mill wrote that English settlers in India thought it "monstrous that any rights of the natives should stand in the way of their smallest pretensions."[27] They, and not the natives, had the ear of the public at home, with predictable results:[28]

> And when the resident English bring the batteries of English political action to bear upon any of the bulwarks erected to protect the natives against their encroachments, the executive, with their real but faint velleities of something better, generally find it safer to their parliamentary intest, and at any rate less troublesome, to give up the disputed position than to defend it.

The phrase "real but faint velleities" is one to bear in mind as we examine the failure of the central government to protect Indigenous interests in Canada, including those of the Musqueam.

Merivale saw only three alternatives for the ultimate destiny of Indigenous peoples: their extermination; "their civilization, complete or partial, by retaining them as insulated bodies of men, carefully removed, during the civilizing process, from the injury of European contact"; and "their amalgamation with the colonists."[29] By amalgamation, he meant "the union of natives with settlers in the same community, as master and servant, as fellow-labourers, as fellow-citizens, and, if possible, as connected by intermarriage."[30] It was to be a process of assimilation and the Indigenous peoples were to become assimilated or amalgamated with the settler society once they had reached a sufficient level of civilization. He was clear, however, that successful amalgamation required acting on "the broad principle that the native must, for their own protection, be placed in a situation of acknowledged inferiority, and consequently of tutelage ... a state of fictitious equality is far worse for him than one of acknowledged inferiority, with its correlative protection."[31] This tutelage would be expressed as a guardian/ward relationship. In order to implement his policy of amalgamation, Merivale saw a need for British functionaries in the colonies who would have higher qualifications than usual: "Such functionaries must be ready, not to perform negative duties only, but to take the initiative –

to act, devise and control. Unless, they are fit to do this, they are absolutely useless."[32] They had to be ambitious "officers of the higher grade and highest importance."

One of the more thoughtful settlers in British Columbia was Gilbert Sproat, who was very active in colonial and early provincial affairs, including acting as a reserve commissioner allocating reserves in the province.[33] He wrote *Scenes and Studies of Savage Life* in 1868 based on his early experiences in Port Alberni on Vancouver Island. Sickness and death had been caused by introduced diseases, the change of food, "and the despondency and discouragement produced in the minds of the Indians by the presence of a superior race: the latter being the principal cause."[34] The "Indian" had lost his motivation and his old way of life. He was "bewildered and dulled by the new life around him for which he is unfitted."[35] Probably, little could be done to prevent the "seemingly appointed decay" but it might be possible "to benefit isolated bodies of savages by civilized teachings and example."[36] Their hunting and fishing places had been intruded upon, their social customs disregarded, and their freedom curtailed. Admitting the right of settlers to the land in spite of the opposition of the "savages," it was a reasonable claim – indeed, of simple justice – that "the injury done to the native population, as a whole, should be counterbalanced, not according to the Indians' poor ideas of gifts of food or blankets, but by a wise and paternal action of the Crown, in some practical way, on their behalf."[37] His suggestion was to place "about five men, carefully chosen in England," in isolated native villages to teach the "Indians" any useful employments and arts that they were capable of learning, to improve their moral ideas, and to instruct them in Christianity.

The most detailed and well expressed justification of colonialism was probably written in 1922 by Lord Lugard, a leading theorist on, and advocate for, colonialism and a former governor of Hong Kong and Nigeria. In his classic book *The Dual Mandate*, he defended European empires as being in the interests of both the Indigenous peoples *and* the colonial power:

Let it be admitted at the outset that European brains, capital, and energy have not been, and never will be, expended in developing the resources of Africa from motives of pure philanthropy; that Europe is in Africa for the mutual benefit of her own industrial classes, and of the native races in their progress to a higher plane; that the benefit can be made reciprocal, and that it is the aim and desire of civilised administration to fulfil this dual mandate.[38]

He placed reliance for this approach on the trust mandate system set up by the League of Nations after the First World War, which will be considered in our discussion of the fiduciary relationship. In 1957, another former governor of an African colony, Sir Alan Burns, wrote *In Defence of Colonies,* concluding:

Many years ago Britain undertook the gigantic task of helping the peoples of various under-developed territories to overcome the handicaps imposed on them by nature and environment; to learn the principles of democracy and honest administration; and to qualify themselves for independence. In many parts of the world the task has not yet been completed and it is inconceivable that we should abandon it half-done.[39]

With the important exception of the reference to independence, these sentiments would have been echoed by most officials in the Canadian Department of Indian Affairs in 1957 – the year in which the Shaughnessy lease was negotiated by the department.

The writer George Orwell, whose views on colonialism changed dramatically during his time as a policeman in Burma, doubted the sincerity of the claim to be helping the Indigenous population. He denounced

the lie that we're here to uplift our poor black brothers instead of to rob them. I suppose it's a natural enough lie. But it corrupts us, it corrupts us in ways you can't imagine. There's an everlasting sense of being a sneak and a liar that torments us and drives us to justify ourselves night and day. It's at the bottom of half our beastliness to the natives. We Anglo-Indians [the British in India] could be almost bearable if we'd only admit that we're thieves and go on thieving without any humbug.[40]

This was a minority view and it seems most colonial officials, including those at the Department of Indian Affairs in Canada, were sincere in their belief in "the dual mandate" of acting for "the mutual benefit of [the colonial power] and of the native races in their progress to a higher plane."[41]

THE COLONIAL SERVICES

The colonial policy towards Indigenous peoples was implemented mainly by colonial officials, although missionaries were also involved, especially through residential schools. We shall review later the role of Canada's Department of Indian Affairs and, in particular, that of the Indian agent, the field officer who had direct contact with Indigenous peoples such as the Musqueam. The department was part of the broader system of colonial administration of Indigenous peoples and their lands implemented by the British Empire and by other European empires.[42] Colonial administration was often part of the military administration, as in central Canada until the 1830s, when it became a separate civil administration, as noted below. It may also have been a part of the commercial operations of large trading firms such as the East India Company, the Hudson's Bay Company, and the British South Africa Company. The East India Company recognized the need for professional administrators and established systems to select them through competitive examinations and to train them. It set up a college at Haileybury that became something of a model for future education of colonial administrators in colonial Asia when the India Office took over administration from the company in 1858.[43] Members of the Indian Civil Service formed an intellectual elite – the so-called heaven-born – and were expected to be familiar with the local language, laws, and customs.[44] In contrast, the rest of the Empire was administered by administrators who glorified the cult of the amateur until reforms were carried out, especially in the 1940s, with regard to the administration of colonies under the Colonial Office.

In her magisterial survey of the British Empire, Jan Morris described administration of the non-Asian colonies known generally as the Colonial Service:

> Jobs in Africa and the lesser tropical colonies went by a kind of patronage. The private interview was the chosen method ... There was no training programme – men were expected to learn their trade on the spot: many subtleties of native life and custom escaped this slapdash novitiate, and British colonial officers were frequently ignorant about complexities like customary law and land tenure. As a whole, the Crown Colonies were ruled by willing all-rounders of very varied quality – what ambitious man, in the days before malaria control, would wish to devote a career to Sierra Leone? They were recruited more for character than brain-power: it was said that a candidate with a first-class degree would actually be regarded as suspect.[45]

This prejudice against professionalism was confirmed by that arch-imperialist Alan Burns, who wrote:

> Basing my conviction on a long experience in several colonies, I feel certain that a strong character and sound common sense are far more valuable assets to a colonial official (and the Colonial Service) than the most brilliant academic distinctions. Those whom Kipling has called the "brittle intellectuals" too frequently "crack beneath a strain," such strains as the loneliness of a "bush" station, the irritations of heat and insects, the perversity of the local people who *will* not realise what is best for them, and the temptations of drink and women ... I believe that an officer of high intellectual and academic qualifications might quite easily be a failure in "the bush."[46]

This opposition to professionalism and the references to "a strong character and sound common sense"[47] and "the perversity of the local people" should be remembered when we review the selection and training of Indian agents in the Department of Indian Affairs and the events of 1957 that led to the signing of the Shaughnessy lease in 1958.

We have many accounts, real and fictitious, of the lives of colonial field officers, especially from Africa.[48] What emerges most clearly is the extent of the power wielded over the Indigenous peoples, and often paternalism and the associated belief in the inferiority of those peoples. Lord Lugard alludes to these in his account of the qualities that must be shown:

> The white man's prestige must stand high when a few score are responsible for the control and guidance of millions ... There is no room for "mean whites" in tropical Africa. Nor is there room for those who, however high their motives, are content to place themselves on the same level as the uncivilised races. They lower the prestige by which alone the white races can hope to govern and to guide.[49]

One district officer based in Sarawak described the range of his responsibilities in 1936:

> The District Officer was in charge of the prisons and had to turn out the prisoners. He was also the magistrate, so that having remanded a chap in prison he then had him come up before him in court and had to decide whether he was guilty or not guilty. He was also responsible for public works, for maintaining such roads as there might be in the district and drains and so forth. And all this quite apart from his main job of generally administering the people in this area – touring around finding out their troubles, resolving their problems, settling their land disputes and collecting the head tax.[50]

In the first half of the twentieth century, with the expansion of the Empire in Africa,[51] Labour governments in Britain, and growing independence movements around the Empire, the role changed in line with the new policy of preparing the Indigenous peoples for self-government or independence within the Empire/Commonwealth.[52] In a break with the long-standing policy that colonies had to be self-sufficient, the central government in London passed legislation in the 1940s to make funds available to promote economic development.[53] Training courses for colonial administrators and the greater professionalism discussed below sought to equip them for the new challenges. One internal memorandum noted the growing presence of educated people within colonial territories and warned of the danger posed by "the Uninstructed White."[54] Paternalism was still present, however, even as it was being denied. In the words of Alan Burns, "the main thing in my opinion is to find out what Colonial peoples want, and if their wants are not too unreasonable to let them have their way ... The time is long past when we can get away with the attitude that 'Daddy knows best'; and we must remember that children are perverse enough to grow up."[55]

As noted, the Indian Civil Service was a professional administration from its early days, whereas the Colonial Service lacked professionalism and preferred to stress character and common sense and a jack-of-all-trades approach. This changed after the First World War and was especially notable after the Second World War as a "Modern Colonial Service" was created. An important part of this development was the recruitment of specialists with professional qualifications and experience. In addition to the Colonial Administrative Service, there were no less than nineteen professional services, such as agriculture, education, forestry, police, and public works. One district officer who joined the Colonial Service after the Second World War observed: "Gone were the days when the District Officer could properly be termed the maid-of-all-work: treasurer, magistrate, prosecutor and defence counsel, road-builder and tax collector all rolled into one. The post-war District Officer was likely to be the leader of a District Team of professionals."[56]

The other major developments in making the Colonial Service more professional were recruitment of better-educated officers and better training rather than learning on the job and relying on character and common sense. At last, steps were taken to bring the Colonial Service in line with the Indian Civil Service. Indeed, applicants who might have applied for the latter began applying to the Colonial Service as the inevitability of early Indian independence became obvious. In his history of district officers in Africa, Anthony Kirk-Greene summarizes the change in their educational background and expected sympathy towards the new goal of preparing for independence: "If 'fire in their bellies' had been a feature, at times almost a qualification of the founding [district officers], from 1930 intellectual competence and personal empathy were prize attributes in the final model of the [district officer] in Africa."[57] Applicants to the Colonial Service were expected to be university graduates, although exceptions were made for ex-servicemen who could show similar intellectual ability.[58] A competitive selection process replaced the earlier system of patronage.

Key to the new professionalism was the development of training programs starting in 1909 for district officer cadets destined for Africa, which were later extended to other colonies.[59] A major advance in training resulted after 1946 in partial implementation of recommendations made by a committee of colonial officials and academics chaired by the Duke of Devonshire and generally referred to as the Devonshire scheme.[60] Successful applicants had to attend and pass a year's postgraduate course at Oxford, Cambridge, or the London School of Economics covering a range of subjects including local languages, economics, law, anthropology, engineering, and geography. Also, mid-career officers could attend university on a year's sabbatical for advanced study. Some of the old-style colonial administrators were not impressed and thought the new training schemes were a waste of time and money: "There is a danger that the courses will produce a number of young men, full of zeal and theory, with more than the usual arrogance of youth, impatient of the slowness of Africans in responding to schemes devised for their benefit, and trying to reach perfection in a few weeks."[61] The professionalism of the Modern Colonial Service provides a good comparison for the state of the Canadian Department of Indian Affairs in 1958 when the Shaughnessy lease was signed, as will be discussed below.

The basic methods used by colonial administrators to rule Indigenous peoples can be divided into three very broad forms: direct rule, indirect rule, and local self-government.[62] Direct rule was administration directly by the colonial authorities. It was used in different colonies at different times. "British India," comprising nearly two-thirds of the country, was under direct rule, while the balance made up of princely states was under indirect rule. Malaya and most of the African colonies were under indirect rule, meaning that British control would be exercised through local bodies such as sultans and chiefs, often using tribal courts to administer what were described as traditional laws. The role of the district officer was supposed to be that of an adviser. Indirect administration was often portrayed as a step towards, or a form of, self-government. It is mainly associated with the activities of Lord Lugard in Northern Nigeria and was described by his biographer, Margery Perham, as "the most comprehensive, coherent and renowned system of administration in our colonial history."[63] In practice, as noted by J.S. Furnivall in 1948, "there is no sharp line between direct and indirect rule, and we find the same power adopting different systems in the same place at different times, and in different places at the same time."[64] In his view, the choice was often governed by convenience rather than by principle.[65] Even where indirect rule applied in theory, colonial administrators often could not avoid the temptation to intervene in administration,[66] advice had to be asked and acted upon in most matters,[67] and supposedly customary Indigenous law was, in part, a creation of colonial institutions.[68]

Self-government was considered a step towards ultimate independence within the Empire and was prominent as part of the reforms to colonial policy in the final decades of Empire.[69] At the time, it was often predicted to take some time. Alan Burns confidently told a group of district officers in 1947: "We are there to teach and to help, not to govern by the strong hand ... Our main job is to teach the Africans and other Colonials to take our places in the administration of the

Colonies. We must try and teach them to do the work that we are doing ourselves, in order that they may replace us. It will be a long time before they are as efficient as we are."[70] He assured them: "Believe me, the Colonial Civil Service, with all its imperfections, will be needed for many years to come."[71] Giving the Reid Lecture to Acadia University in 1959, one historian of the Empire denied that the British were "empire-builders gone out of business": "Is the British Empire liquidated? No, indeed!"[72] Another historian of the Empire later referred to the 1950s as "the grand climacteric for the imperial idea," although he did not know it when he finished his influential book on the imperial idea in 1957.[73] In fact, the end of the Empire came sooner than most expected, with the full independence of major colonies starting with India in 1947, and a second and decisive wave of decolonization between 1957 and 1964, including the Gold Coast (Ghana) and Malaya in 1957.[74]

BRITISH COLONIAL ADMINISTRATION
AND THEORY IN 1954

The changes that took place after the end of the Second World War were reflected in what one authority on colonial administration describes as "a sudden and silent revolution."[75] On the night of 17 June 1954, the Colonial Service, which had existed since 1837, was replaced by Her Majesty's Overseas Civil Service. Although the full implications would take some years to work out, especially as different colonies gained independence at different times, the change symbolized the end of British colonial administration. Members of the former Colonial Service were encouraged by generous financial arrangements to take employment with the governments of the territories involved. They became more like civil servants in London than the archetypal colonial district officers. The British end of administration would become one in which "there would no longer be any regular establishment, only a series of contract or loan appointments."[76] Colonial theory towards Indigenous peoples had also changed: no longer was the colonial mission expressed as one of protection and civilization as with Merivale in 1839, but rather one of economic development and preparation for independence.[77]

CANADA AND COLONIALISM

Many Canadians speak of colonialism as something that was done to Canadians by Britain (perceiving themselves as the colonized), which ended at some vague time in the past. In fact, of course, the non-Indigenous residents of Canada of whatever ancestry are the heirs of the British Empire and the early predominantly British settlers who dispossessed the Indigenous peoples. Political scientist Alan Cairns noted that "our domestic history is intertwined with a global history,"[78] and Cole Harris that "most British Columbians today ... are the heirs of and continuing participants in a pervasive, ongoing colonialism."[79]

Canada is an example of settler colonialism in which the colonizers not only hold the power but also become a majority of the population and intend to change and remain in the colony forever. In the words of Lorenzo Veracini, "settlers exchange countries but also change countries; they literally transform them, aiming for greater productivity and recognizable patterns of land use."[80] To do this, they imported settlers, crops, domesticated animals, laws, technology, and ways of thinking from Britain.[81] This was true for Canada. With the exception of settlers, this was also true for non-settler colonies such as those in Asia and Africa. Studies of the history and law of Indigenous peoples in Canada make very little mention of such colonies and their common history and law as part of the British Empire.[82] Indeed, a former prime minister of Canada even went so far as to claim in 2009 that "we have ... no history of colonialism."[83]

On the contrary, Canada was very much a part of the British Empire and, for most of its history, most Canadians (legally British subjects as Canadian citizenship was not separated before 1947) shared a common view of the benefits of colonialism with the colonial officials and businessmen in Malaya or Nigeria. They were enthusiastic imperialists

and proud of their British heritage.[84] Kipling celebrated Canada's assertion of quasi-independence in his 1897 poem *Our Lady of the Snow:*
"Daughter am I in my mother's house / But mistress in my own."
However, Canada's inclusion as a senior member of the imperial family
was never in doubt. It was included as one of Kipling's "*The Native-Born*"
(1895) that called "old England 'home.'" About four million British
emigrated to British North America between 1815 and 1915 (about
one-fifth of total emigration).[85] Between 1948 and 1957, over four
hundred thousand emigrated from Britain to Canada, and people of
British and Irish ancestry made up 60 percent of the Canadian population in 1871, 50 percent in 1941, and 44 percent in 1961.[86] They
saw themselves as members of the British Empire and would have
agreed with Stephen Leacock, a prominent political scientist, that "our
Empire not only contains in its destiny the chief hope for universal
peace, but the chief opportunity towards that abiding plenty and prosperity on which alone universal peace can permanently rest."[87] In the
words of John Darwin, together with Australians, New Zealanders,
and the English in South Africa, they viewed "empire as a shared enterprise, a white ethnic commonwealth" and their societies as "new
Britains."[88] Canada was an important part of the Empire that had
"dominion over palm and pine" and "lesser breeds."[89] Canadian law
and policy reflected that of the Empire, including with respect to
Indigenous peoples. Canadians served as colonial administrators in
other parts of the Empire, especially after a program was introduced
in 1923 to encourage recruitment from the Dominion.[90]

As noted by Phillip Buckner, Canadians "clearly supported the
imperial expansion across the globe. They were proud to see large parts
of the map of the world painted red."[91] He details the active role played
by Canadians throughout the Empire and argues that it is "patently
absurd" to see Canadians as part of the colonized rather than the colonizers – a self-evident proposition but which, for clarity of debate
over the numerous current misleading references to "decolonization"
and "postcolonialism," needs to be stated. In his words:

Canadian nationalists ... prefer that Canadians be thought of as part of the colonized rather than as part of the colonizers. In fact, as every member of a First Nation is only too aware [this approach is] patently absurd. True decolonization has not and never will take place in Canada, any more than the United States and it is profoundly ahistorical to pretend that Canadians were passive rather than active imperialists. Indeed, Canadians were late converts to the notion of turning the "British" Commonwealth into a multinational Commonwealth. Canada did not endorse the grant of Dominion status to India until after World War Two and then only grudgingly. It did not speak out against South Africa until the 1960s.[92]

An understanding of the imperialist mentality of Canadians during the 1950s is important to a proper understanding of the facts of the *Guerin* case and why the Musqueam are still suffering from the effects of the Shaughnessy lease.

Significantly for the history of colonial or "Indian" administration in Canada, the most senior official in the Department of Indian Affairs in the early part of the twentieth century was Duncan Campbell Scott. A firm believer in forced assimilation of Indigenous peoples, he was also a firm believer in the Empire, imperial values, and imperial federalism. A prominent poet, he extolled the exploits of Empire builders in his poems. As he saw it, the "manifest destiny of Canada is to be one of the greatest powers in the Federated Empire of England."[93] In this vision of an imperial federation, he echoed the views of John Seeley, an influential Cambridge professor,[94] and of Viscount Milner, the intellectual and political leader of British imperialism at its height around the end of the nineteenth century.[95] Milner made a distinction between the Dominions, "new nations sprung from [Great Britain's] loins" such as Canada and Australia with sizeable British settler populations, and "the Dependent Empire" with over four hundred million non-British people to whom Britain had striven to extend the blessings of civilized government.[96] No account was taken of the existence of the Indigenous peoples in the Dominions. Imperial federation had other adherents in Canada who sought closer union between Britain and the Dominions, including representation in the imperial Parliament.[97]

Alan Cairns wrote a penetrating analysis comparing and contrasting the position of Indigenous peoples in former European empires (the Third World) and that of Indigenous peoples in settler colonies (the Fourth World) and especially Canada. In summary:

> Although Third and Fourth World peoples were both subject to the hierarchy of imperialism, the latter were never treated as peoples/nations on the road to independence. In Canada, Indian peoples were placed outside the standard working of the majority's constitutional order, and governed in geographically discrete communities by superintendents [Indian agents] who were the domestic counterparts of district officers in British colonial sub-Saharan Africa. The system of Indian reserves could be thought of as transitional appendages to the mainstream constitutional order, while the policy of assimilation – for which church-run residential schools were key instruments – eroded cultural diversity. In the context of Canadian domestic imperialism, therefore, the governing logic of the state was that indigenous difference was transitional: to be overcome by state pressure and inducements.[98]

The policy of the Canadian government was that "domestic empire and internal colonialism were to end by Indians, as individuals, entering the majority society and its unchanged constitutional order on the majority's terms."[99] Independence has never been an option for Canada's Indigenous peoples, who are a small (approximately 5 percent) minority: "In the Third World, the imperial power formally departs; in the Fourth World what was the imperial majority remains behind, perhaps no longer imperial, but still the majority."[100] Cairns notes: "The global overseas empires of European powers in Africa, Asia, and elsewhere helped sustain the historic Canadian Indian policy of wardship/ assimilation. The pervasive set of assumptions that undergirded the overseas empire made domestic Indian policy in the imperial era appear to be part of the natural order."[101]

The key events of the *Guerin* case took place in the late 1950s. This was a time of change in colonial history worldwide as the "winds of change" blew around the globe. Independence movements were challenging European colonial systems. In 1957, the year when the terms of the Shaughnessy lease were determined, Albert Memmi wrote his classic and searing analysis of the relationship between the colonizer and the colonized, explaining the complex motivations and contradictions and the impacts of colonialism on both.[102] One issue that he described has direct application to the facts of *Guerin:* the inadequacy of colonial administrators who were often unqualified for similar positions in non-colonial situations. Another relevant factor was a paternalism and a corresponding belief that the colonized were incapable of managing their own affairs.

Changes in Canada were slow to come. The identification of Canada with the British Empire and colonial ideology continued well into the 1950s. The country had a "long-standing self-image of itself as a settler dominion, an empire of the north, a British colony that marched progressively and valiantly to its particular version of nationhood."[103] As noted by historian Bryan Palmer, "however much the writing was on the crumbling wall of an antiquated, imperialistic understanding of nationhood, the values and attachments of and to this particular identity were still vigorously in evidence throughout Canada ... the older imperialism was often on display."[104] This was literally the case when the equestrian Durbar statue of Edward VII was removed from India following its independence and re-erected by subscription in Queen's Park, Toronto.[105] José E. Igartua's study of newspapers, parliamentary speeches, history textbooks, and public opinion polls shows how Canadian identity remained mainly British into the 1950s.[106] The *Citizenship Act* of 1946 specifically declared that Canadians remained British subjects and continued the preferred position of all British subjects in matters like elections. Textbooks stressed that Canada's history was part of that of the Empire and that pupils had responsibilities to both the Dominion and the Empire.[107] Historian Arthur Lower wrote in 1958 that "all little Canadian boys and girls have been subjected from the day on which they start school to an unending steeping in the liquid of imperialism."[108] In 1956, the *Toronto Daily Star* pointed out that "alone among the Commonwealth members we have no flag, no national anthem. We were the last to accept a native son as governor-general, and there are still Canadians who would like to see a Britisher as our chief-of-state. We must be the only country in the world that denied itself the right to amend its own constitution."[109] The Suez Crisis of 1956 was an opportunity for imperialist jingoism in some Canadian newspapers, which enthusiastically supported Britain's invasion of Egypt.[110] John Diefenbaker's success in the federal election of 1957 "was at least partly due to a desire by many English Canadians to reaffirm the importance of the British connection."[111] It was not until 1964 that the great flag debate "marked the last hurrah for English-Canadian believers in a British Canada."[112] The sense of Britishness was especially prevalent in British Columbia, as indicated by the histories of the province and its majority British population.[113]

Colonial attitudes towards Indigenous peoples were very evident into the 1950s both internationally and in Canada.[114] Igartua quotes many examples from Canada. One textbook for grades 7 and 8 used in the 1950s said: "The greatest gift we owe to the red man is our broad land which they allowed us to take over without making any great general war against us ... because of being uncivilized, our Indians could not make use of Canada's good farm land, nor of the other rich resources that nature has given her. To use these gifts, Canada needed civilized people."[115] Very relevant to our consideration of the *Guerin* case dating back to events that took place in Vancouver in 1957 was the continuing attachment to the values of colonialism evident in the celebrations of the 1958 centennial of the creation of the province. This is revealed in a history of British Columbia written for the celebrations by Margaret Ormsby, the first woman professor of history at the University of British Columbia.[116] Her conclusion gives a sense of her views: "Yet never, unless the old British stock became diluted by over-whelming numbers of 'aliens,' would British Columbians forget that they were 'British' British Columbians."[117] She barely mentions Indigenous peoples in her history, and the few references are in the context of colonial settlement and are negative: they were "hostile,"[118] "marauders,"[119] or "depraved."[120] Nothing is said about the pre-contact history or the dispossession of Indigenous peoples, and only cursory references are made to the establishment of reserves in the province. It is as though the province had been empty of people at the time of contact – a *terra nullius* – except that, somehow, Indians appeared from time to time, as with the Chilcotin War, to disrupt the smooth path of British settlement. The invisibility of Indigenous peoples is evident in many other publications of the time. For example, there are only a couple of passing references in *The Culture of Contemporary Canada,* published in 1957.[121]

Mia Reimers's detailed account of the 1958 celebrations[122] concludes that "the role of First Nations was virtually overlooked in favour of a whitewashed western and frontier history."[123] They were merely background to tell the story of explorers and pioneers and colonial progress and civilization. During the Queen's extended visit to Canada the following year, it was noted by the press that the purpose of having Native people on the program was to add colour to the local show. No serious consideration of their concerns was allowed. For example, in Stoney Creek, Ontario, a delegation who wanted to express their views was not allowed to see her.[124] The prevailing understanding of settlement was that there had been "a peaceful penetration," an occupation without the violence that had taken place elsewhere.[125] This was reflected in histories as "the benevolent conquest myth."[126] Theories of biological racism resulting in negative views of Indigenous peoples were widespread.[127] In a speech by Prime Minister Pierre Trudeau in 1969, "Indians" were still seen as a "problem."[128]

INDIAN POLICY IN CANADA TO THE 1950s

We saw earlier that colonial policy gave responsibility over Indigenous peoples to the central rather than the local government in order to protect them from the settlers represented by the local government. In the case of the colonies of Vancouver Island and British Columbia, this meant the Colonial Office in London rather than the local legislatures.

Once the combined colony of British Columbia entered Confederation in 1871, it meant the federal government. In practice, both central authorities abandoned their responsibility and gave in to the demands of the local government and local residents. This is demonstrated repeatedly in the history of reserve allocation as documented by Cole Harris in his classic study of this topic.[129] In his words, "the Colonial Office stood aside and the formulation of Native land policy quickly passed into the hands of local officials, all of whom broadly represented the aspirations and values of an incipient settler society."[130] After Confederation, the federal government was equally ineffective in protecting Indigenous peoples and their assets, including their reserve lands, from the demands of local settlers.

According to Noel Dyck, "the history of Indian administration is replete with examples of Departmental personnel being obliged to take account of influential non-Indians' determination to have the government facilitate their interests with respect to Indian lands and trust funds, not to speak of public funds spent on Indians' behalf."[131] Indian agents put pressure on Indians to secure a surrender of reserve lands and, according to Brian Titley, this happened frequently.[132] In 1906, Minister of the Interior Frank Oliver was under pressure from Opposition Leader Robert Borden, who wanted to make large "unused" reserves available for development. Oliver replied that, although Indian rights ought to be protected, they should not be allowed to interfere with those of whites – "and if it becomes a question between the Indians and the whites, the interests of the whites will have to be provided for." This was, in effect, a repudiation of any notion of protection or a trust. He said every effort was being made to obtain the surrender of "surplus" Indian land. Shortly thereafter, changes were made to the *Indian Act* to make it easier to get surrenders.[133] Further changes enabled the expropriation of reserve land for public purposes without surrender, and the removal of Indians from reserves within towns.[134] After the First World War, there were demands for reserve land to be transferred to veterans and the Department of Indian Affairs cooperated most of the time.[135]

Early Indian policy in what is now central Canada was based upon military alliances with Indigenous Nations to defend British interests against France and then the United States, but this changed in 1830. The Indian department had formed part of the responsibilities of the British military. To win and keep the support of Indigenous Nations, it was necessary to assure them that their land was safe from the land hunger of local settlers. In the early 1800s, the threat from the United States disappeared and, in 1828, the Colonial Office began questioning the need for an Indian department. The response of the Indian department took the form of a report, the Darling Report, which promoted what became known as the civilization and assimilation program. It recommended a policy based on establishing reserves where Indians could be educated, converted to Christianity, and transformed into farmers.[136] The plan was approved by the Colonial Secretary in 1830.

A significant change had been made in Indian policy: Indians were no longer to be treated as independent warriors but as wards of the state. The goal of Indian policy was to be civilization and assimilation. The new policy was reflected in legislation such as the *Gradual Civilization Act* passed in 1857. The implementation of the policy was, in practice, left to missionaries and residential schools rather than government officials. The main task of the officials was to keep order on the reserves through Indian agents. By isolating Indigenous peoples, reserves were inconsistent with the stated objective of civilization/assimilation but they were seen by Indian Affairs officials as places of protection against the mainstream society. Over time, officials recognized the inconsistency between "protection" and "advancement." In 1946, the second most important official in the department wrote a complacent article that defended the department's record but acknowledged that "perhaps the time has come when the protective reins are becoming a curb on progress and should be loosened."[137]

The essence of assimilation can be seen from the following quotations. In 1887, Prime Minister Sir John A. Macdonald said: "The great aim of our civilization has been to do away with the tribal system and assimilate the Indian people in all respects with the inhabitants of the

Dominion, as speedily as they are fit for the change."[138] In 1920, the deputy superintendent of Indian Affairs, Duncan Campbell Scott, told a parliamentary committee: "I want to get rid of the Indian problem ... Our object is to continue until there is not a single Indian in Canada that has not been absorbed into the body politic and there is no Indian question."[139] This philosophy of forced assimilation (or "cultural geno-cide," to quote a former chief justice of Canada[140]) was accompanied by a belief that Indigenous people would largely die out as separate peoples. In the words of one of Canada's leading anthropologists, writing of West Coast Indigenous peoples in 1935: "Socially, they are outcasts, economically they are inefficient and an encumbrance. Their old world has fallen into ruins, and helpless in the face of a catastrophe they cannot understand, they vainly seek refuge in its shattered foundations. The end of this century, it seems safe to predict will see very few survivors."[141] The assimilation policy continued despite changes to the *Indian Act* in 1951 that corrected some of its most objectionable features.

In 1867, upon Confederation, the new federal government assumed responsibility for Indian affairs. Under the terms of Canadian Con-federation, "Indians, and Lands reserved for the Indians" are within federal and not provincial jurisdiction.[142] The federal government soon passed legislation to consolidate the civilization and assimilation policy. The first act with the title of *Indian Act* was passed in 1876, which, as consolidated in 1880 and subsequently amended, remained in place until 1951. At the time of Confederation, Indian Affairs was the res-ponsibility of the Secretary of State; in 1873, it became a branch of the Department of Interior; in 1880, it was made a separate Department of Indian Affairs; in 1936, it became a branch of the Department of Mines and Resources; and in 1950, it formed part of the Department of Citizenship and Immigration.

From 1830 to the Second World War, "Indian administration re-mained a backwater government operation that received only sporadic public attention or political scrutiny ... The nineteenth century civil-ization mentality of policy-makers persisted: paternalism, hegemony, and wardship effectively limited policy options and administrative innovation."[143] As acknowledged by the *Hawthorn Report* of 1966, which was commissioned by the department, Indian administration was "a version of colonialism," and the Indian Affairs Branch was, for all practical purposes, "a miniature government, rather than an ordinary civil service branch." It had a reputation for being "particularly authoritarian" and having an "inward looking parochialism" that "laid great stress on field experience for knowing the Indian."[144]

The postwar years saw some efforts to modernize Indian policy and administration in Canada, but nothing like the changes that we reviewed above resulting in a "modern colonial administration" for the British Empire/Commonwealth under the rule of the Colonial Office. These efforts are described in detail by John Leslie in his PhD thesis covering Indian policy from 1943 to 1963.[145] From 1946 to 1948, a special parliamentary joint committee met to consider changes to the *Indian Act*. Leslie notes: "One salient fact quickly emerged: the Indian Affairs Branch possessed neither the staff, financial means, nor expertise to fulfill its mandate of ameliorating Indian conditions and promoting assimilation ... Field administration was a shambles and local record keeping lax."[146] One First Nation chief bravely criticized the poor calibre of Indian agents.[147] The committee made a number of recommendations, including hiring more Indian agents. In 1947, the department finally issued a field manual for agents and made efforts to hire more agents.

A new *Indian Act* was passed in 1951 but, as also noted by Leslie, "the act once again reflected the philosophical assumptions, values, and paternalistic administrative practices that had guided Indian policy since the nineteenth century."[148] The Department of Indian Affairs still had control from "womb to tomb" over the lives of Indians and their reserve lands. "In terms of administrative practice much remained as before."[149] As observed by Dyck, "while some of the most obviously obnoxious features of this system were amended after the war, what remained were many of the lingering assumptions traditionally purveyed by the Department concerning the incapacities and requirements of Indians. What also remained were reserve communities which, from their very inception, had been prevented from determining their own destiny."[150]

The *Indian Act* of 1951 led to initial optimism but it was not to last. More funding was made available for administration. "Indians" were eligible to receive pension and welfare benefits available to Canadian citizens. Amendments were made in 1956 to the *Citizenship Act* to remove any doubt that Indian people were citizens of Canada. A study was commissioned in 1954 from Harry Hawthorn, an anthropologist from the University of British Columbia, and his colleagues on Indian administration in British Columbia and the condition of BC Indians. Tensions arose thereafter, however. Leslie summarizes events during the latter part of the 1950s: "Ministerial speeches hinting that [termination of Indian status] was a hidden policy objective; band membership disputes arising from a provision in the new *Indian Act;* and expropriation of Mohawk reserves to make way for the St. Lawrence Seaway drew unfavourable public attention to authoritarian Indian administration."[151]

Looking back over the period from 1830 to 1960, the fundamental objective of Indian policy did not change: Indians were to be educated on Western civilization to assimilate into mainstream Canada and, until they were considered ready, they were to be protected by isolation on reserves, which were to be managed on their behalf by the Department of Indian Affairs, although subject to the demands for reserve lands from the settler society. According to Leslie, "despite attempts at camouflage by non-Native policy-makers, the basic tenets of post-war Indian policy maintained an eerie continuity with the nineteenth century, particularly in terms of philosophy, policy objectives, and administrative practices."[152] Instead of "assimilation" and "civilization," "integration" and "full citizenship" were used, but the fundamentals had not changed.

We are not directly concerned with post-1960 changes to Indian administration as the events that led to the *Guerin* case took place in 1957 and 1958.[153] We can note that the 1960s did lead to some improved housing and reserve infrastructure as the welfare state approach was applied. The right to vote in federal elections was extended to Indians in 1960. Indigenous leaders began acquiring more power as they organized in opposition to the federal White Paper of 1969 that sought to terminate the special status of Indian people. First Nations have acquired delegated powers over most aspects of administration of membership and assets. Arguably, Canada has finally adopted the system of indirect administration through Indigenous governments so enthusiastically promoted in 1922 by Lord Lugard in *The Dual Mandate*.

The Hawthorn, Belshaw, and Jamieson report on *The Indians of British Columbia* is an important document in our understanding of the background to the facts of the *Guerin* case.[154] It was completed in late 1955 and submitted to the minister of citizenship and immigration, then responsible for the Department of Indian Affairs. We may note in passing the irony of placing Canada's Indigenous peoples under the minister of immigration but it reflects the view that Indigenous peoples, like immigrants, were not true Canadians and needed to be made so. Leslie describes the scope of the report: "The Hawthorn team's research was a monumental undertaking comprising 34 chapters and 1024 pages of data dealing with all aspects of B.C. Indian community life: history; demographics; ethnic relations; natural resources; occupations; fishing, lumbering and agricultural economies; capital and credit; crime and punishment; liquor, housing; social welfare; band council government; family life; education; and government administration."[155] We will note below some key observations and recommendations from the report on the administration of Indian affairs. Before doing so, it should be pointed out that the report was commissioned by the department and the authors were clearly sensitive to the need to take a diplomatic approach towards their clients. However, it was still received cautiously by the department, which resisted publication. It did not lead to any immediate changes.[156] For our purposes, its chief value is the light it casts on Indian administration in British Columbia at the time the Shaughnessy lease was signed. Although not published until 1958, internal copies were circulated for review and comment and it would have been known to those officials involved in the events leading to the lease.[157]

The Hawthorn, Belshaw, and Jamieson report was critical of the policy of direct administration that was "by far the most common in the Province" and of the associated paternalism. Direct administration did nothing to develop initiative and responsibility. Local leadership should be not only recognized but brought into being where it was lacking.[158] The report described the meeting procedures of band councils, noting the limited facilities and the fact that meetings were usually convened by the Indian agent and in his presence. He prepared the agenda and the minutes. The Indian agent did not often approach councils to obtain views on matters of policy.[159] In a passage that has direct implications for the events that led to the Shaughnessy lease and the "manipulation" of the Musqueam reserve, the report declares:

> We have been astonished to find that ... all business of a financial kind is transacted through the superintendent's office, and that officials of the band council seldom come face to face with representatives of the groups with whom they have business. This is one of the most revealing lacks in the administration of Indian Affairs, since it documents with clarity our contention that the focus of administrative action is not the education of the Indian, except in a narrow formal sense, but the manipulation of his property.[160]

Also, "on every major issue, it is the superintendent and his staff who obtain the data, who sign the contracts, who see to it that the band makes no mistakes."[161]

The report made unfavourable comparisons between Indian administration in British Columbia and colonial administration elsewhere. In recommending that a band council's decisions should be acceptable unless on review the minister found reason to object to them, the report added that "this last principle is well established in British colonial policy ... in which a native local authority usually considers its by-laws valid unless specific review action is taken against them. We believe that the Indians of British Columbia should have no reason to consider themselves behind-hand in this regard."[162] The policy of direct rule followed in British Columbia, rather than the indirect rule that was applicable, as we have seen, in Africa and parts of Asia for many decades, was inefficient:

> It is also true that in many parts of the world, such as Africa and India, controlling administrative staffs no larger and often smaller than those in the British Columbia agencies, have carried out more positive and more educative policies for population units that are as great as, and sometimes much larger, than the Indian population of all the agencies in British Columbia, combined. They have been able to do this by delegating responsibility to the local population.[163]

The authors recorded their impression "that the superintendent, like the old-style colonial administrator, is required to know too much about too much."[164]

Echoing the general complaint made decades earlier about colonial administrators in the British Empire, they described the Indian agent as "a Jack-of-all-trades who gains his knowledge from day-to-day experience ... In view of the very special tasks demanded of it, the Indian Affairs Branch depends too much on general experience and too little on training to develop the necessary qualities in its officers."[165] The report concluded with recommendations for training based on "the experience of service training which has been developed in other countries (particularly Britain and Australia) to meet similar problems."[166] Specifically, it recommended training based on the Devonshire Courses that, as we have seen, were introduced for the British Colonial Service in 1946.

THE INDIAN AGENT

It was the Indian agent (sometimes called the Indian superintendent) who was the point of contact for residents of the reserve.[167] As Jarvis Brownlie noted in her study of Indian agents in Ontario in the 1930s, "all contact with Indian Affairs was to pass through the agent and he alone would take care of any issue that arose on the reserve ... The effect of this practice was to entrench Indian agents as power brokers between the department and its 'wards.'"[168] They were not simply passive instruments of central power but could play their own considerable part.[169]

The Indian agent had extensive power over the lives and property of band members, whose independence was correspondingly diminished. That power came formally from the *Indian Act*, which is a federal statute. "In matters of schooling, management of band monies, reserve lands, wills and estates, local by-laws, community improvements, matters of health and welfare, the Department and especially the Superintendent, were the guiding and controlling powers."[170] Underlying this bureaucratic structure and regulation was the belief that Indigenous people were incapable of managing their own affairs. They therefore had to be subjected to what was essentially a colonial system of government, and reserves became "a series of internal colonies."[171] As Rolf Knight observes, the department was "cast in a strongly colonial mould."[172] The Indian agent was, in effect, the Canadian form of the archetypal district officer who ruled Indigenous peoples throughout the British Empire prior to the formation of the Modern Colonial Service following the Second World War. Having set up the system, however, the federal government failed to adequately fund or staff it. Witnesses from the department complained at the *Guerin* trial of insufficient funds to discharge their responsibilities, and officials were often insufficiently qualified and trained.

One role played by the Indian agent that is especially relevant to our consideration of the *Guerin* case was that of intermediary between various types of Indian and non-Indian interests. As pointed out by Vic Satzewich and Linda Mahood, "the nature of 'white' interests revolved mainly around gaining access to Indian land and other natural resources, labour power and souls. These interests were articulated and pursued in a variety of ways and depended on the nature of the communities Superintendents lived and worked in."[173] Brownlie notes that "leasing lands for various purposes tended to be the prerogative of the department. Typically, department officials insisted on negotiating contracts for leases, timber, permits, woodcutting contracts and other such matters, rather than letting First Nations people handle these themselves."[174] An example from the Musqueam was the role of the Indian agent in negotiating leases and the sale of timber from the reserve. The intermediary role even went so far that local tradesmen would send their bills to the department for payment on behalf of band members from band funds.[175] As discussed above, Indian agents and the department often put the interests of non-Indians before those of their "wards."

Indian agents also had a role in the Indigenous community that went beyond their formal powers. Kew states:

> Musqueam people, as did all registered Indians in some degree, came to depend upon the Superintendent for [services under the *Indian Act*] and this dependence extended beyond the sphere of normal business matters and into the inter-personal and even domestic affairs. Complaints about misbehaviour of neighbours' children, visitors who had outstayed their welcome, family discord and so on, were at times taken to the Superintendent. He in turn sometimes took action – issuing orders for non-members to leave the reserve, delivering horticultural lectures or whatever the case and circumstances required. The Indian Superintendent was, within the social system of the village, a figure of authority, a step above that of chief and council.[176]

It is little wonder that some Indian agents let this power go to their heads or became paternalistic. One of them is quoted as writing that "behind all the seeming indifference of the Indians for the officials of the Department, I am glad to say that in their heart, they know the Department is watching with a fatherly eye to their care and protection."[177]

Another wrote in 1935 of his experiences using the classic language of colonial biological racism that might have come straight out of Joseph Conrad's *Heart of Darkness,* complete with reference to Kipling's White Man's Burden:

Possibly another reason may be given why the Indians are increasing, and why their physique is improving, but the reason does not reflect creditably on the white people. It is owing to the infusion of white blood that these results are occurring. A very large percentage of the Indians to-day are not of pure Indian blood, but have a large admixture of white blood, and, as one can imagine, it is not the better class of white men who have thus degraded themselves by intermingling with the Indian women, so that the result morally is not so great as the result physically. However, it will hasten the time when the Indians as such will be no more, but will be absorbed into the white race, and will help to carry the burden that so far has been borne by the white man for his benefit.[178]

In his view, the question of "Indian title" was of recent origin and "originally was not brought up by the Indians themselves, but by the white people who expected to gain financially or achieve notoriety, and the feelings of the Indians were stirred up until they fancied that the Government of British Columbia had stolen their lands, their rights, and their privileges ... selfishness was at the bottom of the whole movement."[179] One power that he had as an Indian agent was that of a magistrate, and he used this power to enforce legislation banning the potlatch.[180]

Sometimes Indian agents went beyond paternalism and became petty dictators, especially if they were opposed. Brownlie calls the whole system "a government-sponsored tyranny" and "a primary source of oppression for aboriginal people."[181] She explains that "agents had many ways to control band councils if they so wished – by deposing individual members, by delaying relief payments, by refusing loan requests, and so on. The agent's range of powers enabled him to exact petty sorts of revenge on those who crossed him."[182] Dyck observes: "The powers held by an agent made him a formidable opponent: direct and unambiguous opposition by reserve residents could trigger unfavourable forms of retaliation."[183] At Musqueam, as on other reserves, it made sense to be on good terms with the Indian agent.[184]

Administration of Indian affairs became a goal in itself, and the primary goal of preparing "Indians" to be assimilated was overlooked. There was a failure to develop specific assimilation policies, especially after the retirement of Duncan Campbell Scott in 1932. It was left to the schools to do whatever was necessary. Brownlie discusses this issue in some detail.[185] She concludes: "Ultimately, what becomes clear is that many officials seemed to have abandoned the hope of achieving assimilation in the near future, although they still had to pay lip service to the policy."[186] There was, of course, a fundamental conflict between the interests of Indian agents and other department officials preparing Indians for assimilation while also preserving their own jobs. This conflict also existed for officials in the Colonial Service as they prepared Indigenous peoples for independence, but with the difference that independence became inevitable as the Indigenous peoples demanded it. In contrast, the Indigenous peoples of Canada did not, generally speaking, support the policy of assimilation and had no prospect of independence.

Indian agents often lacked the qualifications and experience required for the proper exercise of such extensive powers. This lack of qualifications was recognized by Alan Fry in his depressing semi-autobiographical novel about an Indian agent based on his own experiences in British Columbia in the 1960s. The interview process for employment did not require much by way of experience: "He had expected more penetration into what was after all a fearfully limited experience of the people themselves for someone now offering to make a life's work of solving their problems, but his brief association with a few individuals seemed in some ways to be sufficient."[187] Once employed, "he did worry at times about the extent to which he was making decisions in areas where more normally someone with professional qualifications ought to have been in charge." The professional people at regional office "were few in number and spread thin; for much of the work, they could not be available and it was often a case of make your own decision or do without."[188] Brownlie noted that, during the 1950s, there were few formal qualifications for Indian agents and those hired were simply expected to be familiar with the office procedures and filing system of the Indian Affairs Branch.[189] There were "no special programs and no employees trained in long-range economic development. In fact, apart from a few engineers and surveyors, the department's staff had little training for their work."[190] Some department officials were woefully underqualified to adequately represent the interests of those for whom they were responsible. As noted by Rolf Knight, "while [the Indian agents] were often patronizing, arbitrary, and autocratic, their main failing was that they were ineffectual in protecting Indian interests."[191] They fell far short of the ideal described by Merivale of "officers of the higher grade and highest importance" able to take the initiative. Too often, they and their wards were at a serious disadvantage in dealing with better-qualified and experienced businessmen who knew how to look after their own interests.

With the extensive powers granted to the Indian agent came a corresponding lack of power on the part of band councils and a lack of respect for them.[192] Brownlie observes that "Indian agents could exercise authority over meetings of band councils in important ways. It was their role to call council meetings, act as the chair, and express their own views in deliberations. They were excluded only from the voting process."[193] They could also urge headquarters to veto band council decisions they disapproved of. The Indian agent in Fry's novel observes: "Band councils were often a farce. They were frequently elected in indifference, knowing little and caring less what their responsibilities might be. They went through the formalities of their work under [the Indian agent's] persuasion while he carried out all the substance of it."[194] This attitude is criticized by John Steckley in his book on Indian agents: "He was right about the indifference, but not for the right reasons ... The lack of interest in band councils and their representatives was due largely because the substance of leadership had been taken away from them decades before, and had been handed over to Indian agents."[195]

In summary, this chapter has sought to give the context of the *Guerin* case in colonial theory, policy, and administration, including "Indian policy" in Canada. The signing of the Shaughnessy lease in January 1958, which continues to have such a negative impact on the Musqueam, was the direct result of the history of the British Empire not just in Canada but around the world. The imperial legacy was very evident on the day the lease was signed. It was reflected, in particular, in the administration in Canada of Indian affairs and reserve lands that saw "Indians" as child-like wards whose lives and lands had to be managed by often unqualified colonial administrators until they could be assimilated into Canadian society. It was also reflected in the priority given to the interests of the local settler population and especially the powerful and well connected. We shall now narrow our focus a little and, in the next chapter, turn our attention to the Musqueam, their land, the Shaughnessy golf club, the Indian agent who "negotiated" the lease, and the Musqueam Chief whose actions led to the litigation.

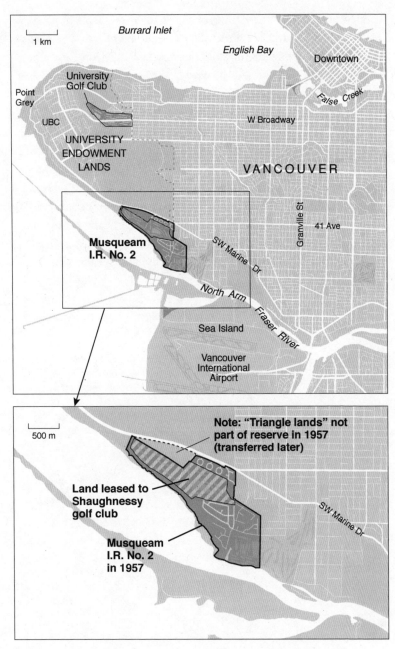

Musqueam reserve and land leased to Shaughnessy golf club

2

The Musqueam and Their Land

THE MUSQUEAM FORM PART of the Central Coast Salish people and are the descendants of the original inhabitants of the Vancouver area of British Columbia.[1] They are named after the river grass that grew in the area. As evidenced by belongings and ancestral burials found in various parts of the city, their presence in the area goes back thousands of years. Such archaeological evidence shows that the present Musqueam village has been occupied for over three thousand years.[2] The main reserve, Musqueam Indian Reserve No. 2, is the site of their main winter village and was the reserve involved in the *Guerin* case. In the words of Justice Brian Dickson, the reserve "was created out of the ancient tribal territory of the Musqueam Band."[3] It is strategically located on the Pacific coast at the entrance to the North Arm of the Fraser River. Musqueam territory extended over much of what is now the Metro Vancouver region.

The Coast Salish depended on the sea and the rivers and the land for their survival. The sea and rivers were the source of fish, sea mammals, and shellfish. The land supported game and provided roots, leaves, shoots, bulbs, and berry crops, as well as bark and reeds used for clothing. It provided the wood used for large plank houses in which extended families lived communally and which made up the winter villages, as well for the canoes made out of dug-out and steam-shaped logs. Susan Roy describes the area before colonization:

This was a rich coastal forest and river geography, an integrated physical, temporal, and spiritual landscape, full of natural and supernatural creatures and punctuated with named places and significant sites. People had lived in a spiritually animated and sometimes dangerous world – a place in which networks of kin with economic and ceremonial obligations extended throughout the region.[4]

Spring and summer were periods of great activity as successive migrations of salmon were fished, game was hunted, and various root and berry crops were gathered. During these seasons, there was intensive use of the economic hinterland beyond the winter villages located on the coast. During the winter months, many families would live together in the plank houses that made up the winter village. Many important ceremonies or "dances" were held at this time of the year. There were exchanges of food and wealth such as blankets and ornaments with other groups, especially those related by common ancestry or marriage.[5] The size of the Musqueam population before contact with Europeans is not known, but it was substantial.[6] The diary of the explorer Simon Fraser in 1808 describes houses that likely could have accommodated several hundred people.[7] Anthropologist Homer Barnett was told by Musqueam members in the 1930s that there had once been three adjacent villages. The largest, Male, was a continuous shed building, five hundred yards long and made up of many segments.[8] As will be seen, that population fell dramatically post-contact.

The extent of sharing and equality among different hunter-gatherer (including predominantly fishing) peoples has been much debated by anthropologists and archaeologists.[9] The existence of social classes and private ownership among the peoples of the Pacific Northwest has also been contested.[10] Part of the difficulty lies in using English terminology and associated concepts to describe Indigenous social and economic relations and differences in understanding as to what constitutes "equality." The Pacific Northwest groups are often used as prime examples of inequality and exceptions to the rule of egalitarianism found in hunter-gatherer societies,[11] but this may ignore significant differences among the groups.[12] In the case of the Coast Salish, including the Musqueam, the situation appears to be that they were essentially egalitarian classless societies in economic but not in social status terms.

Some inequalities existed and "transegalitarian" may be a more appropriate term, suggesting a movement towards greater inequality.[13] There was a relatively small underclass and an even smaller group of captives from other groups (often referred to as "slaves" but not slaves in the sense of the European slave trade).[14] There were no clans, and the community that lived in the winter village was made up of extended families linked by common ancestry through both the male and female lines or by marriage.

Wayne Suttles, a leading anthropologist of the Coast Salish, used the image of an inverted pear to describe the social groupings.[15] The bulk of the population belonged to the main group (the "good people"), from which headmen or leaders of various sorts emerged on various occasions. There was no centralized political authority, no "superior chief" prior to contact with Europeans.[16] The leaders or headmen were an impermanent set of adult males representing their family members and usually possessing more wealth (which grew following contact and which they were expected to redistribute if it was tangible in nature) and prestige than the average person. This wealth and prestige usually arose as the result of practical skill, knowledge of rituals and powers conferred by spirits, or hereditary rights. There were no clear divisions or ranks within this main group, and the differences in wealth were relatively small compared with other forms of society.[17]

A much smaller number of people belonged to an underclass (the "worthless people" or "people without history") upon which the main group imposed its will and that it treated with contempt. Suttles includes illegitimate people, orphans, and "black sheep," as well as refugees, tramps, and freed slaves among this group. It is likely to have included those who were unwilling to work or who were considered anti-social. It has been suggested that the group may have included the descendants of the offspring of slaves and non-slave fathers and of orphans resulting from the smallpox epidemic introduced by Europeans, which suddenly grew in numbers.[18] They were not a class in the usual sense but more of a shunned group or underclass. Movement from this group into the main group was probably difficult but not impossible. A still smaller group of captives or "slaves" lived with their masters, who were always of the main group.

The essential rule governing access to the resources of the area was that all members of the community had a right of access. Barnett observed that "as far as making a living was concerned ... all village members were, for the most part, free to range as they pleased so long as they did not interfere with others. This was particularly true of fishing sites."[19] Among the Coast Salish generally, some extended families had priority rights to access certain resources such as deer, duck, and fish nets (but not fish dams) and sealing rocks. Barnett noted that his Musqueam informant did not remember any family hunting and gathering-land rights. Even if such rights existed, the holder of the rights was expected to give permission to others to use the site, for "although in certain instances title to the places and instruments of exploitation might nominally be vested in him, he was more of a trustee of communal property than a dictatorial owner of it."[20] References to "private ownership" of such resources must be seen in this light: "manager" is a better description than "owner."[21]

In contrast to land and resources, there was private ownership of personal property such as canoes and blankets. There were also exclusive rights to intangibles, such as the right to sing a certain song or perform a certain dance, which are sometimes included as "private property." The extended family normally lived in one large house partitioned by planks that were owned by the nuclear family that had built and lived in that section of it. Subterranean houses were sometimes used as an accessory shelter.

The history of contact between the Indigenous peoples of the Northwest Coast and Europeans can be summarized in the following progression: first the Europeans came to trade, then they came in search of gold, and finally they came to settle.[22] The Musqueam and other Coast Salish had some direct contact with Europeans from the time of the Spanish and British expeditions from 1791 onward.[23] The first Europeans to see the Musqueam were probably those on board the *Santa Saturnina* with Jose Maria Narvaez, who saw Musqueam villages from his vessel in 1791. The journal of a Spanish expedition in 1792 states that "when they came alongside, they at once gave us a salmon without showing that they looked for any return or taking any interest in the beads we gave them."[24] In the same year, Captain George Vancouver had a similar welcome in Burrard Inlet: "Here we were met by about fifty Indians, in their canoes, who conducted themselves with the greatest decorum and civility, presenting us with several fish ... These good people finding as we were inclined to make some return for their hospitality, shewed much understanding in preferring iron to copper."[25] In contrast to these friendly encounters, Simon Fraser's diary for 1808 records a hostile reception from Musqueam "howling like so many wolves, and brandishing their war clubs."[26] His records were used by David Thompson to draw the earliest known map of the region in 1814, which included the location of "Musquiam Village."

After these early expeditions, because of the relative scarcity of the sea otter, which was the basis of the fur trade, the Coast Salish were left very much to themselves until the middle decades of the 1800s.[27] In 1848, the Hudson's Bay Company moved its headquarters from Fort Vancouver on the Columbia River to Victoria. The colonial era began in 1849 with the establishment of the colony of Vancouver Island. In 1858, the colony of British Columbia was declared on the mainland, and in 1866 the two colonies were united. Increasing contact with Europeans brought great changes to the way of life that had existed for thousands of years.[28] The Indigenous peoples were decimated by diseases against which they had no immunity.[29]

THE MUSQUEAM RESERVE

Government action undermined the traditional Indigenous society but did nothing to replace it with a new viable way of life. Central to this action were measures to dispossess the traditional owners by allocation of most of the land to settlers through the process of pre-emption.[30] Pre-emption enabled settlers to claim land, settle on it, and then purchase it at a low rate after having cleared and improved it. The policy of pre-emption in British Columbia differed from the policy followed in most of the country, which consisted of entering into treaties with Indigenous groups, such as the Numbered Treaties on the Prairies, to obtain surrenders of their interests to the Crown before the land was allocated to settlers. The "fundamental understanding – the *Grundnorm* of settlement in Canada," according to Justice Beverley McLachlin in the Supreme Court of Canada's *Van der Peet* decision, was that "the Crown took subject to existing aboriginal interests in the lands," and those interests "were to be removed only by solemn treaty."[31] This understanding went back to the Royal Proclamation of 1763. McLachlin noted that the fundamental principles held sway on Vancouver Island prior to the union with Canada in 1871, and that Governor James Douglas had negotiated a few treaties there before the policy of negotiating treaties was abandoned. His requests for funding were rebuffed by both the colonial legislature in Victoria and the Imperial Government in London. Each agreed that treaties ought to be negotiated, but the former said that the latter should pay and the latter said it was the responsibility of the former. Apart from the extension into the province of Treaty 8, treaty making came to an end for over a century.

In the words of historian Allan Greer, "dispossession is really the essence of colonization."[32] Dispossession in British Columbia began in the 1850s and continued through the rest of the century. "Physical violence, the imperial state, colonial culture and self-interest all underlay it."[33] Dispossession led to the confinement of Indigenous groups to the winter villages, which became reserves.[34] Eventually, the province had about 1,500 small reserves, slightly over a third of 1 percent of the land area.[35] As we saw earlier, such villages satisfied the needs of the population only during the colder months, when economic activity was at a low and people survived on what had been accumulated during the preceding spring and summer. To sustain their economy and culture, they needed access to the rest of their traditional territory, their economic hinterland, to obtain food and supplies to be preserved and stored for the winter months. The winter villages alone were never a viable economic base.

In 1874, the Indigenous peoples of the Fraser River complained in vain to government officials of their treatment by the settlers and the

British Columbia colonial and provincial governments, which represented the interests of the settlers:

> We have been at a loss to understand the views of the Local Government of British Columbia in curtailing our land as much as to leave, in many instances, but few acres of land per family.
>
> Our hearts have been wounded by the arbitrary way the Local Government of British Columbia have dealt with us in locating and dividing our Reserves ...
>
> For many years we have been complaining of the land left us being too small. We have laid our complaints before Government officials nearest to us; they sent us to some others; so we had no redress up to the present and we have felt like men trampled on, and are commencing to believe that the aim of the white man is to exterminate us as soon as they can, although we have always been quiet, obedient, kind and friendly to the whites.
>
> Discouragement and depression have come upon our peoples.[36]

In the case of the Musqueam, the pressure from neighbouring settlers was felt soon after land was surveyed by the Royal Engineers and pre-emption in the area began in 1859.[37] The land east of the main winter village along the Fraser River was pre-empted and sold during the next decade. By the late 1860s, there were over twenty pre-emptions.[38] The land to the north was leased as timberlands to the Hastings Saw Mill Company. Fitzgerald McCleery, who came from County Down in Ireland and settled in 1862 near the village, recorded in his diary that the settlers could go to the winter dances being held there.[39] Once the settlers acquired land by pre-emption, they took steps to have the Indigenous people removed. For example, one William Smith wrote in 1875 to the Indian superintendent to complain about "Indians" trespassing on his lands at the mouth of the Fraser:

> There is some Indians settled on my Preemption and I can not get them off also their dogs are a bothering my Stock and Stealing everything they can get hold of and the Indians are tramping down my dykes and

when I say any thing to them they call me all the mean names they can think of so I think it is time they was moved off with strick [*sic*] orders not to come back on the place any more.[40]

The Musqueam were now considered trespassers on land that they had occupied for thousands of years, land that they had never given up and for which they had received no compensation. The customary law of the Coast Salish relating to ownership of land had to give way to imported English common law concepts.[41] The law of the settlers was now used to support them in their conflict with Indigenous peoples over the land. Cole Harris notes that

> suddenly there were survey lines and fences on the land. There were owners who could identify trespassers, tell them to get off, and know their commands would be backed, if need be, by the full apparatus of the state. Native people suddenly found that they could not go where they had; there were too many watchmen (property owners) backed by too much power.[42]

Although the early colonial administration under Douglas recognized Aboriginal title and entered into a few treaties to acquire land by agreement on Vancouver Island, later administrations simply denied its existence.[43] (It may be noted that the policy of the US government was to enter into treaties with the Coast Salish tribes south of the border.)

No treaties were made with the Musqueam, but they were increasingly confined to the area of their main winter village at the mouth of the Fraser by the pressure of European settlement. The current Musqueam Indian Reserve No. 2 was informally established by the colonial government before the colony entered Confederation in 1871. It was first laid out in 1864 on the orders of Magistrate Brew acting under Douglas's instructions and was to consist of "all the land N. of a line drawn from the Black Stump to the River," but it was not surveyed.[44]

Douglas's earlier, more liberal policies were soon replaced by a harsher policy leading to reduction in the size of reserves. On 28 August 1867, Colonial Commissioner of Lands Joseph Trutch criticized the policy of Douglas and the size of reserves and expressed his opinion that "these reserves should, in almost every case, be very materially reduced."[45] In 1870, the Musqueam reserve was surveyed and reduced in size by another magistrate, and a settler named Bates took over the cut-off lands, making it difficult to restore those lands when the reserve was later formally established in 1879.[46]

After Confederation in 1867, the federal government had jurisdiction over "Indians, and the Lands reserved for the Indians."[47] When British Columbia joined Canada in 1871, the federal government expressly assumed "the charge of the Indians and the trusteeship and management of the lands reserved for their use and benefit."[48] To discharge this responsibility, it attempted to obtain land from the province to be set aside for reserves. For its part, the province took every opportunity to frustrate the process (which was not completed until 1938) and to perpetuate the small size of British Columbia reserves, which were considerably smaller than those in the rest of the country.

During the early discussions between the federal and provincial governments, the former suggested that reserves should be allocated on the basis of eighty acres per family, but the province countered with an offer of only ten.[49] Dr. Israel Wood Powell, the Indian superintendent appointed by the federal government, managed to get a short-lived agreement on twenty acres.[50] In 1874, he completed a survey of the Musqueam reserve and wrote to the chief commissioner of lands and works for the province:

Indian Office, Victoria, July 31st, 1874

SIR, – I have the honour to inform you that the survey of the Musqueam Indian Reserve, lately undertaken by my orders, is now finished, and the quantity of land is insufficient to give each head of a family an allotment of 20 acres. The actual number of families in the

tribe is 70, consequently 1,400 acres of land will be required to make
up the full quantity. Of this the present reserve contains 314 acres, 114
of which is quite useless.

I now make application for 1,197 acres, and request that the surveyor
may be allowed to choose the land in the immediate vicinity, or as near
the present reserve as may be found practicable ...

I have, & (Signed) I.W. Powell.[51]

On the basis of 20 acres for each family and a population of seventy
families, the Musqueam should have received 1,400 acres for their
reserve. In reply to his request for this amount of land, Powell received
a letter from the provincial commissioner of lands and works raising a
number of petty questions clearly designed to obstruct the survey.[52]
The provincial government then changed its position and restricted
the grant of 20 acres for each family to new reserves only. In light of
this reversal of the provincial position, Powell wrote another letter:

Department of Indian Affairs, Victoria, August 15th, 1874.

SIR, – Pursuant to the arrangement of granting 20 acres of land to
every head of an Indian family in British Columbia, I had the honour
of applying to the Honourable Chief Commissioner of Lands and Works
for land to make up deficiency in the present reserves of Musqueam
and Tsowassen ...

As many of the present reserves do not contain *five* acres of land to
each head of a family, the injustice with which the Indians having such
reserves would be treated in case they were not extended, and the serious
complications which would at once be consequent upon such treatment
are so great, that I sincerely trust the interpretation seemingly conveyed
in the Honourable Commissioner's letter, of confining the grant to new
reserves, is not that intended by the Government in lieu of *all* reserves
containing 20 acres to every head of a native family ...

I have &., (Signed) I.W. Powell.[53]

Despite Powell's efforts and the clear wording of the Order-in-Council
making the allotment, the provincial government insisted that its

agreement to allocate twenty acres for each family did not apply to existing reserves such as those for the Musqueam and Tsawwassen.[54] Even Margaret Ormsby, the historian mentioned in Chapter 1 for her negative views of Indigenous peoples, was critical of the province's reserve policy, describing it as "a disgrace" and "completely unenlightened."[55]

The federal government reacted critically but took no effective action. The minister of the interior saw the position as "little short of a mockery" of the claims of the "Indians."[56] He said the policies of the former colonial and the provincial governments "fall far short of the estimate entertained by the Dominion Government of the reasonable claims of the Indians" and expressed concern that discontent among them might possibly lead "in the near future [to] an Indian War with all its horrors."[57] In the face of the provincial government's determined opposition, however, the federal government effectively abdicated its recently assumed "charge of the Indians and the trusteeship and management of the lands reserved for their use and benefit" under the *British Columbia Terms of Union*. It did little to support Powell in his efforts to get more land for existing reserves. In 1875, it agreed with a provincial proposal (made at the suggestion of the missionary William Duncan) to abandon any specific acreage per family.[58] As one writer noted:

> To all appearance the Province had now taken a position that could only lead to a complete deadlock with the Dominion. Most surprisingly, however, the Dominion Government for reasons that seem incomprehensible expressed its readiness to adopt the proposals of the Province. It seems difficult to understand how the Dominion Government so readily yielded this point. It is indeed anomalous that at the very moment when the Canadian Government was in a strong position, when the Imperial Government was roused to action and determined to give every support to the Dominion Government, that the latter should have surrendered almost every point for which it had long contended.[59]

Under the *Terms of Union*, the federal government could have referred the dispute to the secretary of state for the colonies, who had indicated support for its position, but it did not do so. It took no effective action at all to protect the land base of the Indigenous peoples of the province. Within five years of expressly assuming an obligation for BC Indians and lands reserved for them under the *Terms of Union*, the federal government had shown that it did not have the will to oppose the hunger of the local non-Indigenous population for Indigenous land. Its obligation to the Indigenous peoples meant little in practice. So far as the Musqueam were concerned, this was a foretaste of what was to come.

A joint reserve commission consisting of three members was set up to look at each situation individually.[60] The commission began its work at Musqueam in 1876. In 1879, a reserve of just under four hundred acres was formally allocated to the band, including about sixty acres across the Fraser River from the Main Village where Vancouver International Airport is now located.[61] This was just under six acres per family, less than one-third of what Powell had requested. It was also less than what the band had understood it was to receive. In 1913, a Musqueam Chief complained to another joint commission, the McKenna-McBride Royal Commission, which finally settled the boundaries of reserves in the province, that "since these posts were put down by Sir James Douglas for the Indians, the land has been lessened twice. The Indians were not notified or consulted ... and after that three persons came here to Musqueam and told some of the Indians that the posts ... meant nothing at all."[62]

From the beginning, the reserve provided an insufficient land base. Some effort was made by band members to become farmers, and in 1877 twenty-two acres were under cultivation.[63] Such cultivation had never been part of the Coast Salish way of life, however, and band members were not equipped to support themselves by agriculture. In any event, the size and quality of land that the band was permitted to retain as a reserve were simply inadequate for farming. In 1913, the McKenna-McBride Commission determined that it consisted of 416.82 acres, or 4.11 acres per capita.[64] The average for the New Westminster Agency, of which it formed a part, was 16.30 acres per capita.[65] In fact, the Musqueam reserve had the lowest per capita acreage in the agency and almost in the entire province, and almost certainly among the lowest in Canada since British Columbia reserves were considerably smaller than those in the rest of the country.[66] This was based, in part, on the thinking that Indigenous peoples on the Pacific coast did not need such a large land base since they were fishing peoples.[67]

The quality of much of the land was also poor. The McKenna-McBride Commission effectively confirmed Powell's assessment that 114 acres was "quite useless,"[68] noting that "approximately one-third" was "low and marshy – good if drained."[69] Other traditional Musqueam villages, located in what is now much of Greater Vancouver, were not given reserve status and so received no protection at all from the demands of settlers. They soon ceased to exist.[70]

Indigenous people were also denied the opportunity to acquire interests in land under the newly introduced legal system based on European legal concepts.[71] Governor Douglas had seen the pre-emption of land by Indigenous people as the means by which they could integrate into settler society. This changed, however, when Joseph Trutch was appointed chief commissioner of lands and works for British Columbia in 1864.[72] He thought that Indigenous people were not capable of using land in a productive way and should be given only minimal amounts. Under his administration, much of the land set aside by Douglas for reserve lands was taken away. It was his opinion that to allow Indigenous people to pre-empt land would create an "embarrassing precedent."[73] In 1866, a land ordinance prevented "Indians" from pre-empting land without the written permission of the governor.[74]

By 1875, there was only one case of an Indigenous person pre-empting land under this provision.[75] In that year, Attorney General George Walkem noted that the provision "is now in force, but the practice of giving these permissions has been discontinued, lest it should interfere with the Dominion policy of concentrating the Indians upon Reserves."[76] Meanwhile, Trutch was implementing measures that would increase the amount of land that a settler could acquire. An 1865 land ordinance allowed each settler to purchase up to 480 acres in addition to a pre-emption of 160 acres.[77] At the same time, Trutch expected an "Indian" family to subsist on 20 acres of reserve land, and even less in the case of bands such as the Musqueam.

Parallel to their exclusion from the new system of land ownership was the exclusion of Indigenous peoples from the new system of ownership and regulation of the fishery that was so important to them. The story of this exclusion has been told by Douglas Harris. He summarizes the situation at the end of the nineteenth century:

> Native fishing was confined on all sides. Indians could still fish for food, but that right was increasingly circumscribed [by regulations], and when they attempted to join the industrial commercial fishery they were thwarted by discriminatory licence restrictions. Licences were allocated to white settlers to encourage settlement. A few Natives received licences, but most were told they could either fish for food or work for the canneries as employees. In the early years, cannery work was plentiful, but increasingly it went to immigrants.[78]

In the case of the Musqueam, their traditional control of the fishery was lost in the 1880s. In 1892, the Musqueam Chief complained to the British Columbia Fishery Commission about his people's inability to get licences and about overfishing by white fishers, who threatened the salmon. He said that during his lifetime, the runs had declined dramatically to the point where they were dangerously low. Only ten licences had been issued to the band.[79] In 1913, another Musqueam Chief complained to a Royal Commission that they had to buy licences from both the provincial and federal governments: "When I want to go fishing, the two parties are also holding on to each end of my boat ... I know that I own the water ... I don't want to have a licence to do anything. When I want to catch fish for my living I don't want to be interfered with at all."[80]

Writing in 1955, just three years before the lease over the main Musqueam reserve was signed by the Department of Indian Affairs with the Shaughnessy Heights Golf Club (now the Shaughnessy Golf and Country Club), Homer Barnett gave this gloomy summary of the state of the Coast Salish:

At present the old culture is practically dead. There has been very little displacement of the Indian population, and reserves for the most part comprise the traditional village locations; but the material basis, the technology, and the spirit of the aboriginal economy are gone. The plentiful sources of salmon, once so easy to exploit, have gradually receded to the north under the onslaught of cannery operations, and most of the young men go in summer to Rivers Inlet north of the Salish territory for the commercial fishing season. Others, with their families make annual excursions to the hop fields of Washington. Dugout canoes are still made, but "gas boats" and row boats have taken the field. Houses are built in the modern manner. The ancient handicrafts are modified or have ceased altogether to be practiced. Wood and fiber working, formerly foundation crafts, have given way to wage labor and ready-made products. I have seen (during six summer months) three men making canoes, one woman making baskets, and three others carding wool for sweaters. Utensils and furnishings are of white manufacture and pattern, and today it is not easy to find even wooden spoons of a simple type.[81]

One sign of the changes was the disassembly in that year of the last surviving above-ground mortuary houses at Musqueam and the burial of about a hundred rewrapped ancestral remains in the community cemetery.[82]

It is not surprising that many of the Musqueam's traditional forms of economic activity and social organization broke down under the pressures created by the city growing next to them. Dr. Michael Kew, another eminent authority on the Coast Salish, gave evidence for the band at the trial of the *Guerin* case based on his doctoral thesis and subsequent work with the band.[83] As he pointed out, "within the span of a single lifetime the timbered peninsula of Point Grey gave way to modern city suburb."[84] The Musqueam could no longer go into their traditional economic hinterland to hunt, obtain wood and other materials, or gather berries and other crops. Their access to fish was severely limited both by the declining salmon stocks noted by Barnett and by legislation in existence since 1888 that permitted "Indian" people to catch fish for their own consumption but prohibited them from selling or trading fish without a commercial fishing licence, as noted above.[85] Such restrictions undermined the rationale for allocating such small reserves based on the ability to fish. The Musqueam obtained some seasonal part-time jobs at the bottom end of the new economy as unskilled or semi-skilled workers in fishing and the canneries and saw mills.[86] As a result, Kew commented, "the Musqueam population of 1960 contained within its ranks virtually no persons with work experience or skills in such fields as commerce, accounting or business management. It was not prepared by experience for developments to come."[87]

Most of the people at Musqueam were converted to the Catholic religion, but, perhaps because of the relatively small population, the Musqueam village never attracted sufficient attention from the missionaries to have a permanent mission or school such as those established by missionary William Duncan in Port Simpson for the Tsimpsean.[88] There were no schools on the reserve and relatively few children attended schools off the reserve because of lack of space, resistance from parents to sending children away from the family to attend residential schools, and the non-acceptance of "Indian" children by local public schools. Provincial and Vancouver city schools were not generally open to Indigenous people until 1958, and by 1955 only two or three Musqueam youths had graduated from high school and only one had acquired a little university experience.[89] Part of the difficulty was that the public schools required payment for "Indian" children, which the Department of Indian Affairs refused to provide for off-reserve schooling.

Those who attended public schools faced discrimination. Writing in 1965, Wilson Duff referred to "the social barrier which still discourages many of these people from entering fully into the social life of the communities which surround them ... Any impartial observer can see that some degree of prejudice still operates to segregate the Indians socially."[90] An editorial in the Vancouver *Province* of 5 June 1941 gives some indication of the prevailing attitude towards "Indian" settlements such as the Musqueam village as obstacles to progress to be relocated to some unstated destination:

Kids on bikes on Musqueam reserve, 1958. *Left to right:* Roberta Louis, Basil Point, and Harvey Louis. *Vancouver Public Library, VPL 1994*

The reserves, by the very fact of their existence, stand in the way of orderly community development. Town-planning cannot be made completely effective while these areas lie athwart the path of development.

It is not good for the Indians to be domiciled on undeveloped tracts in the centre or on the outskirts of a big city and it is certainly not good for the City to have them there.[91]

This overt racism may have been toned down somewhat by the time of the Shaughnessy lease in January 1958. However, the marriage of a Musqueam woman to a non-Indian was considered newsworthy enough for the 6 May 1958 issue of the *Vancouver Sun* to have a headline declaring "Indian Marries White Man." The wife's parents complained of her difficulty in finding employment and the extent of the prejudice against "Indian" people.

Although limiting their advancement in the wider society, this prejudice, together with the strength and resolve of the community, may have helped keep alive some aspects of Musqueam culture, such as the winter ceremonies ("spirit dancing") and gift-exchange cere-monies ("potlatching"), which continue to be part of Coast Salish and Musqueam life.[92] According to Bruce Miller, "Coast Salish culture was permeated with the spiritual concerns and their universe full of spirit beings who intersected with humans. From the moment of birth until long past death, Coast Salish practices are informed by this perspec-tive."[93] In their 1955 study *The Indians of British Columbia,* Harry Hawthorn, Cyril Belshaw, and Stuart Jamieson note that "considerable cultural conservatism" existed at Musqueam.[94] As Kew comments, "in the face of segregation and social restriction encountered in the larger community, [cultural practices] provided Musqueams of all ages with rewarding and compensating roles and statuses. They have been essential means of providing positive self-images for Musqueams."[95] He points out the contrast that still exists in the lives of many Musqueam people: "Musqueams may pass through the automatically opened doors of a bustling, air conditioned supermarket and within five minutes step into a dirt floored, fire-lit structure where painted Indians are singing and dancing under the instructions of guardian spirit powers."[96]

These ceremonies exist as an unbroken link to a culture that still survives despite, or perhaps in part because of, the pressures of the larger community to which the Musqueam also belong. Legal restrictions on spirit dancing and potlatches ended only in 1951 but, despite the restrictions, some Musqueam "kept the fires burning" and continued their practice. They were very influential in the revival that took place in the 1950s and 1960s.

INDIAN AGENT EARL ANFIELD

The traditional system of governance broke down in the face of pressures from the wider society and was replaced by government imposed by the colonial and federal authorities. A commissioner for Indian Affairs was the senior officer for Indian Affairs in the province of British Columbia; at the time of the negotiations for the lease with the Shaughnessy golf club in 1957–58, William Arneil filled this position.[97] Reporting to him were the Indian superintendents (commonly referred to as Indian agents) in charge of the twenty agencies existing at the time. The Musqueam came under the Vancouver Agency; Frank (Earl) Anfield was Indian superintendent for that agency for most of the negotiations, although he was promoted to assistant Indian commissioner towards the end of the negotiations and replaced by Jack Letcher. (Anfield subsequently became the Indian commissioner for British Columbia and died in 1961.) Department officials in Ottawa also had some involvement in the negotiations. At the *Guerin* trial, Anfield's assistant, William Grant, recalled that Anfield would often say that, from the womb to the tomb, the "Indians" were his responsibility. He described Anfield as very paternalistic. The combination of power, paternalism, and poor qualifications for his responsibilities was to have dramatic and still continuing consequences for band members.

Anfield appears to have been concerned for the interests of Indigenous people under his care. In his autobiography, Chief Simon Baker describes how, as senior teacher of the St. George's Residential School in Lytton, British Columbia, in the 1920s, Anfield took an interest in what he did and always seemed to help and encourage him. He was invited to be a pallbearer at Anfield's funeral.[98] Anfield was principal of the Anglican residential school for "Indian" children in Alert Bay from 1927 to 1943 and was sometimes referred to as the "Reverend Anfield," although he does not seem to have been an ordained minister. In his history of residential schools, J.R. Miller singles him out as an exceptional example of a principal who respected the Indigenous community, understood its language, and treated children under his care considerately.[99] He "showed sensitivity to Native culture and enjoyed

Frank (Earl) Anfield poses with staff members on front lawn of St. Michael's
Residential School in Alert Bay, BC, in the 1940s. Anfield is standing on the
far left. *Courtesy of General Synod Archives, Anglican Church of Canada,
P7538-1142*

good relations with the Kwagiulth community."[100] During his time as
principal, two totem poles were erected on either side of the school's
driveway. They had been refurbished during "manual labour classes."
Anfield saw such work as "fundamental needs in any programme that
aims, as does that of this school, at the emancipation of the Indian
children to Christian citizenship in this great country, and of which
they form no unimportant part."[101] In her account of her experiences
as a teacher/nurse on Village Island, the winter home of the
Mamalilikulla people, Hughina Hughes describes how Anfield announced the prizewinners at the celebrations in Alert Bay to mark
the coronation of King George VI in 1936 and helped install a radio.
She also says that he was instrumental in helping James Sewid become
the first Native fish captain to buy his boat. She comments: "Principal
of the residential school, Earl Anfield, was widely respected by both
his peers and annual enrolment of 150–200 students."[102]

As principal in 1934, Anfield was enthusiastic about residential schools and the foundation they laid for "good homes, clean villages, home arts and crafts, industry and interest."[103] Later, after he had become an Indian agent, he expressed some doubts, suggesting that "it is quite possible that the Residential school system as we have it to-day should be abolished."[104] As Indian agent, he maintained his interest in education. While at Bella Coola, he requested a travelling library service from the department, explaining that "the reading material of most villages consists almost entirely of the type of magazines found on the coastal steamship newsstands, generally speaking a far from appetizing type of reading material for Indians." A well-chosen travelling library "would deter young members of the coastal villages from reading such morally inappropriate material."[105] He was later involved in the first initiative to integrate Indigenous students into the provincially run school. This was examined in some detail by Helen Raptis, who concluded that it had less to do with integration policy than with a multitude of local and regional factors, including inability to find a teacher for the Indian school.[106] A local newspaper quoted Anfield in 1961 as saying that education would be the "salvation" of Indian people in the province as it constituted "the key to what lies ahead. You need trained leaders with educated minds."[107]

Judged by the standards of the day, he seems to have been relatively enlightened and progressive. In their history of the laws against spirit dancing and the potlatch, Douglas Cole and Ira Chaikin refer to an incident where he chanced upon an illegal dance at a cannery.[108] Based on his own account, he seems to have handled the matter in good humour and, instead of prosecuting the offenders, made them take up a collection for the Red Cross. He then "chased them all off to their boats" and admonished them to get a permit for dances off the reserve next time. Compared with some of the agents described by Cole and Chaikin, he was relatively moderate in his approach to enforcing the laws. In 1934, he wrote a letter to the *Vancouver Sun* in which he defended customary marriages, in which "divorce was practically unknown and unfaithfulness rare."[109] On the other hand, he was criticized in the

Truth and Reconciliation Commission's report on residential schools for writing a letter to former students in 1943 encouraging them not to participate in potlatches, implying that such ceremonies would make them "slaves to debt, to unsatisfactory marriages, to poverty, poor health and bad living conditions."[110] Victor Satzewich also cites him as an example of blaming the victim, for saying that "the Indian problem is basically psychological and the removal by uplift of a racial inferiority complex must be paramount in any approach to Indian rehabilitation."[111]

When Anfield was transferred to the Vancouver Agency in 1954 and became responsible for the Musqueam, he demonstrated some vision and regard for the interests and views of the band members. Before he became involved in the negotiations for the Shaughnessy lease, he clearly recognized the department's lack of expertise and the value of the lands to the members of the band:

> It seems to me that the real requirement here is the services of an expert estate planner with courage and vision and whose interest and concern would be as much the future of the Musqueam Indians as the revenue use of the lands unrequired [*sic*] by these Indians. It is essential that any new village be a model community. The present or any Agency staff set up could not possibly manage a project like this, and some very realistic and immediate plans must be formulated to bring about the stated wish of these Musqueam people, the fullest possible use and development for their benefit, of what is undoubtedly the most potentially valuable 400 acres in metropolitan Vancouver today.[112]

The band never did receive the benefit of the "expert estate planner with courage and vision" concerned with their future. Anfield himself obviously lacked that expertise.

Anfield knew the standard that he should have met in his handling of the Shaughnessy lease, including the active involvement of the band members. In 1946, he told the minister of Indian Affairs, "too much has been done for the Indian; not enough with him."[113] Just a year before the surrender of the lands by the Musqueam, at a conference for Indian agents, he stressed the need to go over every step of a surrender meeting with the band council: "If you can get the Council to fully understand what is going on, that is a great help. You are dealing with a mass of people who have no education at all." He told his fellow Indian agents to let the Indians "feel that you are not there to push something across or through." He added: "For the benefit of the newer men among us, you can't go wrong in taking your Councils into your confidence. Let them know what is going on. There has been a tremendous change in thinking on the part of the Indians – don't be afraid to take them into your confidence." He encouraged them to "spend a lot of time in the development of Council conversations – that's part of the education process."[114] He played an active role in discussions at the conference about the many aspects of Indian administration, about which he was clearly knowledgeable. He appears to have been respected by his peers, to whom he gave his advice and on behalf of whom he ended the conference by proposing a vote of thanks to William Arneil, the Indian commissioner, who had chaired it.

Because he was not alive at the time of the trial to explain his actions, one can only speculate on why no expert advice was obtained to protect the future of the Musqueam and why he failed to follow his own advice and took the action he did in connection with the Shaughnessy lease. As found by the trial judge, he failed to disclose all the terms of the proposed lease to the government appraiser, leading to an opinion that the appraiser testified at the trial he would not have given had he known all the facts, and then "over-stated" the opinion to the band.[115] Anfield gave information on the appraised value to the representatives of the club during the negotiations that he did not disclose to the band and ignored expressions of interest from other potential lessees of the land that would have generated a higher return for the band.[116] He told William Guerin, a member of the band council at the time, that if the band was "unreasonable" in its demands, the department could lease the land without a surrender (something that would have violated a requirement of law going back to the Royal Proclamation of 1763[117]) and for any sum it wished.[118] Once he obtained the surrender of the lands from the band members, he did not return to them to explain that some of the terms of the proposed lease were not the terms approved by the band.[119] In particular, he did not tell them of the proposed restrictions on rent increases, although he knew they were strongly opposed to any restrictions.[120]

During the Penner Inquiry into self-government, which heard evidence on the Musqueam litigation in 1983 prior to the decision of the Supreme Court of Canada, one Member of Parliament expressed his view that "the Indian people have been cheated" and "somebody must have had his fingers in the till."[121] However, the trial judge ruled out fraud in the sense of deceit, dishonesty, or moral turpitude.[122] One is therefore left wondering whether this was a case of a mid-level civil servant being unknowingly affected by the rare opportunity to meet and rub shoulders with the wealthy and powerful representatives of an exclusive club.[123] Another possibility is that he was acutely aware that an officer of the club had contacted a deputy minister to lobby on the club's behalf. The deputy minister then told his subordinates to report on the progress of the negotiations.[124] Subconsciously, Anfield might have been anxious that his actions would be closely and critically scrutinized if the club were to complain to his superiors about his conduct towards them. His subsequent rise to Indian commissioner for British Columbia might have been thwarted.

There are many questions surrounding Earl Anfield. How did someone born in England end up in the remote Indigenous community of Alert Bay in British Columbia in the 1930s as principal of St. Michael's Residential School? Why did he leave the school to become a bureaucrat in the Department of Indian Affairs? Why did he behave as he did during the Shaughnessy lease negotiations? Although lacking relevant professional training and experience, he was clearly not a stupid man and saw the need for an "expert estate planner with courage and vision" who would keep in mind the future of the Musqueam. He would likely have been aware that the 1955 Hawthorn, Belshaw, and Jamieson report on *The Indians of British Columbia* criticized the lack of training of department officials. (The report was referenced at the 1956 conference of Indian agents in which he participated.) As we have seen, he acknowledged that "the present or any Agency staff set up could not possibly manage ... the fullest possible use and development ... of what is undoubtedly the most potentially valuable 400 acres in metropolitan Vancouver today." Why did he assist in throwing away so much of this value for the next seventy-five years to the benefit of the club? He must have realized that a lease with rents at below market value could never be in the best interests of the Musqueam. He would or should have been aware of a report completed at the same time as the appraisal showing the value of neighbouring lands at more than double the value ascribed to the proposed leased lands.[125] Why did he depart from his expressed concern for those subject to his control and actively assist in obtaining a lease that was so clearly unfavourable to them?

Was it again the conflict between theory and practice? The theory was easy: the federal government had to protect the interests of the band. The practice was very different. As we have seen, in the face of the determined opposition of the settler society represented by the provincial government, the federal government failed to take any effective steps to protect the interests of the band by obtaining a reserve of adequate size for its needs. The result was that the Musqueam reserve was less than a third of the twenty acres per family sought by the federal government in 1874, which was already much smaller than the eighty acres per family that it had originally sought and that was the standard in other provinces. In the same way, Anfield's recommendation for vision and courage in the planning of the Musqueam lands was abandoned. The federal government again failed to protect the interests of the band and leased over a third of the reserve at much lower than market rent. The value of the limited land base of the Musqueam became substantially less. They will live with the consequences of that breach of fiduciary duty until the lease ends in 2033.

The other side of the coin to the extensive powers of the department was the powerlessness and dependency of the band. The Indian agent directed the affairs of the band council.[126] He called and chaired meetings and drew up the agenda. He arranged for the minutes to be typed. It was not until 1963 that council meetings were held without the presence of the Indian agent.[127] The band did not have a band office at the time of the Shaughnessy lease negotiations.[128] It lacked private telephones and typewriters. As noted above, members also lacked formal education and relevant experience. Legally, their powers were limited by the *Indian Act* and the need to obtain department approval to do any number of things, particularly for any use of reserve lands. They had no say in the passage of this legislation. Except in very specific cases, such as war veterans, "Indians" were denied a vote in federal elections until 1960. The first federal election in which they were eligible to vote was that of 1962. They had no political power and were unavoidably dependent on the department, which had long ago taken control over their limited assets, including the reserve.

The result of this bureaucratic control of band assets was that band members had little or no opportunity to manage their own affairs, including use of their reserve. The Indian agent handled all important land and other business transactions on the reserve, including leases and contracts. Writing of long-term contracts negotiated by the Indian agent for the use of Musqueam reserve lands by Chinese market gardeners, Alexandra Pleshakov comments that "Musqueam people were all but eliminated from the process of administering these contracts."[129] Reflecting this lack of power as wards of the government, when the Shaughnessy lease – involving 162 acres of the best land out of a total of 416 acres, one-third of the whole reserve, for seventy-five years – was made on 22 January 1958 between Her Majesty The Queen in right of Canada and the Shaughnessy Heights Golf Club, the band was not even a party to the agreement. During negotiations with the experienced negotiators of the golf club, the band was represented by bureaucrats from the Department of Indian Affairs, primarily by an ex-residential school principal without any business experience. No legal advice was made available to either the bureaucrats or the band.

THE GOLF CLUB

On the other side of the negotiating table, representing the Shaughnessy Heights Golf Club, were vice presidents of the leading corporations of the province who had contacts at the highest levels of the federal

Shaughnessy Heights Golf Club, 1960. *Vancouver Archives*

government. They also had available to them the services of a leading law firm, which prepared the lease that was ultimately signed without any significant amendments. It was a complete mismatch, with predictable results.

The Shaughnessy Heights Golf Club was, and is, an exclusive golf club with sizeable admission and green fees. Membership is subject to approval and a strict dress code is enforced. The club has always been *the* club for Vancouver's business elite, where discreet dealmaking is every bit as important as hitting golf balls around the manicured fairways, which are kept always green and lush. It was the Vancouver symbol of the clubs of the Empire. As noted by Jan Morris, "the gentleman's club, its membership strictly limited, had been exported from London to every part of the Empire ... Wherever they were, though, whatever their pretensions, the clubs of the Empire had this in common: that they made the Right People feel more important, and made the Wrong People feel small."[130]

In 1956, the club was located in the Shaughnessy area of Vancouver, which is an area of larger homes and generally upper-income people. Shaughnessy Heights was part of a large amount of land acquired by the Canadian Pacific Railway (CPR) in return for bringing the railway to Vancouver and so providing a link to the rest of the country, which was the condition of British Columbia's agreement to join Confederation. The Shaughnessy area was designed as Vancouver's "Nob Hill" and the golf club was part of that design to provide recreation for the wealthy residents.[131] By the 1950s, however, the surrounding area had become too developed for the golf club to remain and the CPR wanted to develop its lands. Witnesses at the trial spoke of golf balls having to be retrieved from neighbouring Oak Street, which had become a busy road. The club was told by the CPR that its lease would not be renewed beyond the end of 1960. It was also told that the CPR was willing to sell the lands, but the club decided not to purchase them and began looking for an alternative location. According to the club's website, the members determined that the $2 million price tag was too high.[132] The Musqueam reserve became the object of their interest. Reserve land was generally cheap, and their negotiators were to make Musqueam lands incredibly cheap.

It was clear from the witnesses for the club at the trial that they were very concerned at the prospect of having to relocate to the suburbs.[133] They did not want members to have to drive from their homes on the west side of Vancouver to the suburbs for their recreation.[134] This was the fate of another nearby prestigious golf club, the Quilchena Golf and Country Club, which was forced to move to the suburb of Richmond in 1956. That club also leased its lands from the CPR, and the railway wanted to sell those lands. There was an attempt to get the city of Vancouver to purchase those lands as a replacement for the eventual loss of the municipally owned Exhibition Golf Club, which closed in 1953. According to the website of the BC Golf House Society, "the City Planner squashed this idea by arguing the potential land assessment the City would receive on this development far out weighed the value the City would receive if the land remained a golf course."[135] Clearly, the City Planner was well aware that a golf course was not the highest and best use of lands on Vancouver's west side in the 1950s. Another major concern of the Shaughnessy members was the restriction on having alcohol on the reserve, and it successfully lobbied senior officials for a waiver. In short, the terms of the lease were tailored to their concerns and their "own selfish point of view, what we felt we could pay, taking a long gamble."[136]

It was also clear from that evidence that the Shaughnessy golf club's negotiators were concerned that membership fees should not rise and so the rent had to be kept low.[137] For this reason, they successfully negotiated a restriction on any increase in rent of 15 percent for the second rent period of fifteen years, and a restriction for all rent periods that the lands were to be valued on the fiction that they were uncleared and unimproved and with limited use as a golf and country club rather than market rents based on highest and best use, which all the experts at trial accepted as residential. This would have resulted in significantly higher rents. The club also insisted on a provision that would give it a unilateral right to terminate the seventy-five-year lease on six months' notice, and another provision that permitted it to remove the improvements at the end of the lease.

A CLASH OF CULTURES AND POWER

The band members had little involvement in the lease negotiations, which were primarily conducted between the department and the club. There is, however, one poignant account of the clash of cultures in the evidence of Ed Sparrow, who was Chief at the time of the negotiations. He describes a social meeting he attended with Councillor Gertrude Guerin at the old clubhouse, a "tea party" in his words.[138] A witness from the golf club said that it was a chance "to discuss and be on social terms with our very delightful friends from the Reserve."[139] It was clearly an awkward meeting, with representatives of the impoverished, powerless band sitting at the table opposite the representatives of the affluent, powerful business elite at their exclusive club. The imposing clubhouse, where the meeting took place, stood as a silent monument to that affluence and power – a world away from the poverty of the nearby reserve.

At the trial, Chief Sparrow described the meeting:

We ... we were just talking across the table, chatting away, nothing in particular. Then we had our tea and cookies, whatever we had there, and we got finished. Anfield gathered up his papers and left the room. He left the room first before – before the Golf Club people did, and left us sitting there. They finally all went in to a lounge room and left us sitting there ... they left Gertie Guerin and I sitting right at the table, and there was one man waiting at the door. And then Gertie says, "Well, I guess that's all. I guess we're not wanted," and we walked off. They didn't even bid us good-bye or anything ... They went to see [Anfield] in the room.[140]

Gertrude Guerin's son, Delbert, recalled how she arrived home furious at the treatment she and Chief Sparrow suffered at the hands of their prospective tenants. She never forgot the insult. She felt humiliated both as an individual and as a representative of her people, a people who had always placed great value on personal dignity and hospitality. This incident brings to mind the scene from the heyday of the Raj in E.M. Forster's novel *A Passage to India,* in which members of the European club invite Indian guests to a party on the lawn but then keep strictly to themselves. As the visitor from England exclaims: "Fancy inviting guests and not treating them properly!"[141]

DELBERT GUERIN

Delbert Guerin was nineteen at the time of the fateful meeting on 6 October 1957 when Anfield held the pencils of adult band members as they voted on the surrender of a large part of the reserve for lease to the golf club.[142] He was too young to vote. Also, as his wife, Fran, testified at the trial, those under twenty-one were expelled from the meeting by Anfield when they started to object to his use of a proposed Christmas distribution of monies as a reason to vote in favour.[143] This occurred even though some of them, like Fran, had been specifically asked to attend by the Elders, who did not understand English too well and wanted them to explain what was involved in the surrender. Delbert stood outside the band hall where the meeting was held and was joined by the others when they were told to leave. They all looked in through the window as their future and that of the next two generations of band members was decided.

Delbert Guerin was born in 1938 and passed away in 2014. He was impressive in appearance, with a physique reflecting a lifetime as a longshoreman on the Vancouver docks. A serious accident in 1975 left him with a permanent limp, but he rarely missed a day's work. He usually worked the evening or graveyard shift to have time to devote to band business. He also continued to fish over the years. The work ethic was drilled into him as a child. From the age of ten, he delivered newspapers on the Squamish reserve, where he was raised by his parents because of the housing shortage at Musqueam until the family moved back to Musqueam in 1953. It was delivering papers that introduced him to some of the issues confronting Indigenous people.

On his newspaper route lived Andrew Paull, a member of the Squamish Nation and an outstanding Indigenous leader. In 1916, he had been a founder of the Allied Tribes of British Columbia, one of the earliest intertribal Indigenous organizations in the country, which he led with the Reverend Peter Kelly, a member of the Haida Nation.[144] The Musqueam and other Coast Salish nations were members of the Allied Tribes. The organization kept alive the issue of unextinguished Aboriginal title in the province, especially in opposition to the recommendations of the McKenna-McBride Commission to "finally" settle the question of reserves in British Columbia.

In 1927, Andrew Paull and Peter Kelly had appeared before a hearing of joint committees of the Senate and the House of Commons to present a petition for judicial determination of the validity of their claim.[145] Unfortunately, the hearing turned out to be little more than a farce as committee members blatantly displayed their prejudice and constantly insulted the counsel for the Allied Tribes, Arthur O'Meara.[146] Their report rejected the request for a judicial determination and they took it upon themselves to deny the existence of Aboriginal title in the province of British Columbia.[147] Although legislation was then passed to make it almost impossible for litigation to be undertaken, strong views about Aboriginal title remained into the 1950s, when the Shaughnessy lease was signed.[148]

Andrew Paull took a liking to the young newspaper boy and they had many conversations together about Paull's experiences before the joint committees and in advancing the interests of his people.[149] He talked of some of the things he had done and what he thought should be done to help Indigenous people. In this way, Delbert was introduced to some of the issues that would be so important to him for the rest of his life.

Delbert had direct experience of the power and influence of the Indian agent during the 1940s and 1950s. He recalled climbing up, at the age of eight or so, into the attic of the Squamish meeting hall with other children in order to witness a meeting attended by the Indian agent, Mr. F.J.C. Ball, Anfield's predecessor. The Chief and council were dressed up in their best suits and greeted him with such formality that Delbert thought Ball was the king.

As a day student at St. Paul's Indian Residential School from grade one to grade eight, he also had first-hand experience of an educational system that had such a devastating effect on generations of Indigenous people.[150] After the family moved back to the Musqueam reserve in 1953, Delbert enrolled in a public school off the reserve, one of the first Indigenous children to be accepted in the provincial system. He had mixed feelings about the move from the Indian residential school to the public school system, where he and other Musqueam students now faced racist taunts and became involved in fights with some of the non-Indigenous children as a result. Some of the Musqueam children could not take the abuse and dropped out, but he "fought it right through" and graduated from high school. He had some hopes of going on to further education, but financial pressures forced him to find employment.

One of his earliest jobs as a twenty-year-old in 1958 was helping in the development of the reserve for the Shaughnessy golf course. He worked on the drainage system as a manual labourer and drove a backhoe, and his abilities won praise from his supervisors. They became upset, however, and could not understand when he gave notice so he could help his uncle fish during the fishing season at River's Inlet. They did not understand that Delbert and his people had fished in this way for centuries and that, however incompatible it was with the wage economy, he could not let his uncle down – again, a clash of cultures.

Delbert was not critical of band members who voted in favour of surrendering land for the lease. He understood the pressure exerted by Anfield, who had overstated the appraiser's opinion and failed to disclose to them all the terms of the proposed lease. He also noted the financial pressure they were experiencing. They were living in Third World conditions on the doorstep of Canada's third largest city, lacking facilities that Vancouver residents took for granted.[151] Sometimes this had tragic consequences. On Christmas Eve 1957, just a few weeks before the Shaughnessy lease was signed, six children died in a fire caused by an overheated wood heater at a house on the reserve. One of the chief factors in the loss of life was the failure of the Department of Indian Affairs to provide long-requested fire hydrants. The coroner noted that the cause of death could be ascribed to a form of neglect.[152] There were no public buildings except a church and the band hall (which was actually a house converted into a band hall when the owner died without heirs and the property came into the hands of the band). The houses had no running water, no electricity, and no municipal services.

One Musqueam member, Rose Sparrow, who was married to Ed Sparrow, the Chief at the time of the Shaughnessy lease negotiations, described the situation before running water came to the reserve:

The city was far up, up there and we had no money to put in water pipes or anything to get water. Our drinking water was up in the spring up here, the spring water up here. In the early evening the boys would go pack water. Send the boys and they'd go up there, get pails of water. We'd always send them up there. That's for cooking and drinking. But for washing clothes we used to come to this well over here. We didn't want to drink that in the well that was up there. We just use that for washing.[153]

The road to the reserve was a rough dirt road full of potholes. An article in the *Vancouver Sun* in 1962 reported on the squalid living conditions:

Women wash their clothes in buckets after carrying water from outside taps near their homes. The wooden houses are badly in need of repair ... There's no drainage system, few families have bathroom facilities and the only toilets are ramshackle shacks behind the houses ... Many are elevated basementless homes and you have to literally climb, or walk along narrow strips of plank to reach the front door ... Jack Campbell, a 53-year old carpenter who lives in a 10-year old home at the west end of the reserve overlooking the Fraser River, said: "It floods here every year to a depth of about three feet and there's a swamp under the house but we can't do anything about it. There's no plumbing inside, the place needs fixing up, there's no drainage and the toilet is over there."[154]

Overcrowding was also a problem, with about thirty tumbledown houses for the 250 or so band members.

There was no economic activity on the reserve, no sources of employment.[155] Only a handful of men had regular employment, so band members had very limited income: an average annual income of about $2,000 for each wage earner.[156] The only band income was the low rent received from Chinese market gardeners who had informal, or "buckshee," leases. Social assistance was under a hundred dollars a month. Members received some income from seasonal fishing and did a variety of things to make ends meet. As a child, Delbert went beachcombing to find things that he could sell. He recalled Musqueam women going down to Washington state to pick berries and, when the season was over, returning to go to Sardis and Sumas to pick hops. Many were involved in weaving baskets. Some members would go to the neighbouring University Endowment Lands to strip bark off the barberry bushes, dry it, and then chop it into chips, which were sold to traditional

Chinese herbal shops in Chinatown. Delbert recalled even his blind grandfather picking berries and hanging fishing nets.

Because of the poverty of the people on the reserve, the temptation was overwhelming when Anfield pressured them into leasing land to the Shaughnessy Heights Golf Club, especially when he told them that, after the low rent during the first rent period, they could "hit" the club for a large increase.[157] Band members were not informed about restrictions on rent increases written into the lease (which they had strongly opposed), or that the club had the right to remove the improvements at the end of the lease. Delbert remembered the shock of his mother and the other members of the band council at the time of the negotiations, Ed Sparrow and Bill Guerin, when he finally obtained the lease and told them what it contained. They were totally aghast and said that they had no idea that the lease contained such terms. It was the discovery of the lease by Delbert Guerin in 1970 that led to the commencement of the *Guerin* case in 1975.[158]

Delbert was first elected to the band council in 1964. One of his early responsibilities was to represent the band in negotiations with the City of Vancouver over tax sharing and the provision of municipal services to the reserve. The British Columbia Court of Appeal held in the *Chow Chee* case that the city could tax the non-Indian lessees of reserve lands.[159] The band had objected to such taxation as an infringement on its own taxation jurisdiction (such jurisdiction was not expressly recognized until amendments were made to the *Indian Act* in 1987), and said in its submission to the city that "if there is any tax to be paid by the said Chinese it should come to the Musqueam Reserve for the benefit of the Reserve." Despite the band's objection, the city continued to be the exclusive beneficiary of the reserve tax base for some time, so that in 1967, in the case of the Shaughnessy golf club, the city was collecting property taxes of $33,000 while the rent paid to the band was only $29,000. The city was deriving a greater benefit from these reserve lands than the band!

Starting in 1966, the band commenced a campaign to get a share of the taxes received from the reserve. Its claim was rejected by the mayor with the racist comment "They're trying to scalp me."[160] Delbert and other members of the band's negotiating committee met with Harry Rankin, a socialist opposition member of city council who supported their claim and Indigenous peoples generally.[161] Rankin suggested that the band consider a protest demonstration outside City Hall, and Delbert and the others agreed. Delbert remembered the protest as an exciting example of the protest politics of the sixties. He was especially encouraged by the support received from passing motorists.

Faced with this pressure, the city changed its position and the band obtained an agreement in 1970 under which it would finally receive some basic municipal services in return for a payment of about a quarter of what the city had initially demanded.[162] The neophyte politician had learned the importance of determination and persistence. It would serve him, the Musqueam, and other Indigenous people well as he turned his attention from negotiations with the city to the upcoming negotiations with the Shaughnessy golf club on the amount of rent to be paid in the second rent period of the Shaughnessy lease. We shall follow these developments in Chapter 4.

3

The Government as Fiduciary

CHAPTER 2 PROVIDED BACKGROUND to the facts of the *Guerin* case. As discussed in the next two chapters, the case established that there is a fiduciary relationship between the Crown (the federal and provincial governments) and Indigenous peoples. This means that there is a duty to act in their best interests. This chapter discusses the broader historical and legal background to this relationship. Its focus is on the history and development of the fiduciary concept, especially as it has been applied to Indigenous peoples in Canada and other parts of the British Empire and internationally. It also gives a brief overview of fiduciary duties.

The idea that governments are fiduciaries and so have duties to act in the best interests of their citizens has a long history. It can be traced back in Western philosophy and politics to Greek and Roman times and the writings of Plato and Cicero. Around 400 BC, Plato's *Republic* described an ideal state.[1] Plato said that it should be ruled by guardians consisting of men and women, specially chosen for the task by senior guardians, who were to put the interests of other citizens above their own. They were to be educated in wisdom, courage, justice, and temperance, and trained in gymnastics to help prevent illness and weakness. Their duty was to defend the citizens and govern in the light of what they knew to be beautiful and good. They were to be the very best in the community and dedicated to defending other citizens. To prevent corruption, they were to live in common and not have any private wealth.

The idea of governments as fiduciaries continued through Western thought, in the writings of theorists of international law such as Hugo Grotius and political theorists such as Thomas Hobbes and John Locke.[2] Republican writers used it to criticize the monarchy and American revolutionaries to support their own views on democracy and the constitution. John Adams, one of the US Founding Fathers, wrote that "rulers are no more than attorneys, agents, and trustees for the people."[3] In 1783, in a debate on the governance of India, Edmund Burke, a father of modern conservatism, submitted to Parliament that rights and privileges derived from political power "are all in the strictest sense a trust."[4] The fiduciary concept was extended to office-holders that same year in a prosecution for fraud of an accountant in the Paymaster's Office. Lord Mansfield, the Chief Justice of England, ruled that the accused held "an office of trust and confidence concerning the public" and that a breach of this trust was a criminal offence.[5]

The concept of governments as fiduciaries is enjoying a resurgence in both international and domestic law.[6] It has been described as "a burgeoning field of legal scholarship" and "one of the most exciting developments in legal and political philosophy in recent years."[7] Sometimes, the fiduciary model is advanced metaphorically by analogy with the role of non-government fiduciaries such as private trustees and agents, and it is argued that governments have moral or political obligations but it is not intended that they are liable in law. Sometimes, it is argued that governments and government officials have, or should have, binding obligations as fiduciaries in law.

Evan Fox-Decent is a leading Canadian proponent of the government as fiduciary. He argues in his book *Sovereignty's Promise – The State as Fiduciary*:

> The state is a fiduciary of the people over whom it exercises power. As a fiduciary, the state owes its people a single but complex legal obligation, one which arises solely from the fiduciary character of its relationship

to the people. The state must govern its people in accordance with the demands of legality, which is to say, in accordance with the rule of law.[8]

Accordingly, state institutions "must exercise their powers on behalf of the legal subject and in accordance with the demands of legality, or, as Hobbes might put it, consistent with the demands of equity and the other laws of nature."[9] If they fail to do so, the state's legitimacy "comes into question, and so too does the obedience it can reasonably expect from its people."[10] To support his argument, Fox-Decent examines in some detail the fiduciary obligations owed to Indigenous peoples in Canada derived from the *Guerin* case. In his view, "the First Nations case is significant because it demonstrates that public and far-reaching fiduciary obligations are possible."[11] He acknowledges the "ongoing neglect of the fiduciary standing of public decision-makers" in other areas of the law but argues that this cannot be justified.[12]

In *Fiduciaries of Humanity,* Fox-Decent and Evan Criddle extend the argument of governments as fiduciaries to international law:

> This book takes up the idea that states serve as fiduciaries for their people and, collectively, for humanity at large. Indeed, we shall see that in many contexts states are fiduciaries of humanity generally, as well as discrete agents of the people within their territorial jurisdiction. As fiduciaries of humanity, states owe various context specific duties to foreign nationals, including, in some cases, extraterritorial foreign nationals.[13]

An important implication of their theory is that "the time has come to retire the traditional, but increasingly embattled, conception of state sovereignty as exclusive jurisdiction. In its place, we propose a new relational model that views sovereignty as emanating from a fiduciary relationship between states and the people subject to their jurisdiction."[14] They argue that "the relationship between a state and its people is distinctively fiduciary because it shares constitutive features common to all fiduciary relationships, including trust, discretionary power, and vulnerability."[15] Under the fiduciary model, "sovereignty serves people rather than states. Consequently, a state's claim to exercise sovereign authority is derived from, and wholly dependent upon, the satisfaction of its relational duties to the people subject to its legal powers."[16] The state-subject fiduciary relationship is a distinctive legal relationship. The state's authority to govern its people and represent them internationally is held in a fiduciary capacity for them. Accordingly, a state is obligated under international law to work towards the establishment of a regime of secure and equal freedom for its people (the purpose for which international law entrusts the state with sovereignty), and it must respect, protect, and fulfill human rights (its core substantive fiduciary duties) to qualify for the rights and privileges associated with sovereignty.[17] It should be noted that the authors do not claim that contemporary international law fully embraces the fiduciary model.

The concept of the colonial power being a parent, protector, guardian, tutor, or trustee of Indigenous people was frequently used in international law to justify colonialism around the world.[18] Historian John Darwin traces the concept in the British Empire to colonization of India in the late eighteenth century and contrasts it with the semi–self-government enjoyed by settlers in North America.[19] Another historian, Klaus Knorr, discusses it in the context of the Humanitarian movement of the time, which also led to the campaign against the slave trade and the missionary enterprise. He notes that "the idea of the Trusteeship over coloured people obviously was a powerful phenomenon in the thirties and forties of the nineteenth century."[20] In his poem *The White Man's Burden,* Kipling praised the imperial ideal of selfless service to ungrateful Indigenous peoples: "To seek another's profit / And work another's gain." Joseph Chamberlain, Colonial Secretary from 1895 to 1903 and an architect of imperial expansion, declared: "We develop new territory as Trustees for Civilisation, for the Commerce of the World."[21] The idea of trusteeship was reflected in colonial policies and, in 1940, one commentator claimed that "the governing principle behind all colonial administration is that of trusteeship."[22] In the final days of the Raj, as the British were arranging to leave India, the last governor, Lord Mountbatten, told Gandhi, "We are only trustees. We have come to make it over to you."[23] However, the concept had started to fall out of favour in some parts of the Empire. In a memorandum prepared for the British War Cabinet in 1944, it was noted that doubts had grown whether the term sufficiently recognized the increasing role played by some colonial peoples. "Trusteeship" had, therefore, been largely superseded by "partnership."[24]

The fiduciary concept was used by imperial powers to justify continuation of control over Indigenous peoples under Article 22 of the *Covenant of the League of Nations.*[25] It declared that the well-being and development of "peoples not yet able to stand by themselves under the strenuous conditions of the modern world ... form a sacred trust of civilization." It then continued: "The best method of giving practical effect to this principle is that the tutelage of such peoples should be entrusted to advanced nations who by reason of their resources, their experience or their geographical position can best undertake this responsibility, and who are willing to accept it, and that this tutelage should be exercised by them as Mandatories on behalf of the League."[26] The provision was used to justify the transfer of German colonies in Africa and the Pacific to Britain, Australia, and New Zealand. Jan Morris describes how the British Empire shrewdly used Article 22 and the trustee concept to extend its coverage of the globe:

> This concept served the Empire usefully. In theory the League of Nations retained supervisory rights over the territories: in effect the British ruled their Mandated acquisitions as parts of the Empire, administering them like any other Crown Colonies, and colouring them red, or at least red-hatched, on the map of the world.[27]

In a memorable expression that could be generally applied to the cynical use of fiduciary language to disguise colonialism, historian H.A.L. Fisher declared: "The crudity of conquest was draped in the veil of morality."[28] Article 22 was eagerly seized upon by Lord Lugard, former colonial governor and a leading theorist for British imperialism, to justify colonialism throughout the Empire, and not just for the mandated territories taken from Germany. He argued that it was a much better justification than "the naked deception of 'treaty-making,'" referring to the treaties signed with African chiefs "which were either not understood, or which the ruler had no power to make, and which rarely provided an adequate legal sanction for the powers assumed."[29] He much preferred the mandate system of the League of Nations to the "make-believe" of treaties:

> The civilised nations have at last recognised that while on the one hand the abounding wealth of the tropical regions of the earth must be developed and used for the benefit of mankind, on the other hand an obligation rests on the controlling Power not only to safeguard the material rights of the natives, but to promote their moral and educational progress.[30]

This "dual mandate" constituted "not only a pledge in respect of Mandate territories, but a model and an aspiration for the conduct of those already under the control of the signatory Powers."[31] In practice, all the talk of trusteeship and promotion of the progress of "the natives" was largely empty talk. Harold Laski wrote in 1938 that the idea of trusteeship was too flattering to the results obtained: "It is a word whose sound is too noble for the squalid results often obtained."[32] As historian B.R. Tomlinson concludes in the *Oxford History of the British Empire*, "British rule did not leave a substantial legacy of wealth, health or happiness to the majority" of their ex-colonial territories in Asia and Africa.[33]

The colonial concept of wardship extended to Canada. In 1868, Gilbert Sproat, an early settler in British Columbia, referred to "a wise and paternal action of the Crown" on behalf of the Indigenous peoples.[34] Joseph Trutch, the colonial official who was active in reducing the size of reserves in the province, wrote in 1870 that "the Indians have, in fact, been held to be the special wards of the Crown, and in the exercise of this guardianship" the government had set aside the reserves.[35] This reference to wards under the guardianship of the government was to be a standard way of describing the status of Indigenous peoples in Canada until at least 1969.[36]

In 1942, the Musqueam band council stated in a letter to the prime minister and the Department of Indian Affairs opposing the inclusion of the reserve within the city limits of Vancouver: "We are wards of the Dominion government ... The Department of Indian Affairs is our guardian and we rely upon them for protection, not the City of Vancouver."[37] During the hearings of the Special Committee of the House of Commons on Indian Self-Government held in 1983, one of the members told the Musqueam witnesses: "Certainly for years and years there was a presumption that the minister held a trust responsibility with respect to Indian people and Indian land, and even the government spoke that way. You see it in documentation, in speeches and whatever, that there is a trust."[38] Indeed, many statements were made that governments were trustees for Indigenous peoples in Canada and throughout the Empire/Commonwealth. What was not clear was whether any weight could be attached to these statements. One critic suggested that the use of trust or similar fiduciary language by colonial authorities was merely "a vague and decorative notion to which anyone can attach any meaning he pleases" so that it could be cynically used to hide exploitation.[39] Were the statements merely empty words or did they have legal significance? Were they enforceable in the courts?

THE HISTORICAL RELATIONSHIP

When the British first encountered Indigenous people on the east coast of North America, they found groups such as the Mi'kmaq and the Iroquois, organized in societies and occupying the land as their forefathers had for generations.[40] At the time, which lasted roughly from contact until the early nineteenth century, the British were mainly interested in trading for furs,[41] and they relied on the knowledge and capacity of the Indigenous people, who harvested the pelts. In the event of a conflict with their European competitors, particularly the French, the British wanted assistance from, or at least the neutrality of, the Indigenous peoples. It only made sense for them to enter into alliances to establish peaceful relations and encourage Indigenous peoples to place themselves under the protection of the British Crown.[42] As the fur trade gave way to settlement of European populations, the Crown placed itself between the settlers and the Indigenous peoples in order to protect the latter from exploitation.[43] No settler could take title to land directly from "Indians." Title had to be acquired from the Crown, but only if the Indigenous group was first prepared to surrender its Aboriginal title in the land to the Crown. Gradually, reserves were established. Legal title to reserve lands was held by the Crown for the benefit of the Indigenous people so there would be some protection from land-hungry settlers.[44]

The contemporary fiduciary relationship between the Crown and Indigenous peoples has its roots in this early history. As Chief Justice Brian Dickson (who gave the leading judgment in *Guerin*) explained in the subsequent decision of the Supreme Court of Canada in *Mitchell v Peguis Indian Band:*

> The recent case of *Guerin* took as its fundamental premise the "unique character both of the Indians' interest in land and *of their historical relationship with the Crown*" (at p. 387, emphasis added). That relationship began with pre-Confederation contact between the historic occupiers of North American lands (the aboriginal peoples) and the European colonizers (since 1763, "the Crown"), and it is this relationship between aboriginal peoples and the Crown that grounds the distinctive fiduciary obligation on the Crown.[45]

This "historical relationship" was explained by law professor Brian Slattery.[46] He noted that most Indigenous peoples were never conquered by the Crown. In a passage that has been quoted with approval by the Supreme Court of Canada,[47] he said:

> This general fiduciary duty has its origins in the Crown's historical commitment to protect native peoples from the inroads of British settlers, in return for a native undertaking to renounce the use of force to defend themselves, and to accept instead the protection of the Crown as its subjects. In offering its protection, the Crown was animated less by philanthropy or moral sentiment than by the need to establish peaceful relations with peoples whose friendship was a source of military and

economic advantage, and whose enmity was a threat to the security and prosperity of the colonies.[48]

Until the constitutional recognition of existing Aboriginal and treaty rights in section 35 of the *Constitution Act, 1982,* the most important legal protection for Indigenous peoples was found in the Royal Proclamation of 1763 issued by King George III.[49] This document prohibited private purchases of "Indian" lands, prevented colonial governments from issuing patents for unceded "Indian" lands, and required settlers to remove themselves from such lands. It referred to "the several Nations or Tribes of Indians, with whom We are connected, and *who live under Our Protection*" (emphasis added).

The Supreme Court of Canada in *Guerin* regarded the Royal Proclamation as operable in British Columbia.[50] The early colonial administration there initially pursued the same policy of making treaties with the Indigenous peoples as that followed in most of the rest of the country.[51] Subsequent administrations refused to follow this policy, which has led to claims of unextinguished Aboriginal title to much of the province.[52] Even in the absence of treaties, the settlement of the province was largely peaceful.[53] In short, the "historical relationship" between the Crown and Indigenous peoples existed in British Columbia as much as in the rest of the country: the Indigenous peoples allowed peaceful settlement and, in return, the Crown extended its protection to them.

FIDUCIARY OBLIGATIONS IN THE LAW

In his article "Demystifying the Fiduciary Mystique," Justice J.R. Maurice Gautreau wrote:

> The origin of the fiduciary concept is to be found in equity. The original fiduciary was the trustee and trusts being creatures of the Court of Chancery came under its exclusive jurisdiction. Because of the dependence and vulnerability that was involved in trust situations, equity imposed special duties on the trustee which were known as fiduciary

duties. These duties included such rules and obligations as: the trustee must act solely in the interests of the trust, he must avoid all conflict of interest and he is not to profit from the position entrusted.[54]

Over the years, courts recognized that other relationships involved similar elements of trust and vulnerability as those found in express trusts.[55] As a result, those relationships were also classified as fiduciary relationships, and similar fiduciary duties were imposed. Although fiduciary duties were originally exemplified by the obligations owed by a trustee to act in a selfless manner for the benefit of the beneficiary of the trust, trustees are now only one example of a fiduciary. There are many other examples, such as agents, company directors, partners, parents, and solicitors. What they have in common is that the law holds them to a high degree of loyalty and good faith in order to protect the beneficiary.

Justice Gérard La Forest, writing for the majority of the Supreme Court of Canada in *Hodgkinson v Simms*,[56] commented extensively on the rationale for the imposition of fiduciary obligations in certain relationships. He stated that the unique function of the fiduciary principle is that it "monitors the abuse of a loyalty reposed."[57] He also commented on the important social function of fiduciary principles:

> The desire to protect and reinforce the integrity of social institutions and enterprises is prevalent throughout fiduciary law. The reason for this desire is that the law has recognized the importance of instilling in our social institutions and enterprises some recognition that not all relationships are characterized by a dynamic of mutual autonomy, and that the marketplace cannot always set the rules. By instilling this kind of flexibility into our regulation of social institutions and enterprises, the law therefore helps to strengthen them.[58]

It was noted by Justice Ian Binnie in *R v Neil* that "fiduciary duties are often called into existence to protect relationships of importance to the public including, as here, solicitor and client. Disloyalty is destructive of that relationship."[59]

FIDUCIARY OBLIGATIONS AND INDIGENOUS PEOPLES: THE LAW PRIOR TO *GUERIN*

In 1975, the year in which the *Guerin* action was commenced, an article was published that considered the tendency of some of those concerned with the rights of Indigenous peoples "to claim that the rulers of these peoples stand in the position of trustees." Professor L.C. Green reviewed the American and Canadian case law on the trust obligation of the governments towards "Indian" peoples and then examined a trusteeship based upon treaties or international law. His conclusion was that "it is hardly possible to regard the relation between the Government and the Indians as one based on trusteeship, whether it be legal or political in character – unless, of course, the words ward and guardian and trust are to lack all meaning – legal, equitable or moral."[60] Although our brief review of the US law later in this chapter will suggest that Green was only partially correct in this conclusion, it cannot be said that he was incorrect in his statement that Canadian law did not recognize an enforceable trust obligation, or indeed any other type of fiduciary obligation, of the government towards Indigenous peoples. Prior to *Guerin,* there was no clear judicial authority in support of such an obligation, and the weight of authority denied its existence.

Legislation and other documents, however, indicated the existence of some type of trust. As with the references to fiduciary concepts in the imperial, international, and other Canadian contexts noted earlier, the critical legal issue was whether this "trust" was one that could be legally enforced or was simply political in nature. Early legislation affecting "Indians" often referred to the Crown being a trustee of their lands. For example, legislation enacted in 1849 for Crown lands in Upper Canada applied to such lands "whether the same be held in trust or in the nature of a trust for the use of the Indians or of any parties whomsoever."[61] In 1850, *An Act for the Better Protection of the Lands and Property of the Indians in Lower Canada* provided:

> That it shall be lawful for the Governor to appoint from time to time a Commissioner of Indian Lands for Lower Canada, in whom ... all

land or property in Lower Canada which are or shall be set apart or appropriated to or for the use of any Tribe or Body of Indians, shall be and are hereby vested, in trust for such Tribe or Body.[62]

Clause 13 of the 1871 *British Columbia Terms of Union* stated that "the charge of the Indians, and the trusteeship and management of the lands reserved for their use and benefit, shall be assumed by the Dominion Government."[63] The early *Indian Acts* contained similar provisions: section 4 of the 1876 act provided that "all reserves for Indians or for any band of Indians, or held in trust for their benefit, shall be deemed to be reserved and held for the same purposes as before the passing of this Act, but subject to its provision."[64] Other examples of trust wording can be found in the *Ontario Boundary Act* and its Quebec equivalent, stating that "the trusteeship of the Indians in the said territory, and the management of any lands now or hereafter reserved for their use, shall remain in the Government of Canada subject to the control of Parliament."[65]

However, the case law prior to *Guerin* was not clear as to the legal nature of this relationship, particularly whether the "trust" was one that could be legally enforced against the Crown or was merely a political or moral obligation without any effective remedies available from the courts for its enforcement. The law was sketchy and far from certain. There were only a few cases and they failed to provide any clear guidance, but they appeared to give a negative answer to this question.[66]

Attorney-General for Canada v Giroux was a 1916 decision of the Supreme Court of Canada that touched on the possibility of the Crown's being a trustee for Indigenous peoples.[67] Justice Lyman Duff, speaking for himself and Justice Francis Anglin, said of a surrender of lands:

The Indian interest being ... ownership is by the terms of the surrender a surrender to Her Majesty in trust to be dealt with in a certain manner for the benefit of the Indians. The Dominion Parliament, having plenary authority to deal with the subject of the "Indian Lands" and having authorized such a transfer of the Indian title, it is difficult to see on what ground the transfer could be held not to take effect according to its terms *or on what ground the trusts, upon which the transfer was accepted can be treated as non-operative.*[68]

Five years later, however, in *Attorney-General for Quebec v Attorney-General for Canada* (the "*Star Chrome* case"), the same judge, speaking for the Privy Council, denied that the legislation in question in both cases created "an equitable estate in lands set apart for an Indian tribe of which the Commissioner is made the recipient for the benefit of the Indians."[69]

In the 1935 case of *Dreaver v The King,* Justice Eugène Angers of the Exchequer Court held that the Crown was liable for certain breaches of trust in the administration of funds generated from the sale of reserve lands surrendered by the Mistawisis Band of Indians to the Crown in trust.[70] The surrender documents were signed after the band's adhesion to a treaty in 1876, and involved the surrender of some of the lands set aside under the treaty as reserve lands. The proceeds of disposition of the surrendered lands were to be held by the Crown for the band. The Crown made various charges against the monies. For example, it charged for drugs and education, which the band considered should be provided under the treaty without charge. The Crown denied that any charges were improper. It also defended on the grounds that the band had delayed too long in bringing the action, which was therefore outside the relevant limitations period. Angers rejected the Crown's defence of limitations, awarded the band part of its claim, and ordered the return of monies wrongly charged to the band. He also restrained the Indian agent from farming part of the band's reserve without its approval. Although the case does not contain any explicit discussion of the Crown's fiduciary duty, it is notable for giving a legal remedy for wrongful administration of band assets.

The issue in *Re Kane,* decided five years later, was whether "Indians" working off-reserve in Sydney, Nova Scotia, were required to pay a municipal poll tax and were liable to imprisonment for failure to do so.[71] Justice McArthur of the Nova Scotia County Court held that they did not have to pay the tax. He explained his decision on the basis of wardship:

For reasons which are quite apparent, the Indian has been placed under the guardianship of the Dominion Government. He is its ward, so long as he remains unenfranchised, and the Minister of Interior, as Superintendent General of Indian Affairs, is given the control and management of all lands and property of Indians in Canada. They are looked upon and treated as requiring the friendly care and directing hand of the Government in the management of their affairs. They and their property are, so to speak, under the protecting wing of the Dominion Government, and I do not think in such circumstances, it was ever contemplated that the body of an Indian should be taken in execution under a civil process pure and simple.[72]

Chisholm v The King, decided in 1948, was brought by the widow and executrix of a solicitor to obtain payment of her husband's account for legal services rendered to an Indian band.[73] She sued the Crown in order to obtain payment out of funds held for the band. Justice O'Connor held that the action could not succeed for various reasons, including a failure to obtain the written approval of the superintendent-general of Indian Affairs to the contract to provide the services, as required by the *Indian Act*. He did state, however, that "the Minister of Mines and Resources [who was then also the minister of Indian Affairs] is and has been at all times material the trustee of the Indians." It is not clear whether he would have provided a legal remedy for breach of this trust responsibility.

The 1950 case of *Miller v The King* was an action brought by the chief councillor of the Six Nations of the Grand River, suing on behalf of all members of his tribe, including himself.[74] It was alleged, among other things, that the Six Nations had surrendered certain lands to the Crown in trust on terms that the Crown would sell the surrendered lands and hold the sale proceeds in trust for the benefit of the tribe. Further, it was alleged that the Crown breached this trust by investing $160,000 of the sale proceeds in the stock of a company that subsequently became insolvent. The case came before the Supreme Court of Canada on the preliminary point of law of whether an action could be brought against the Crown for the relief sought. The court held that the Crown could be an express trustee and that equitable relief would be available to enforce the trust obligation against the Crown, and referred the matter back for trial.

The decision has a special significance since the Crown advanced the defence of "political trust," as shown in the following passage from the judgment of Justice Roy Kellock:

> On behalf of the respondent it is first contended that the allegations of fact in the petition and particulars do not show any agreement by His Majesty or anything held by His Majesty in trust. It is said that reference to the Crown (presumably in documents or statutes) as trustee for the Indians and to the Indians as wards of His Majesty is not a technical use of such terms but such references are merely descriptive of the general political relationship between His Majesty and the Indians.[75]

This contention was not considered by the court, however.

Just a couple of months before the commencement of the trial in the Federal Court of *Guerin*, in *Pawis v The Queen*, Justice Marceau of the same court considered and rejected a claim that the Lake Huron Treaty of 1850 created a trust.[76] The subject matter of the trust was said to be the hunting and fishing rights confirmed by the treaty. Marceau held that the rights could not be considered trust property. He also applied the political trust doctrine, which we will now consider.

THE POLITICAL TRUST DOCTRINE

In order to understand the decision in *Guerin* and how it changed the law, it is necessary to understand the political trust doctrine, which was a major issue in that case, especially in the Federal Court of Appeal.[77] The basis of the political trust concept is a line of cases holding that, where the Crown is called a trustee, it may be a trustee in a political sense only. This means that its obligations are not enforceable in the courts. It is the legal doctrine used to deny enforceable rights to Indigenous peoples who were treated as child-like wards of the government. Prior to the *Guerin* case, the status of the commonwealth law on the political trust doctrine was reflected in the following cases.

The leading case was the 1881 decision of the English House of Lords in *Kinloch v Secretary of State for India* concerning claims to certain booty of war arising out of the Indian Mutiny.[78] Lord Selborne LC said:

> Now the words "in trust for" are quite consistent with, and indeed are the proper manner of expressing, every species of trust – a trust not only as regards those matters which are the proper subjects for an equitable jurisdiction to administer, but as respects higher matters, such as might take place between the Crown and public officers discharging, under the directions of the Crown, duties or functions belonging to the prerogative and to the authority of the Crown. In the lower sense they are matters within the jurisdiction of, and to be administered by, the ordinary Courts of Equity; in the higher sense they are not. What their sense is here, is the question to be determined, looking at the whole instrument and at its nature and effect.[79]

In this strangely worded passage, he is saying that there are two classes of trusts: trusts "in the higher sense," which are trusts imposed on public officers and not legally enforceable, and trusts "in the lower sense," which are trusts that can be enforced by courts. Citizens who are told that they have no legal recourse for the misdeeds of a public officer may be forgiven for wondering in what sense the trust is "in a higher sense."

An example of the application of the political trust doctrine can be seen in a case from another part of the history of the British Empire, *Rustomjee v The Queen,* which arose out of the *Treaty of Nanking* in 1842 between Britain and China.[80] The Emperor of China paid Queen Victoria to compensate British subjects for debts owed to them by Chinese merchants. The petitioners sought to recover some of this money on the basis that it was received by the Crown on their behalf. The claim was rejected by the English Court of Appeal with some indignation:

The notion that the Queen of this country, in receiving a sum of money in order to do justice to some of her subjects, to whom injustice would otherwise be done, becomes the agent of those subjects, seems to me really too wild a notion to require a single word of observation beyond that of emphatically condemning it. In like manner, to say that the sovereign becomes the trustee for subjects on whose behalf money has been received by the Crown appears to be equally untenable.[81]

A few years prior to the *Guerin* decision, the doctrine of political trust had been applied by Vice Chancellor Megarry in the English case of *Tito v Waddell*, where he held that South Sea Islanders were not entitled to claim as trust funds certain royalties payable to the local colonial official as the result of mining operations on their land.[82] Placing particular reliance on the distinction recognized in *Kinloch*, he held that an agreement and certain ordinances did not create "a true trust" or impose any other fiduciary obligation on the Crown:

> When it is alleged that the Crown is a trustee, an element which is of special importance consists of the governmental powers and obligations of the Crown; for these readily provide an explanation which is an alternative to a trust. If money or other property is vested in the Crown and is used for the benefit of others, one explanation can be that the Crown holds on a true trust for those others. Another explanation can be that, without holding the property on a true trust, the Crown is nevertheless administering that property in the exercise of the Crown's governmental functions. This latter possible explanation, which does not exist in the case of an ordinary individual, makes it necessary to scrutinise with greater care the words and circumstances which are alleged to impose a trust.[83]

Another application was the 1978 decision of the House of Lords in *Town Investments Ltd v Department of the Environment*, where the issue was whether premises occupied under leases entered into by a minister of the Crown were occupied by the Crown or by the minister in trust for the Crown.[84] Lord Simon noted that:

In public law even a phrase like "in trust for" may not betoken at all
the relationship of trustee and cestui que trust [i.e., a beneficiary], but
rather the imposition of a constitutional duty the sanction for which is
political or administrative not legal (cf. Lord Selborne L.C. in *Kinloch
v. Secretary of State for India,* 7 App. Cas. 619, 625, 626).[85]

On the other hand, prior to *Guerin,* there were a few isolated cases
going against the concept of a political trust and imposing a fiduciary
obligation on municipal governments in favour of ratepayers when
judges disagreed with the policy of the municipality. *Roberts v Hopwood*
was a controversial decision of the English House of Lords.[86] A municipality had paid a wage to its employees that was above the market
rate, and ratepayers challenged the payments. Upholding the challenge,
the members of the House of Lords held that a municipality owed a
fiduciary duty to the ratepayers. In the words of Lord Atkinson:

> The indulgence of philanthropic enthusiasm at the expense of persons
> other than the philanthropists is an entirely different thing from the
> indulgence of it at the expense of the philanthropists themselves. The
> former wears quite a different aspect from the latter, and may bear a
> different legal as well as a moral character. A body charged with the ad-
> ministration for definite purposes of funds contributed in whole or in
> part by persons other than the members of that body owes, in my view,
> a duty to those latter persons to conduct that administration in a fairly
> businesslike manner, with reasonable care, skill, and caution, and with
> a due and alert regard to the interest of those contributors who are not
> members of the body. Towards these latter persons the body stands
> somewhat in the position of trustees or managers of the property of
> others. This duty is, I think, a legal duty as well as a moral one.[87]

Several years later, the House of Lords reached a similar decision in
Bromley London Borough Council v Greater London Council.[88] This
involved the question of whether the Greater London Council could
implement a reduction in bus fares under the relevant statutory provision that governed its powers. In the course of the judgment, Lord

Wilberforce noted that the council "owes a duty of a fiduciary character to its ratepayers who have to provide the money."[89] Lord Scarman said that the statutory provisions had to be considered "bearing in mind the existence of the fiduciary duty owed by the GLC to the ratepayers of London."[90] Critics have pointed to these decisions as examples of judicial lawmaking that substituted the more conservative views of the judges for those of the democratically elected bodies. J.A.G Griffith said of the *Bromley* case that "the application of the doctrine of fiduciary duty in this case was a gross interference by the judiciary in the exercise of political responsibility of an elected local authority."[91]

The "political trust" concept developed from British imperial law was echoed in judgments of the Supreme Court of Canada. In *Hereford Railway Co v The Queen,* the Supreme Court of Canada applied the *Kinloch* decision and held that money that the plaintiff railway company said the Crown had agreed to grant to it as a subsidy was not held by the Crown on its behalf in a trust that could be enforced in the courts.[92] But the Canadian law also provided some support for a fiduciary duty owed by a municipality to the ratepayers. In *MacIllreith v Hart,* a decision of the Supreme Court of Canada, a municipality refused to sue for the return of certain payments wrongfully paid to one of its officers.[93] Justice James Maclennan based his decision on the fiduciary position of the municipality:

> The right of the inhabitants to compel the city corporation, that is, the city council, as a body, to do its duty, rests on this: – That the corporation is a trustee for the inhabitants ... The city corporation is composed of all the inhabitants and not merely of the ratepayers ... whether inhabitants or not, all the ratepayers are also *cestui que trustent* [beneficiaries] of the city corporation.[94]

However, in the subsequent case of *Norfolk v Roberts,*[95] the Supreme Court affirmed the decision of the Ontario Court of Appeal that it was "erroneous to treat either the corporation or its council as trustees for the ratepayers."[96] This decision reflects the political trust doctrine: "They are, no doubt, in the sense in which the Sovereign is spoken of as a trustee for the people, trustees for the inhabitants of the municipality, but they are, in my opinion, in no other sense trustees."[97]

Two of the Supreme Court's judgments dealing with political trusts involved Indigenous peoples.[98] In *St Catherine's Milling and Lumber Co v The Queen*, Justice Jean-Thomas Taschereau stated:

> The Indians must in the future everyone concedes it, be treated with the same consideration for their just claims and demands that they have received in the past but, as in the past, it will not be because of any legal obligation to do so, but as a sacred political obligation, in the execution of which the state must be free from judicial control.[99]

It may be noted that, although the case concerned the legal position of Indigenous peoples, they were not represented in the litigation.

In *St Ann's Island Shooting and Fishing Club v The King*, one of the members of the court referred to "political trust" and wardship, although it is not clear if he was intending to exclude legal liability.[100] The Chippewa and Pottawatomie Indians of Walpole Island had surrendered reserve lands to the Crown. The lands were subsequently leased to the St. Ann's Island Shooting and Fishing Club by the superintendent-general of Indian Affairs through a series of leases. Only the first lease had been authorized by an Order-in-Council as required by the *Indian Act*. The Supreme Court of Canada upheld the trial judge's ruling that the subsequent leases were void. In giving his judgment, Justice Ivan Rand said:

> The language of the statute embodies the accepted view that these aborigines are, in effect, wards of the State, whose care and welfare are a political trust of the highest obligation. For that reason, every such dealing with their privileges must bear the imprint of governmental approval, and it would be beyond the power of the Governor in Council to transfer that responsibility to the Superintendent General.[101]

Such was the law of Canada prior to the *Guerin* case.

UNITED STATES LAW

In any consideration of Canadian Aboriginal law, it may be relevant to review the law developed in the United States.[102] Although the details of the law may differ, we share a common early history and a predominantly common law tradition.

The trust responsibility of the United States has been recognized as a central concept in American Indian law. It has been described as "one of the cornerstones of Indian Law,"[103] and another writer has noted that "much of American Indian law revolves around the special relationship between the federal government and the tribes."[104] Another has commented that "there is no responsibility more venerable and more important than the trust responsibility."[105] It has a long history stemming from the comments of Chief Justice John Marshall of the United States Supreme Court in the 1831 decision in *Cherokee Nation v Georgia:* "[The Indians] are in a state of pupilage; their relation to the United States resembles that of a ward to his guardian. They look to the government for protection; rely upon its kindness and its power."[106]

Some of the subsequent decisions of the Supreme Court emphasized the legislative jurisdiction of Congress over Indians resulting from the duty of protection recognized in the *Cherokee* case. As the court commented in *United States v Kagama,* "these Indian tribes are the wards of the nation. They are communities dependent on the United States ... From their very weakness and helplessness ... there arises the duty of protection and *with it the power.*"[107] The court accordingly upheld a statute giving the courts of the United States the jurisdiction to try and punish an Indian who had killed another on an Indian reservation. Another leading decision was *Lone Wolf v Hitchcock,* in which the plenary power of Congress to manage Indian property was held to entitle it to abrogate treaties.[108]

On the other hand, there is another line of cases that hold that the trust relationship creates legally enforceable fiduciary duties for federal officials in their dealings with Indians. These cases indicate that an action may be maintained against officials of the executive branch of government for equitable or declaratory relief for breach of trust.[109] For example, in 1937, the US Supreme Court decided *Shoshone Tribe v United States*.[110] The government had allowed the Arapahoe to occupy part of the Shoshone reservation despite the objections of the Shoshone and in breach of a treaty. The court found in favour of the Shoshone.

Perhaps the most significant of this line of cases was the decision in *Seminole Nation v United States,* decided in 1942, which involved claims based on various treaties, agreements, and acts of Congress.[111] The claims related to payments made to Seminole tribal officials who were allegedly corrupt and misappropriated the funds. The following quotation shows the high fiduciary standard expected of the government:

> Furthermore, this Court has recognized the distinctive obligation of trust incumbent upon the Government in its dealings with these dependent and sometimes exploited people ... In carrying out its treaty obligations with the Indian tribes the Government is something more than a mere contracting party. Under a humane and self-imposed policy which has found expression in many acts of Congress and numerous decisions of this Court, it has charged itself with moral obligations of the highest responsibility and trust. Its conduct, as disclosed in the acts of those who represent it in dealings with the Indians, should therefore be judged by the most exacting fiduciary standards.[112]

CONCLUSION

The situation in 1979, when the trial of the *Guerin* case commenced in the Federal Court of Canada, was that there were no Canadian precedents in favour of a ruling imposing legally enforceable obligations on the Crown with respect to its relationship with Indigenous peoples. US law provided support for such a ruling, but US law is not binding on Canadian courts. Such Canadian decisions as existed were not conclusive but tended to the opposite conclusion, including the decision earlier in that year in *Pawis,* in which Justice Marceau of the same court applied the political trust doctrine to reject a claim of an enforceable trust.[113] He interpreted the role of a judge in a narrow, conservative

fashion: "As a Judge of this Court, I am not called upon to pass judgment on the legitimacy of the Indian people's grievances as these have
been lately so often formulated. I must leave to others the task to deal
properly and fairly with the so-called 'Indian cause' in all its political
and social aspects."[114] In the opinion of Douglas Sanders, "it was clear
that Musqueam had to lose the case. The First Nation had to lose if the
prior judicial decisions were respected."[115] Another leading Aboriginal
law scholar, Richard Bartlett, observed that "at the commencement of
the 1980s, it remained unclear under what circumstances and to what
extent the Crown was accountable at law to the aboriginal peoples ...
The matter required further consideration by the Supreme Court of
Canada."[116] The *Guerin* case was to provide the opportunity for such
further consideration. As Bartlett also noted, "the decision [would]
indicate judicial attitudes to the degree to which the Crown should be
held accountable for the past."[117]

PART 2

THE CASE

4

The Trial and Federal Court of Appeal

THIS CHAPTER WILL EXAMINE the commencement of the litigation leading to the Supreme Court of Canada's *Guerin* decision and the working of the case through the Federal Court Trial Division and the Federal Court of Appeal.[1] The next chapter will look at the Supreme Court decision. These chapters describe events that took place between the signing of the Shaughnessy lease and that decision. Before looking at those events, we will briefly consider the changes in Aboriginal law and the constitutional reform that were taking place during this period in order to provide some further context to the litigation and the legal decisions.

ABORIGINAL LAW AND CONSTITUTIONAL REFORM FROM 1960 TO 1984

Aboriginal law has changed greatly over the last forty or so years.[2] The *Guerin* decision was an important and early step in that development. The outcome was likely influenced by the political and constitutional developments that had taken place in the years between the signing of the Shaughnessy lease in 1958 and the Supreme Court of Canada's decision in 1984, although these developments were not expressly referenced by the judges. The decision should be considered in that context.

In 1969, the federal government issued the *Statement of the Government of Canada on Indian Policy,* popularly known as the White Paper, as part of its "Just Society" program.[3] It rejected any unique legal status for "Indians," which it saw as the cause of their disadvantaged position. The pressure for more self-government powers and greater legal recognition of treaty and Aboriginal rights started as a protest against the White Paper and the attempt of the federal government to remove special legal status for "Indian" people.[4] This created momentum for Indigenous people to seek constitutional protection for an inherent right of self-government and Aboriginal and treaty rights.

It was in the midst of the political upheaval over Aboriginal and treaty rights that the early breakthrough cases on Aboriginal rights, including *Guerin,* were decided.[5] The case that started the rapid growth of Aboriginal law in 1973 was *Calder v Attorney-General for British Columbia,* in which the Supreme Court rejected the claim of the Nisga'a people for Aboriginal title on the grounds that any claim had been extinguished by legislation or on procedural grounds.[6] Although not free from doubt, a majority appeared to accept that Aboriginal title had existed in law prior to extinguishment. *Guerin* was to prove an important stepping stone in the path leading from the decision in *Calder* to unanimous recognition of Aboriginal title in the *Delgamuukw* and *Tsilhqot'in* decisions of the Supreme Court of Canada.[7]

The White Paper spurred Indigenous leaders to lobby for greater legal rights. This lobbying influenced the debate on the repatriation of the Canadian Constitution in 1982 and led to the inclusion of section 35(1) of the *Constitution Act, 1982,* which recognizes and affirms the "existing aboriginal and treaty rights of the aboriginal peoples of Canada."

THE LITIGATION COMMENCES

The Department of Indian Affairs was aware, at least as early as 1968, that the terms of the Shaughnessy lease did not reflect a fair market rent. A confidential report prepared for the department contained a severe criticism by a firm of valuers of the rents to be received under the lease. The report was especially critical of the restriction on rent increases. It was never given to the band and became public only when it was leaked to the press in 1972 by Frank Howard, MP.[8] In 1970, Delbert Guerin and other members of the band council did not even know of the terms of the lease substantially drafted by the solicitor for the Shaughnessy Club and signed by the government in 1958. They were anticipating a large rent increase on the first rent review date in 1973 in order to obtain a market rent based on the highest and best use of the land, which was residential. At a meeting in March 1970 with Graham Allen, who was then a lands officer with the department, Chief Guerin mentioned that he expected to be able to negotiate a significant increase in the rent at the rent review. Allen checked the lease and wrote him a letter to say that there was a 15 percent restriction on the permitted increase for the period from 1973 to 1988.[9] This came as a great shock to Guerin and the other members of the band, who had no idea of this restriction and the other unfavourable provisions in the lease. He remembered being "totally vehement, wild over it."[10]

Guerin insisted on getting a copy of the lease and, after some initial resistance, he was permitted by department officials to go down to the "cage" in the basement of the department's building to look for the lease and related documents. He recalled the look of horror on Earl Anfield's former secretary as she heard him demand a copy of the lease. She was about five feet tall but he described her as "bouncing off the ceiling." He felt she knew that, at long last, the band would find out the truth. The "cage" was a cramped wire enclosure about ten feet long by ten feet wide, full of boxes, including some marked "Musqueam," which he eagerly opened. He later explained his surprise at finding documents that he had been told earlier had been destroyed in a flood or fire: "The thing that was surprising to me was that all the documentation that had been destroyed in floods and fire was all of a sudden all there."[11] His head swam as he tried to make sense of them. He described his feelings of "bitter surprise,"[12] then growing anger and amazement as he read document after document dealing with Musqueam lands.

Guerin spent hours looking at the documents and trying to copy them on an old-fashioned copying machine, which was "tormentingly slow." By the time the other department officials had left for the day, leaving Graham Allen behind, he had copied only a few of the documents. Finally, Allen said that he would have to leave and would be back in a few minutes to lock up the "cage," and Guerin would have to do what he had to do before he came back. Guerin took this as a hint that he should take away the relevant documents. He seized the opportunity, scooped up a pile of documents, and left the department's office with an armful of papers. He had offered a lift home to Allen, who lived on the route back to the reserve. On the half-hour journey, they never discussed the lease and Allen never once mentioned the pile of papers occupying the back seat, which was as inconspicuous as an elephant. True to his English background, he turned a blind eye in the best tradition of Admiral Nelson.

Guerin read the documents over the next few days with growing despondency. He and the other members of the band gradually realized just how badly band members had been misled on the terms of the lease. It did not contain the terms that the members had voted on but terms that were much less favourable. The first rent increase was limited to 15 percent; rent periods after the first were fifteen years, not ten years as understood by the band; the subsequent rent increases were based not on the market rent for residential lands or even a developed golf course but on the fiction that the lands were uncleared and unimproved and restricted as to their use; the club had a unilateral right to terminate the lease on six months' notice and could take the improvements. The practical and immediate result was that, instead of the sizeable rent increase they had expected to receive starting in 1973 (the "big raise" Anfield had promised to band members before they voted[13]), they were going to receive an increase of just over $4,000, so that the annual rent for the second term of the lease, from 1973 to 1988, would be $33,500. This was about the same amount as the city of Vancouver was receiving in property taxes.

The question for Chief Guerin and other members of the council was what could be done about it. Their energies were initially focused on the rent review in 1973. For a couple of years, the band council put pressure on the Department of Indian Affairs in an unsuccessful attempt to get it to negotiate a change in the terms of the lease. The band council then tried to negotiate directly with the golf club to get it to waive the 15 percent restriction. The club refused. In a letter dated 9 April 1973, the club's solicitor said the lease was not the subject of negotiations. Articles in the *Province* on 8 and 9 May 1973 reported that the band had written directly to club members appealing for the rent to be increased and pointing out that, based on recent appraisals, a market rent would be $800,000 yearly. The plea fell on deaf ears. A club member was quoted as saying that he believed the membership was not inclined to be sympathetic with the band's point of view because of high membership costs. At that point, the club had an annual income of about $419,000, so at an annual rent of $29,000, it was paying only approximately 7 percent of its income on rent to the band. In another letter, dated 11 May 1973, the club's solicitor threatened legal action after a band member hinted that the band might organize a demonstration at the entrance to the club. The government lawyer wrote back on 30 May 1973 to say that the band had no authority to negotiate the renewal of the rent on behalf of the Crown. The club then refused to deal with the band. The 15 percent restriction was applied.

Having failed to negotiate an increase outside of the lease terms, the band council sought legal advice on whether it could obtain a remedy for the failure of the government to ensure that the lease contained the terms understood by members of the band before they voted on the surrender of lands for the purpose of the lease. The band's solicitor was Garde Gardom, later attorney general and then lieutenant-governor of British Columbia, who was in partnership with Jack Volrich, later mayor of Vancouver. They said there was nothing that the band could do. A successful action was impossible and the band would only be wasting its money to pursue a claim.

At the time, Delbert Guerin was attending meetings in different parts of the country to discuss Indigenous issues and he came to know several lawyers advising Indigenous groups. He took every opportunity to buttonhole them on the potential case against the government or the golf club. Over time, he became something of a nuisance. At the end of the meetings, he would seek out lawyers in bars or coffee shops and ask for their advice. One by one, they would excuse themselves to go to the washroom but they never came back. Many lawyers just turned him away. Others were clearly reluctant to get involved. They had no desire to take on the federal government or the powerful members of the golf club. Those who were willing to consider the claim at all were worried about how they would be paid. If they looked at the matter in any detail, they saw insurmountable legal problems. He was repeatedly advised that the band would not be successful.

Although concerned at the difficulties, some of the lawyers Guerin consulted were excited by the prospect of establishing in Canadian law that the Crown owed enforceable duties towards Indigenous peoples. They were aware of the importance of a favourable decision and what it would mean for Indigenous peoples generally. However, they also tempered their enthusiasm with strategic advice to attempt to downplay the impact of the case. Lawyers involved in cases raising undecided issues are usually very concerned about the timidity of judges who fear that expanding legal liability will "open up the floodgates." In this case, a finding of liability could lead to numerous large claims against the government. Guerin was advised to stress the special facts and note the improvements in the land management practices of Indian Affairs since the 1950s.

A major problem was the delay in bringing any action. There were statutes of limitation that required actions to be brought within six years. It was over twelve years since the lease was signed. The events leading up to the case took place in 1957–58 with the surrender of the lands by the band on 6 October 1957 and the signing of the lease on 22 January 1958. One lawyer consulted by the band expressed his views as follows: "I have agonized over the Statute of Limitations problem in this case and reluctantly have come to the conclusion that there is no legal answer to the defence that [you] have not brought this case in time. In my opinion success in the lawsuit is barred by the Statute of Limitation ... I cannot advise that you proceed with this case." Even if the statute of limitations could be overcome, courts still had a discretion to refuse a remedy on the grounds that the band had delayed too long in bringing the claim.

The passage of time also meant that it might be difficult to prove the claim. The band's claim rested on the recollection of members involved in the surrender. Some of them had died or were elderly and in ill health. Nobody knew at the time that government documents and witnesses would support the band's claim when the case was finally heard. The costs of bringing the action were a major consideration, as well as the possibility of being ordered by a court to pay the costs of the government if the band was not successful. (The Federal Court of Appeal did, in fact, make this order but it was reversed by the Supreme Court of Canada.) Expensive expert witnesses would have to be retained to give evidence on the loss suffered. It was impossible to give any reliable estimate of costs, and early estimates proved very wrong as the government dug in its heels and raised numerous defences using the unlimited amount of money available to it. Discussions about the government's contributing towards the band's costs in recognition of the importance of resolving the issues of law for all parties went nowhere. Some other Indigenous groups made contributions but the ongoing legal costs were almost entirely borne by the band until partial reimbursement was received from the government following an order of the Supreme Court of Canada at the end of the nine years of litigation.

As we saw in the last chapter, no band had ever obtained a judgment against the Crown for breach of trust or other breach of fiduciary obligation. The matter had never been squarely dealt with by the courts in Canada, but actions against the British Crown had been rejected on the basis that any obligation of the government was political and not legal. The courts would not enforce such obligations. There were cases from the United States that supported the claim, but they were not binding on Canadian courts, and the constitutional law of that country was quite different.[14] All in all, the consensus of those with whom he spoke about the claim was that Chief Guerin was being quite unrealistic and unreasonable in thinking he could succeed in any action. His ultimate success provided further proof of the truth of George Bernard Shaw's maxim that all progress depends on the unreasonable man who perseveres when a reasonable man would have given up.[15]

Eventually, after being repeatedly advised to drop the case by several lawyers, including many experienced in Aboriginal law, Guerin obtained the opinion of Doug Sanders. Sanders was then a young lawyer, but he had gained some experience in the practice of Aboriginal law and had taught the subject. He was the editor of and the person primarily responsible for the first edition of *Native Rights in Canada,* a pioneering study of Aboriginal law, published by the Indian-Eskimo Association of Canada in June 1970. The band had retained him to assist them in preparing their land claim. He was a sole practitioner and did not have the resources to take the matter to trial. He also had serious concerns about the defence of limitations. He made it very clear that his involvement would be restricted. In order to limit the chance of a successful limitations defence, however, he agreed to file the statement of claim and so commence the action within the period of six years from the band's knowledge of the terms of the lease. This period would expire early in 1976.

The claim was filed and served just before Christmas, on 22 December 1975. Guerin drove Sanders to the Federal Court Registry in Vancouver and then to the offices of the Department of Justice, where government lawyers could accept service for the government. He spent some time tracking down someone who would accept service. Finally, he persuaded a somewhat disgruntled Department of Justice lawyer to interrupt his Christmas party to do so.

The full name of the *Guerin* case is "*Delbert Guerin, Joseph Becker, Eddie Campbell, Mary Charles, Gertrude Guerin and Gail Sparrow, suing on their own behalf and on behalf of all other members of the Musqueam Indian Band versus Her Majesty The Queen.*" The action was therefore brought in the name of all the members of the band and not just in the name of Delbert Guerin. The names of all the then council members were listed in the Statement of Claim commencing the action because the legal status of a band was uncertain. The action was therefore commenced in the names of the council members as representatives of all the band members. Delbert Guerin was then the Chief, so his name came first, and the case is consequently referred to by his name, as is common practice. Having said that, it is also appropriate that his pivotal role in bringing the case be acknowledged. It was his persistence that led to the true terms of the lease being known to the band and to the commencement of the action. Without him, there would have been no case.

Since Sanders was not in a position to pursue the matter to trial, Guerin still had to find a lawyer able and willing to do so. Robert Banno, a solicitor at Davis & Company, had been advising the band on other matters. Guerin was involved in a motor vehicle accident and called Banno to get a referral to a litigation lawyer who could act for him. The lawyer Banno recommended was unable to make the appointment and Banno decided to refer Guerin to a new lawyer at Davis & Company, Marvin Storrow. Storrow had recently joined the firm after handling tax litigation at the Department of Justice in Ottawa, and was free to take on new work. He had been both a prosecutor and defence lawyer and had extensive trial experience. He agreed to meet Guerin to discuss the motor vehicle case. When they met, Guerin was a bit nervous, and to put him at ease, Storrow asked what else was happening with him. Guerin explained his frustration at not being able to find a lawyer willing and able to take the claim against the government to trial. As Guerin explained the facts, Storrow became more and more fascinated and agreed to take the case.

Marvin Storrow has been recognized as a leading litigation lawyer who has successfully advanced high-profile cases in many areas of the law. The former chief justice of British Columbia, Lance Finch, praised him for his ability, tenacity, courage, and conviction.[16] His success has been due in part to his ability to read and charm judges. More than one lawyer has commented to me that Marvin could get away with things that others would not have dared try. Subsequently, other lawyers at Davis & Company joined the legal team, including me (I was also counsel at all levels of the case), Lewis Harvey (who was counsel at the Supreme Court of Canada), and Steve Schachter (who appeared at the trial and the Federal Court of Appeal). Robert Banno remained an active member of the team. Our knowledge, experience, and skills complemented each other and we functioned well as a team.

Davis & Company was then the largest law firm in Vancouver (this was before the city had national, let alone international, law firms) and firmly part of the local establishment. Founded in 1892 by Edward Pease Davis, who appeared as counsel before the Privy Council in London over a dozen times, it represented the largest logging companies and banks as well as the Guinness family, famous for its beer, which owned and developed much of the mountain in West Vancouver on which was located the prestigious development known as the British Properties.[17] Representing an Indian band in a case involving the lease to the Shaughnessy golf club, *the* establishment club, was not a routine piece of litigation and did generate some comments. To their credit, however, the partners allowed the firm to act for the band. In part, this may have been because the case was perceived not so much as an Aboriginal rights case with potential adverse consequences for other clients but as a claim against the government for breach of trust/fiduciary duty. Also, some partners recalled that the firm had a history of taking on unpopular litigation. It had acted in the 1940s for Japanese Canadians who faced deportation following internment outside of the province and confiscation of their lands.[18]

Davis & Company had all the modern facilities required to take on a case of the complexity of *Guerin*. There were about 85 lawyers and 160 support staff – small by today's standards, when firms number lawyers in the hundreds, but very large back then. There was a comprehensive library with many shelves of books and legal journals: the internet and online materials did not exist. This meant that we could do much of our legal research in the office with occasional trips to the Supreme Court of British Columbia Courthouse or University of British Columbia libraries for more obscure materials. The equipment was

Members of the legal team and the Musqueam Band at the Supreme Court of Canada building during the *Guerin* hearing, June 1983. *Left to right:* Lewis Harvey, James Reynolds, Leona Sparrow, Andrew Charles, and Marvin Storrow. *Courtesy of the Musqueam Indian Band Archives*

state-of-the-art, with word processing machines, early computers (for secretaries, not lawyers), telexes, and recently introduced fax machines, although emails and cell phones were still in the future. I recall handwriting early drafts of our legal argument, which were then typed and retyped, with lengthy changes shown by handwritten attachments – "cut and paste" was very literal then. Old-fashioned photocopying machines were in use although temperamental and prone to failure just when a deadline loomed and they were most needed. The firm occupied about five of the nineteen floors of the Burrard Building in the downtown area. In order to ensure adequate room and prevent too many distractions, space was rented for the legal team on a lower floor, which became known as "the basement." It was here that much of the work on the case was done. The firm had moved into the building and signed its lease in early 1958, about the same time that the Shaughnessy lease was signed.

The following words of the lead counsel for the successful Indigenous plaintiffs in the Australian *Mabo* case on Aboriginal or native title are equally applicable to the *Guerin* legal team and the almost ten years of litigation in that case:

> Over the ... ten years [of *Mabo*] those involved ... have been severely tested in their willpower, persistence and determination to see the case through to its conclusion. There were numerous critical moments at which it seemed the case was doomed, or at which decisions had to be made which were critical to the survival of the litigation. Ultimately, there are some moments in every lawyer's career where it is felt that a decision must be made about one's priorities in life and a balance reached on how far one is committed to see through a professional obligation. I think it is fair to say the plantiffs' representatives including solicitors, law clerks, law students, researchers and others, were highly persistent, stubbornly determined and wholly committed to see the case through many hazards to a final hearing at which all issues could be raised.[19]

The Crown was represented during the pretrial proceedings and at the trial by Gunnar Eggertson, Alan Louie, and Carol Pepper of the local office of the Department of Justice. Eggertson practised with the Department of Justice in Vancouver from 1970 to 1995. His obituary noted that "he conducted a wide range of litigation and was counsel at the trial level in the *Guerin* case which, of course, later went on to the Supreme Court of Canada and set an important precedent in the area of aboriginal law." It also noted that he was "a kind, considerate and caring man without a mean bone in his body" and "the antithesis of aggressiveness, yet through his tireless hard work, his compassion and stubbornness he was indeed a successful litigator."[20] His representation of the Crown during the *Guerin* trial certainly showed his positive qualities.

The pretrial proceedings were complex and involved much legal wrangling. The government served a list of about 1,700 documents. It took a great deal of time for the band's legal team to review each document and try to relate them to each other and to the information provided by the band members. In the view of the legal team, many of the documents were of only marginal relevance; in fact, only 186 exhibits were entered at the trial.

Possible witnesses had to be tracked down and interviewed. Some had since died, such as the former Chief, Willard Sparrow. Some had moved away from the reserve. Others were elderly and in poor health, such as the Chief at the time of the lease, Ed Sparrow, who was born in 1898. Delbert Guerin's wife, Fran, was very helpful in assisting the legal team to locate and interview witnesses. We were impressed by the account provided by the witnesses, which was consistent in its main points with the documentary evidence obtained from the department. It seemed that proving the facts would not be a major problem. The challenge would lie in persuading a court to adopt the band's legal argument that those facts gave rise to a legal remedy.

THE TRIAL

The trial commenced on 18 September 1979, before Justice Frank Collier of the Federal Court of Canada Trial Division. He had been primarily an insurance defence counsel prior to his appointment in 1971 to the Federal Court of Canada Trial Division, where he served for twenty-one years. Probably as the result of his insurance background, he suggested that the Musqueam take out insurance on his life to cover the costs of a rehearing if he should die before giving judgment. Coverage of $300,000 was obtained.[21] He was known as a lawyer with a scholarly bent and is described in his obituary as a "gentle, austere and very private person."[22] During the *Guerin* trial, his sense of humour and love of sports became apparent. He kept control of what were sometimes spirited exchanges among the lawyers with firmness, humour, and occasional sporting analogies. His obituary notes that he "became known for the clarity and precision of his reasons (if not always for their timeliness) and for the breadth and depth of his knowledge of the law." At times, he could be quite testy, especially when he thought lawyers were wasting time. He reminded them of the cost of the trial and estimated that the time of everyone involved in the case amounted to about $1,000 an hour, "a cost everyone in this courtroom is paying."[23]

A sense of the scene in the courtroom can be gleaned from the following newspaper report:

> At the opening of the trial last week ... justice department lawyers and aides wheeled nine cartons of document into Federal Court Room 1. By late in the week the count had increased to 14 containing an estimated 14,000 documents.
>
> ... Spread across a table seating four aides to Crown counsel Gunnar Eggertson are stacks of thick, bound copies of the materials in use or expected to be needed – piled, at times, high enough to impede the vision of those sitting behind them.
>
> Nevertheless, the flurry to find others when they've been required, or make additional copies has kept three or four people hopping most of the time.[24]

There were times when we thought the Crown's strategy was to literally bury us in paper.

As we shall see, the trial had its moments of drama when the Crown sought to produce evidence to show that the band knew of the terms of the Shaughnessy lease but delayed too long in bringing its action and so should be barred from litigating its claim. However, most of the trial proceeded as anticipated on the basis of documents known to the lawyers on both sides, which were formally included as exhibits and thus evidence for consideration by the trial judge. There were the predictable objections as to admissibility relying on rules of evidence that had obscure justifications. The time spent on such matters must have frustrated some of our witnesses from the band as well as the occasional band member or member of the public who came to watch.

The start of the hearing of a trial consists of an opening. These are designed to explain to the court how the parties will present their case, the evidence to be called, and what legal issues will be covered. In his opening for the band, Storrow stated that, to his knowledge, it was the first case of its kind to be brought before the courts of Canada.[25] He itemized the misrepresentations made by government officials regarding the terms of the lease that led the band members to agree to surrender the land for lease. He also described other breaches of the government's duty, including failure to advertise or inform band members of other parties who had indicated an interest in leasing the lands for residential development, which would have led to a higher rent. According to expert witnesses for the band, the loss suffered by the band was in excess of $40 million. The band was seeking this amount plus exemplary damages, given the high-handed and willful nature of the government's breaches of duty.

In his opening for the Crown, Eggertson stated that the evidence demonstrated that "the Crown was to negotiate and have the freedom to negotiate the lease that was actually signed," and further that

> the Crown will show that the Plaintiffs' position is so improbable that they must have deceived themselves, given the long passage of time and all the benefits of hindsight into believing that a state of facts existed which do not exist.[26]

He also stated that, if there were any damages, they amounted to less than $1.5 million. Eggertson caught the attention of the press with his unsuccessful attempt to place in the court records a letter from the lawyers for Anfield's family that said a newspaper article detailing the allegations in the suit had defamed him and caused them pain.[27]

The first witness for the band was anthropologist Dr. Michael Kew.[28] His report outlined some of the band's history, culture, and socio-economic background and is referenced in Chapter 2. A respected scholar of local Indigenous groups, he had written his doctoral thesis on the Musqueam and their ceremonies. He was also married to a band member. His evidence was invaluable in providing the necessary context for the facts. Decades later, he wrote that giving evidence was one of his most rewarding experiences.[29] Another witness, Bud Kelly, a real estate developer, gave evidence that he had expressed to the Department of Indian Affairs interest in developing the land for residential purposes. This would have generated far more than the initial rent of $29,000 each year from the lease to the golf club.[30] He expressed his anger at the way he was treated by department officials. Eventually, adjacent lands on the reserve were successfully developed on the basis that he had proposed.

A number of band members were called as witnesses. Andrew Charles had been band secretary at the time of the surrender in 1957.[31] One press report described him thus: "Short, bespectacled and balding, he smiles often and just as often offers more of an answer to an Eggertson question than the government's lawyer might want."[32] Outspoken and a stickler for correct use of the English language, he did not hesitate to correct Eggertson. Indeed, in my many years of working with him subsequently, I became used to his kindly criticism, accepting that he was probably correct (if a little pedantic!). He was a very capable person and an important witness for the band. On the stand for over two days, he never buckled under cross-examination and often appeared to have the upper hand.

Charles described the circumstances of the band in the 1950s and explained that they lacked any band office and that his bedroom was used for that purpose. There was no typewriter and no private telephone. Much to his embarrassment, band business had to be discussed over a public telephone located in a store. The Indian agent had great power over band affairs. He called and chaired meetings of the band council and typed the minutes. Charles described what took place at the various meetings relating to the Shaughnessy lease and the terms of the lease as understood by the band members present. Their understanding differed significantly from the lease as signed. He also described their repeated requests to obtain a copy of the lease and the reply of the department officials that "we were not allowed to have a copy of the lease."[33] Band members were not told of the interest expressed by other potential lessees, nor were they informed of the communications between the department and the appraiser and the golf club. They were told that they were "not allowed to engage professional people outside of the Department of Indian Affairs."[34] He explained how, during the vote on the surrender, Anfield marked the ballots as each voter held the eraser-end of the pencil. At the end of his evidence, it was clear that the essential facts had been proven through both his testimony and the documents introduced through him.

Ed Sparrow, the Chief at the time of the surrender, also gave evidence.[35] In her master's thesis, his granddaughter, Leona Sparrow, describes his varied background and that of his wife, Rose.[36] Although primarily a commercial fisherman, he worked a number of other jobs – in canneries, hop fields, logging camps, and Chinese market gardens. He acquired his first fishing boat in 1928. During the 1950s, he was active in the Native Brotherhood and was a member of their strike committee. He also became a member of the Musqueam band council. With no formal education beyond grade 4, none of his work experience equipped him to question what he was being told by the Indian agent, who had the power and the responsibility to negotiate the lease with the experienced businessmen representing the club. Eighty-two years old and in ill health at the time of the trial, he needed assistance to hold the book of documents to which he was referred, and giving evidence clearly put a strain on him. But he was mentally very alert, and his humour was evident on occasion despite the gruelling cross-examination. His voice had a distinctive guttural sound to it, which revealed that his first language was hәn̓q̓әmin̓әm̓, the language of the Musqueam, rather than English. His recollections regarding the surrender and the lease were consistent with those of Andrew Charles. He also provided insight into the relationship between the band, the golf club, and the Department of Indian Affairs. During his examination, he described the tea party with officials from the golf club at the old clubhouse, and how he and Councillor Gertrude Guerin had been summarily dismissed without a word.[37] Later in his evidence, he confirmed that a major concern of the club was to get the removal of a restriction on selling liquor on the reserve.

Other band members who gave evidence were William Guerin, Fran Guerin, and Chief Delbert Guerin. William Guerin was a member of the band council from 1957 to 1958, and his evidence was consistent with those of Andrew Charles and Chief Ed Sparrow.[38] He testified that, at a meeting on 17 September 1957, Anfield told him that if the band was "unreasonable" in its demands, the department could lease the land without a surrender and for any sum it wished.[39] Fran Guerin was too young to vote at the surrender meeting, but she objected at the meeting to the references made by Anfield to a possible distribution of lease monies before Christmas, which she saw as a blatant attempt to bribe members to vote in favour of the surrender.[40] Anfield ruled that she was out of order and asked her to leave the meeting. Delbert Guerin was already outside the meeting hall and observed some of what was going on by looking through the window, not realizing the influence that those events would have on him and the other members of the band. He described his excitement at finding the lease in the basement of the Department of Indian Affairs building, his efforts to obtain legal advice, and the filing of the statement of claim.[41]

Chief Guerin's evidence was supported by Graham Allen, the former Department of Indian Affairs officer, who had provided the lease to him. Allen also expressed concern at its contents.[42] For example, in his opinion, which was based on years of involvement in leases and his qualification as a professional appraiser, the provision saying the rent had to be based on the lands in their unimproved condition created "something of a travesty in trying to look at land separated from its improved condition."[43] The 15 percent ceiling on the first rent increase "was a reckless provision ... an extremely unfortunate thing to include in the lease and [he] hadn't seen it in any of the other leases."[44] The tenant's unilateral right of termination was "a rather remarkable concession."[45] He was familiar with over eight hundred department leases and had not seen another lease that gave the tenant the right to remove improvements.[46] Another witness who gave evidence on the unusual and pro-tenant provisions of the lease was the director of lands for the department, Peter Clark. He contrasted the department's standard practices with those in the case of the Shaughnessy lease.[47] He had not seen restrictions on rent renewal similar to those in that lease.[48] He said that he would have ensured that the conditions specified by the band were included in the lease, and bring other offers, as well as the appraisal and the lease, to the band council.

The band produced expert witnesses to quantify the loss suffered, estimated at over $40 million. George Oikawa was the band's appraiser.[49] In his opinion, a realistic annual market rent as of the last rent review date of 22 January 1983 would have been $1,884,563 instead of the $33,500 that the band was forced to accept. According to Oikawa, if the land had been developed in 1958 at its highest and best use, the band would have been the owner, at the end of a ninety-nine year lease, of a subdivision of 438 first-class houses together with the associated subdivision services.

After the band closed its case, the Crown produced its witnesses, starting with Dr. Michael Goldberg, a professor in the Faculty of Commerce at the University of British Columbia.[50] He had been asked by the Crown to produce a report on the microeconomic environment surrounding the lease negotiations. In his view, given that environment and the trends in real estate during that time period, "the lease entered into by Anfield appears reasonable."[51] Under cross-examination, he testified that he had been out of the country for most of the time since the report was commissioned and that an assistant had worked on it under his direction. His attention was directed to a very important report, the Turner Report, written in 1956 on the potential development of the adjacent University Endowment Lands, which gave a value of $13,000 an acre for neighbouring lands, more than twice the value given in the appraisal that was done for the Shaughnessy lease. Despite the reference to it in the report submitted under his name, Goldberg testified that he had not read Turner Report in detail and had not had a chance to critique it.[52]

The Crown also called George McIntosh, the solicitor for the golf club, who was a partner at a big downtown law firm.[53] McIntosh had substantially drafted the lease, including the rent restriction clause.

Under cross-examination, he described the backgrounds of those negotiating for the club. They were representative of the Vancouver business establishment. One was vice-president of BC Telephone Company, another was vice-president of a leading forestry company, and another owned a printing business. He confirmed that no members of the band were present when he met with officials from the Department of Indian Affairs. He had assumed that department officials were reporting back to them, which in fact was not the case. No other lawyers were present at those meetings. McIntosh also confirmed that the club had contacted a federal government minister to make sure that things moved quickly.

Some golf club officials also gave evidence and claimed that Anfield drove a hard bargain to benefit the band.[54] They recalled a meeting at the reserve where they were asked to wait outside while the band council discussed the lease with Anfield. Their recollection of the "tea party" at the clubhouse with Chief Ed Sparrow and Councillor Gertrude Guerin was vague, but one witness recalled Mrs. Guerin as "a most charming and delightful person to talk with."[55] It "was a chance to discuss and be on social terms with our delightful friends from the Reserve, from the Band."[56] Their concern was the ability of the club to pay the agreed rent and avoid moving out to the suburbs as they could no longer stay at the current location in the Shaughnessy area of Vancouver, where most of the club's members lived. "We had truly our own selfish point of view, what we felt we could pay, taking a long gamble."[57] The department officials had not tried to increase the rent by telling them of the other offers for the land. They had met for a "lunch or two" with Anfield at the golf club, but Anfield felt that "he should not accept club lunches where he had no opportunity of signing a chit, indefinitely" and refused a lunch invitation to the Yacht Club.[58] One former director of the club described his visits to Ottawa, where he lobbied a senior Department of Indian Affairs official.[59]

The Crown called Alfred Howell, who had prepared the appraisal report for the department in 1957.[60] His evidence turned out to be very favourable to the band. His original report gave a value for the lands of $5,500.00 an acre and then used a capitalization rate of 6 percent, which gave a rent of $53,450 each year. (It is important to note that this value was based on the standard appraisal approach of highest and best use, which all experts at the trial agreed was residential use, and not on a reduced use as a golf course.) Anfield gave that value to the golf club officials but not to the band. The club countered with $25,000, less than half the initial annual rent in Howell's original report. Instead of terminating the negotiations because of the club's failure to come anywhere close to the appraised rent, Anfield wrote Howell to ask whether a rent of $25,000 for the first fifteen years of the lease would be "just and equitable." Howell was not given any other details of the proposed lease, particularly the restrictions limiting future rents and giving the club the right to terminate the lease and remove the improvements.

Of critical importance, in giving his opinion he had assumed that there was nothing to prevent the rent from being renegotiated on the basis of the land's highest and best use, which he confirmed was residential.[61] He thought the renegotiation of the rent would be based on the highest-and-best-use principle, and was not aware of the rent restrictions. He expressed shock at the ultimate terms of the lease limiting the initial rent increase to 15 percent.[62] As he stated in his letter giving the revised opinion, he had thought "the Department will be in a much sounder position to negotiate an increase in rental in fifteen years' time when the Club will have invested a considerable amount of capital in the property."[63] This was not the case due to the restrictions proposed by the club and included in the lease. Howell stated that if he had known the improvements would not revert to the band, he would have recommended a rate of return of 4 to 6 percent.

The next witness for the Crown, William Grant, also greatly aided the band's case.[64] He was Anfield's assistant and had accompanied him to the surrender meeting. His account of the meeting and the understanding of the band members supported that given by the witnesses for the band. In particular, he said that the band members did not approve the rent restriction provisions that appeared without their knowledge in the lease as signed. They strongly opposed any restriction on the rent payable.[65] Anfield had told the band members that in ten years the band could "really hit the Golf Club with a big raise" based on the best rent possible for the use of the land.[66] Grant was clear that the position of the band members was that no lease was to be signed except on the terms as understood by them – "the Band didn't give him [Anfield] authority to change things around after."[67] He agreed that there was "very little resemblance" between the lease terms approved by the band members and the lease as signed.[68]

Anfield had died in 1961, but witnesses for the Crown, including Grant, provided some insight into his background and personality. (More details are provided in Chapter 2.) He was born in England in 1900 and was the principal of an Anglican residential school for "Indian" children in Alert Bay for a number of years. He was known at the time as the "Reverend Anfield," although he does not seem to have been an ordained priest. He subsequently joined the Department of Indian Affairs and served as Indian agent at Prince Rupert and Bella Coola before joining the department in Vancouver. According to Grant, after twenty-five to thirty years in the residential school system and at the Department of Indian Affairs, Anfield had become very paternalistic, although he meant well. He was fond of saying that "the Indians are my responsibility from the womb to the tomb."[69] He liked "to have things done his own way, whether it was with [Grant] or the Band or anyone else."[70] As confirmed by other witnesses, this paternalistic attitude was apparent in the voting procedure at the surrender meeting, when Anfield made the mark for the voter who held the other end of the pencil. Asked whether he found this procedure to be incredible, Grant said:

> It ... yes, I imagine incredible would be a word that would describe it, it's a – but knowing Mr. Anfield, a different ... it was part of his makeup that rather than use the ballot box and these people were familiar with the ballot box ... [he] reverted back to the father/child attitude, this paternalism, and you know, it was decided it was better to do it that way.[71]

The Crown called witnesses from Ottawa to explain the handling of Indian monies, the different roles within the Department of Indian

Affairs, and the policy of the government on the retention of records. As explained by witnesses, it was not the practice of the department to provide copies of documents to bands.[72] The band obtained a copy of the lease only as the result of the persistent efforts of Delbert Guerin, who was the Chief in the early 1970s.[73] Another witness was Jack Letcher, who had succeeded Anfield.[74] He had finished up some of the administrative work that had to be completed with respect to the lease with the club. When asked whether anyone had asked for a copy of the lease, he referred to a request in 1964 from Professor Philip White of the University of British Columbia, who was acting for the band in connection with another lease.[75] White had been provided with a copy of the lease with the club together with other information. This was a very significant and potentially damaging piece of evidence as it could have supported a successful defence that the band had not acted reasonably in trying to obtain the lease and had accordingly delayed too long in bringing its claim. Letters between Letcher and White regarding the transmittal of documents, including the lease with the club, were produced from a government file.

During a short mid-morning break in the proceedings, we obtained the file from the government's lawyers and reviewed these letters. We also found another that, through oversight, had not been listed by the Crown in its List of Documents. This letter from White, dated 15 April 1964, was very critical of the department's lack of cooperation in providing a copy of the lease being proposed to another tenant and the department's insistence that the tenant had to consent to a copy being given to White. He had tried several times to obtain the terms of that proposed lease but had been put off by officials. He referred to the department's "absurd and irregular proceedings" and said:

> I fail entirely to understand these procrastinations and excuses ... As I understand the position, the land in question belongs to the Band, and I regard it as nothing short of monstrous that the person asked by the Band to advise them as to the disposition of their property is denied access to the terms of the disposition by those who have acted on their behalf.[76]

He stated in the letter that he would hold the department responsible for its lack of cooperation. Gunnar Eggertson, counsel for the Crown, had said that the relevance of the letter he had entered into evidence was that the Court could draw the inference that, since Letcher had made the Shaughnessy lease available to Professor White on request, it would have done the same if the band members had made such a request. The letter dated 15 April 1964, buried deep in the government's file and not listed on its List of Documents, showed that, in fact, White's request for a copy of the lease that he was interested in had been rebuffed on several occasions and it took a strongly worded and somewhat threatening letter from a well-qualified person able to make trouble for the officials to obtain essential information as to the lease terms. Far from supporting the Crown's position, the evidence regarding White supported the band's claim that requests from band members for a copy of the Shaughnessy lease had been denied.

After the Crown had entered evidence through its experts on the value of the lands and the maximum loss suffered by the band, the trial closed on 8 November 1979 with legal argument. The Crown urged the defence of political trust, namely that any obligation that it had was not enforceable by a court. In reply, Marvin Storrow said:

> By defending this action on the basis of "Political Trust" the Department is essentially saying to Indian peoples across this country that we as a Government can control your lives through the Indian Act, that we can control your lands, that we can do things to affect your lives that we cannot do to any other group in Canada and when we do these things you have absolutely no recourse to the courts of this Country.
>
> It is submitted that this position is one which cannot be condoned by the courts of this Country.[77]

Storrow also submitted that the Crown had failed to plead the defence of political trust. Justice Collier agreed that the defence should have been pleaded by the Crown. He gave leave to do so but on condition that either the minister of Indian Affairs or the minister of justice be made available for examination for discovery on that point.[78] This was a significant ruling and would have enabled the band to cross-examine a senior minister on government policy, which might have been very revealing. Perhaps to avoid this possibility, the Crown withdrew the defence.[79] The environment minister and local Member of Parliament, John Fraser, was quoted as saying that the political trust doctrine was "obnoxious ... and most improper to raise."

Three months after the trial closed, the Crown was successful in a motion to reopen it so that the evidence of John Ellis, a real estate developer, could be given.[80] Ellis claimed that during his negotiations with the band in 1963 on a subsequent lease of adjacent lands, someone on the band council had asked for a 15 percent limit on rent increases "because this was the limit that they had on the Shaughnessy lease."[81] He thought the statement about the limit in the Shaughnessy lease had been made by the late Willard Sparrow. Witnesses were called on behalf of the band to rebut this new evidence as to the band's knowledge of the terms of the Shaughnessy lease. Each denied knowing of the lease and having any reason to think that the late Willard Sparrow knew of the lease terms. In his Reasons for Judgment, Collier accepted the evidence of the band members over that of Ellis.[82] He pointed out that it was not in the interests of the band for the band council to propose a 15 percent limit on rent increases as Ellis had testified.

THE JUDGMENT

After about thirty days of evidence and argument, the trial finally came to an end on 25 March 1980. Justice Collier reserved judgment, which was not delivered until 3 July 1981.[83] The judgment takes up fifty-nine pages in the official law report. Except for the disappointing amount of compensation, it was a great victory for the band. Collier rejected the Crown's contention that the band's claim was based on hindsight and that band members had convinced themselves of things that did not happen. He found the witnesses from the band "to be honest, truthful witnesses. They did not, in my assessment, conjure up the key evidentiary matters disputed by the defendant. Nor, in my view, was their evidence based on hindsight and reconstruction. On some matters

... the Band members' testimony is, on analysis, supported by other evidence."[84]

After a careful and detailed review of the evidence given at the trial both orally and in documentary form, he concluded that:

- the band was not told of any interest in or proposals for development of the land other than that of the golf club[85]
- during the negotiations on the rent, Earl Anfield gave information on the appraised value of the land to the golf club but not to the band[86]
- not all the terms of the club's proposals were given to the band council by Anfield[87]
- Anfield did not give all the details of the club's proposal to Alfred Howell when he asked Howell for his opinion on the rent being proposed[88]
- Howell would not have expressed his opinion the way he had if he had had all the facts before him[89]
- Anfield's advice to Chief Sparrow that Howell considered a 3 percent return to be "a very satisfactory return" was "an overstatement"[90]
- before the band members voted to surrender the lands for leasing, they understood that:[91]

  (1) apart from the first rent period, the lease would have rent periods of ten years
  (2) there would be no 15 percent limitation on rental increases

- band members also had no knowledge that the club had the right to remove improvements at the end of the lease, that the future rents were to be based on the uncleared and unimproved condition of the lands with a restriction as to its use rather than on its market value, and that the club had a unilateral right to terminate the lease[92]
- after the surrender meeting, the department failed to consult the band on the provisions increasing subsequent rent periods to fifteen years, restricting the increase for the second period to 15 percent, restricting future increases to the uncleared and unimproved condition, allowing the club to take the improvements, and giving the club the unilateral right of termination[93]

- the terms of the lease that was ultimately entered into "bore little resemblance to what was discussed at the surrender meeting"[94]
- the balance of probabilities was that the majority of those who voted at the surrender meeting "would not have assented to a surrender of the 162 acres if they had known all the terms of the lease of 22 January 1958"[95]
- despite requests for copies of the lease, the band was unsuccessful in obtaining a copy until March 1970[96]
- the band had no reason to think that a lease with terms different from what they had been led to believe would be the case had been entered into.[97]

In short, the band's account of what took place, including the misrepresentation and concealment by Department of Indian Affairs officials, was held to be correct.

After the above findings of facts were reached, the next issue was to determine their legal effect. Collier reviewed the cases on whether the Crown could be a trustee. He concluded that there was, in the case before him, a legal trust created between the Crown and the band.[98] The Crown had become a trustee effective on the date of the surrender of the 162 acres and the band was the beneficiary.[99] He referred to the defence of political trust and said that since the Crown had not amended the pleadings to add this defence, he would not deal with it.[100]

He then considered the terms of the trust upon which the lands were to be leased, which he found to be those understood by the band members at the time of the surrender vote:

(a) A total term of seventy-five years;
(b) The rental revenue for the first 15 years to be $29,000;
(c) The remaining 60 years of the lease to be divided into six 10-year terms;
(d) Future rental increases to be negotiated for each new term; no provisions regarding arbitration or the manner in which the land would be valued;

(e) No 15 % limitation on rental increases;

(f) All improvements on the land, on the expiration of the lease, to revert to the Crown.[101]

Since the lease contained terms that were substantially different from those authorized by the band and the Crown had failed to get authorizations for those changes, there had been a breach of trust.[102]

Collier next considered the defences of the Crown based on the alleged unreasonable delay of the band in bringing the claim.[103] The lease was entered into on 22 January 1958 and the claim was commenced almost eighteen years later, in December 1975. The Crown said that it was prejudiced in being able to make a defence since key witnesses such as Anfield and William Arneill, the commissioner of Indian Affairs for British Columbia at the time of the lease negotiations, had died before the trial. It attempted to demonstrate through the evidence of John Ellis and Professor White's report in 1964 that the band either knew of the terms of the lease or, acting reasonably, could have known and so should have brought the action much earlier. It submitted that the action was barred by either the six-year limitations period in the statute of limitations or the equitable doctrine of laches, which defeats a plaintiff who "sleeps on his rights."

Collier rejected those defences on the basis of his finding that the band did not know the terms of the lease until March 1970. It had been unsuccessful in obtaining a copy of the lease until then despite its requests. Department officials had failed to return to the band after the surrender meeting to advise members of the true terms of the lease or to get another authorization for the changes. This conduct was "unconscionable" and "a concealment amounting to equitable fraud," which prevented the defences being used against the band.[104] He found, however, that there was no fraud in the sense of deceit, dishonesty, or moral turpitude.[105]

He also considered and rejected the Crown's request that it be granted relief under a provision in the *Trustee Act* that enables a court to relieve a trustee from personal liability if the trustee has acted honestly and reasonably.[106] In his view, this provision applied only to the Supreme Court of British Columbia, not the Federal Court. Even if he had jurisdiction, however, he would not grant relief in the circumstances. The Indian Affairs officials had acted honestly but not reasonably in signing the lease without first going back to the band. It would not be fair to excuse the Crown.

Finally, Collier considered the "extremely difficult question of damages."[107] As he pointed out, a great deal of evidence at the lengthy trial was on that subject and given by experts in various fields. Having found that the band would not have accepted the terms that appeared in the Shaughnessy lease, he turned his attention to how to put the band in the position it would have been in if the lease had not been signed. One of the most difficult questions was what would have happened to the land if the lease had not been signed. He reviewed a number of possibilities, including a development based on a ninety-nine-year prepaid lease for residential use as proposed by the band's appraiser, George Oikawa. The three appraisers called by the Crown did not agree that this was a possibility at the time. After considering the proposed development at around the same time of the adjacent University Endowment Lands in the Turner Report and the interest expressed by potential developers in leasing the lands, Collier accepted the opinion of Oikawa over that of the appraisers for the Crown. He was not persuaded, however, that the area would have been developed as quickly as Oikawa had opined. The land may have remained undeveloped for a few years after 1958. "Development might have been, at first, slow, limited, and somewhat experimental. In my view, the area would probably have been well on the road to full development, on a leasehold basis, by approximately 1968 to 1971."[108]

The band had put forward four suggested approaches that estimated losses at between $45 million and $71 million. In Collier's view, "none of those suggested approaches are completely unrealistic. The calculations, based on acceptance of all the plaintiff's evidence as to damages, are, to my mind, relatively conservative."[109] However, he could not accept these calculations because of two factors. None of the approaches took into account "a very realistic contingency in 1988, or at a later rent review period, the golf club may decide, because of the obviously high rents in sight, to terminate the lease."[110] Also, they were based on Oikawa's opinion on the possibility of a development in 1958 as opposed to the later date found by him. Having rejected full acceptance of the band's calculations, he considered the Crown's submissions on the loss suffered and also rejected them. He summarized his views thus: "My views are, in effect, somewhere between those of the plaintiff and those of the defendant. But I have no doubt the plaintiffs, by the breach of the trust by the defendant, have suffered a very substantial loss."[111]

He referred to cases that said that a court has to assess damages as best it can even if it involves guesswork, and then assessed the damages at $10 million.[112] He said he had experimented with various approaches to set out some, perhaps even vague, mathematical basis for coming to this sum – "but I found myself unable to set out a precise rationale or approach, mathematical or otherwise. The dollar award is obviously a global figure. It is a considered reaction based on the evidence, the opinions, the arguments and, in the end, my conclusions of fact."[113] He then set out some of the factors and contingencies that he had in mind, including the contingency that the area might not have been satisfactorily developed; the astonishing increase in land values; inflation and interest rates since 1958; the possibility that the lease would remain in effect until its expiry in 2033; "the very real contingency" that it might be terminated at some future rental review period; the monies already received and to be received by the band under the lease; and finally, the value of the improvements.[114] He rejected the band's claim for exemplary damages. The actions of the department officials could not be seen as "oppressive or arbitrary conduct, warranting punishment by way of exemplary damages."[115]

REACTION

The decision was welcomed by band members. Delbert Guerin was described in the press as elated, and quoted as saying, "I'm just getting higher and higher. I won't be able to keep my feet on the ground soon."[116] However, the award of only $10 million rather than the minimum amount claimed of $45 million came as a big disappointment to the band and its legal team, and was to lead to more litigation in future years to seek a more just remedy, as discussed in the next chapter. With respect to Justice Collier, his rejection of the band's "relatively conservative" calculations on the basis of the contingency that the club might move in 1988 or later was untenable. As we have seen, he referred to the "obviously high rents in sight" as a reason why the club might do so. Yet, unknown to the band members at the time they approved the surrender of land for the lease to the club, the lease ties the rent throughout its duration to the fiction that the lands are to be considered as if "in an uncleared and unimproved condition ... considering the restricted use" rather than the market rent as understood by the band and the government's appraiser, Alfred Howell. The band did not have the ability to "really hit the Golf Club with a big raise" based on the best rent possible for the use of the land as promised by Anfield.[117] It seems that Collier overlooked the effect of this restriction on the rent and the other terms of the lease, which were so favourable to the club, in his consideration of the contingency that the club might move before 2033, the termination date of the lease. Many of the witnesses at the trial, including the director of lands for the Department of Indian Affairs and a former lands officer for the department, demonstrated just how unusually pro-tenant the lease was.

It is difficult to see why the club would want to move or where they could hope to find a more favourable lease. The lease has achieved for them exactly what they set out to achieve, namely, artificially low rents, a long-term security of tenure that they alone can terminate on six months' notice, and the ability to continue operating in the west side of Vancouver without members' suffering the inconvenience of driving out to the suburbs, which was the fate of other clubs similarly situated.[118] The club has not moved, of course, and there is no reasonable basis to think that they will do so until they are forced to in 2033, when the lease expires.

INTEREST ON THE AWARD?

In August 1981, the band sought interest on the award from 22 January 1958 (the date of the lease) to 12 July 1981, the date the award was formally made, and post-judgment interest at an increased rate.[119] It was estimated that these amounts would add another $60 to $90 million to the $10 million awarded.[120] At the time of the hearing, the Crown was represented by Ian Binnie and Cindy Roth. Binnie was a prominent Ontario lawyer who had lectured on Aboriginal rights at Osgoode Hall Law School and who was to be counsel for the Crown before the Federal Court of Appeal and the Supreme Court of Canada. From 1982 to 1986, including during the *Guerin* appeals, he was associate deputy minister of justice for Canada.[121] As counsel for the Crown in the *Guerin* case before the Supreme Court of Canada, he was accompanied by Mitchell Taylor and M. Freeman.

Giving judgment from the bench, Justice Collier rejected these applications.[122] He found that section 35 of the *Federal Court Act* prohibited the award of interest against the Crown unless a contract or statute authorized the award. In his view, there was no contract or statute that provided such authorization. He also held that he had no power to vary the rate of post-judgment interest.[123] This ruling added to the disappointment of the band and its legal team over the monetary aspect of the decision. Still, the band had won a great victory in obtaining a ruling that it had a legal remedy for the Crown's failure to live up to its obligations. The sum of $10 million, although only a fraction of the loss suffered and to be suffered by the band due to the Shaughnessy lease, was still significant to the financially struggling band.

FEDERAL COURT OF APPEAL

The Arguments
After receiving Collier's decision, the band tried to negotiate a settlement with the federal government to avoid the risk and costs associated with an appeal.[124] These efforts were unsuccessful. Minister of Indian Affairs John Munro refused to discuss the case, and the Crown appealed the

judgment to the Federal Court of Appeal.[125] The band cross-appealed, seeking an increase in the amount of damages, a reversal of Collier's refusal to award pre-judgment interest, an increase in the post-judgment rate of interest, and costs at a higher rate.

Many legal arguments were advanced by the government to persuade the Federal Court of Appeal that the trial judge had been wrong.[126] Despite its withdrawal by the minister of justice at the trial, the political trust doctrine was strongly pursued,[127] and reliance was placed on cases such as *Kinloch, Tito,* and *St. Ann's Island Shooting and Fishing Club* (these and other cases referenced below are discussed in Chapter 3).[128] Reference was made to the practical consequences flowing from the imposition of a legally enforceable trust obligation on the government. The decision to revive the political trust defence was probably connected to the change of federal government from the short-lived Progressive Conservative government of Joe Clark to the Liberal government of Pierre Trudeau.

On behalf of the band, the political trust defence was opposed both on procedural grounds and on the merits.[129] It was submitted that, if the Crown disagreed with the trial judge's ruling disallowing the defence except on terms, it should have appealed that ruling. It was not free to simply ignore the ruling, and so it could not raise the defence now. It was argued that the cases relied upon by the Crown to support the defence were not applicable, and reliance was placed instead upon *Miller, Dreaver,* and a recent decision of the Federal Court, *Kruger v The Queen,* in which Justice Mahoney held that the Crown had title to a reserve under "a true trust" and not "a political trust."[130] It was pointed out that when the alleged breaches of trust took place, "Indian" people (save for limited exceptions) were forbidden to vote in federal elections:[131] "The doors of Parliament were then closed to our Native people, the Appellant now seeks to close the doors of the Courts of Justice."[132] Further, it was argued that a defence of political trust would deny "Indian" people equal protection of the law, contrary to the *Canadian Bill of Rights* and the spirit of the *Canadian Charter of Rights and Freedoms,* which had recently been passed as part of the *Constitution Act, 1982* but which was not yet in force.[133]

One argument of the Crown was to dispute the judge's statement that the reserve lands were the lands, the potential investment, and the future of the band. In the government's submission, the federal government could terminate the interest of the band in the reserve lands at its pleasure. Therefore, there could be no legally enforceable trust because the band owned no interest in the reserve lands that could form the subject matter of a trust.[134] This was an important argument that helped turn the case from a breach of trust/fiduciary obligation case (similar to many situations where vulnerable groups such as widows and orphans have been deceived by trustees or other fiduciaries) to a case raising fundamental issues of Aboriginal rights and, in particular, the nature of Aboriginal title. The theory of the case and legal research had revolved around issues of general trust and fiduciary law. Now the Crown's argument that the band lacked any legal interest in the lands forced the lawyers for the band to consider and raise issues of Aboriginal law. Our job had become much harder. It was a very troubling development – adding the insult that Indian bands had no interest in reserve lands (let alone traditional lands) to the injury of the political trust argument.[135] The stakes had been dramatically raised – a loss on this point would result in a severe setback to Aboriginal rights. Although the Nisga'a had been unsuccessful a few years earlier in *Calder,* that case had opened up the possibility that a majority of the Supreme Court of Canada might find that Aboriginal title still existed.[136] The Crown was now seeking to foreclose that possibility but, in doing so, it was running a huge risk that the possibility might become greater.

In reply to this new argument, it was argued for the band that "Indian" peoples *do* have a proprietary interest in their lands.[137] It was also argued that, in any event, the cases cited by the Crown to deny such an interest did not relate to reserve laws but Aboriginal title lands and so could be distinguished by the court. Section 18 of the *Indian Act,* which provides that reserves are held by the Crown "for the use and benefit" of the band, recognizes the band's beneficial interest in the reserve and rendered the Crown a trustee. Even if those cases were relevant, the nature of Aboriginal title was not to be found by an analysis using common law concepts but by way of an inquiry into the actual form of enjoyment of land by the people in question.[138] In the case of the Musqueam, there was expert evidence that the occupants of their villages held a general proprietary interest in the lands and waters in the vicinity of the villages. Cases from the United States indicated that "Indians" had sufficient interest in lands set aside for their exclusive occupation to make a taking of these lands compensable under the Fifth Amendment.[139]

There were other arguments. In particular, the government said that all terms of the proposed lease had to be set out in the document that had been prepared by it for the band to give up its interest in the golf course lands (the surrender document) if they were to be binding on the government.[140] In reply, it was argued that the rule of law relied upon by the government (the parol evidence rule) did not prevent the band from relying upon the oral terms of the trust under which the surrender document was delivered to the government.[141] Cases were cited where courts had permitted evidence to be given that a document that was unconditional on its face had, in fact, been delivered subject to a condition that had to be satisfied before it became effective.[142] Further, it was submitted that to ignore the oral terms would, in effect, reduce the surrender meeting to a mere sham and constitute a gross fraud on the band members.

The Judgment

The appeal was heard in June 1982 and the Federal Court of Appeal handed down its unanimous judgment, written by Justice Gerald Le Dain, on 10 December 1982.[143] Le Dain was a former dean of Osgoode Hall Law School and had chaired the commission of inquiry into the non-medical use of drugs, which attracted some publicity as it recommended that cannabis be removed from the narcotic control legislation, a controversial recommendation that was ignored by governments for decades. He was appointed to the Federal Court of Appeal in 1975.[144]

The Federal Court of Appeal allowed the government's appeal, rejected the band's cross-appeal for greater compensation, and awarded costs to the government. The judgment can be summarized in three statements:

1 The interest of the band in reserve lands is in the nature of a property right and so could be the subject of a trust.
2 The terms of the trust were contained only in the surrender document and there could be no oral terms to the trust.
3 Neither the provisions of the *Indian Act* nor the surrender created a legally enforceable trust, but only a governmental obligation or "political trust."

On the issue of whether the Indian title or interest in reserve lands was a property right, Le Dain reviewed prior judicial commentary, especially in the *St Catherine's Milling, Star Chrome,* and *Calder* cases.[145] He also referred to US cases holding the interest of "Indians" in certain reservations to be property within the Fifth Amendment;[146] to the Privy Council decision in *Amodu Tijani,* which dealt generally with the concept of Native title;[147] to cases dealing specifically with the *Indian Act* provisions relating to reserve lands;[148] and finally to an article in which Professor K. Lysyk expressed the view that the Indian title amounts to a beneficial interest in the land.[149] Based on this detailed analysis of Indian title, he concluded:

> For the reasons suggested by Viscount Haldane in *Amodu Tijani,* to which Professor Lysyk also makes reference, if the Indian title cannot be strictly characterized as a beneficial interest in the land it amounts to the same thing. It displaces the beneficial interest of the Crown. As such, it is a qualification of the title of the Crown of such content and substance as to partake, in my opinion, of the nature of a right of property. I am, therefore, of the opinion that it could be the subject of a trust.[150]

So far as Aboriginal title is concerned, the decision of the Federal Court of Appeal in *Guerin* can be seen as a significant recognition of that title as being in the nature of a property right, and a firm rejection of the argument that the Crown had chosen to raise.

The finding that the terms of the alleged trust were to be found only in the surrender document was based upon an analysis of the provision of the *Indian Act* dealing with the surrender of reserve lands,[151] particularly the requirement that the surrender be accepted by the governor-in-council.[152] The oral terms of the surrender found by the trial judge had not been accepted by the governor-in-council, nor was there any evidence that any official of the Department of Indian Affairs had accepted the oral conditions, even assuming that such conditions could be validly accepted by a departmental official. No reference was made to the band's argument on this issue save for a reference to the decision of the Ontario Court of Appeal in *R v Taylor and Williams,* which allowed oral terms as part of a treaty.[153]

The third and, for present purposes, most important issue dealt with by the Federal Court of Appeal in the *Guerin* case was whether either the *Indian Act* or the surrender document created a legally enforceable equitable obligation. Before considering this issue, Le Dain noted:

> The appeal raises squarely and unavoidably the question whether the legal relationship of the Crown, or the Government to the land in a reserve and to reserve land which is surrendered "in trust" for the purpose of lease, is that of a trustee in the private law sense, that is, whether it is an equitable obligation enforceable in the Courts.[154]

He pointed out that there was nothing in principle to prevent the Crown from acting as a trustee,[155] and then proceeded to note the distinction between "a true trust" and a trust "in the higher sense" or "a government obligation" in cases such as *Kinloch, Hereford Railway Co v The Queen, Tito,* and *Town Investments Ltd v Department of the Environment*[156] (which were considered in Chapter 3).

The band's argument that the Crown was not free to plead governmental obligation or "political trust" was rejected, as was the contention that *Miller v The King* supported a finding of a true trust.[157] With respect to the band's argument that the *Kinloch, Hereford Railway,* and *Tito* cases could be distinguished and so were not binding on the court, Le Dain said:

The [band] insisted that the facts in *Kinloch, The Hereford Railway* and *Tito v. Waddell* are quite different and distinguishable from the facts in the present case. There can be no doubt of that, but the distinction that is affirmed in those cases and the policy considerations which underlie it are relevant to the issues in the present case.[158]

Section 18 of the *Indian Act* was considered. Subject to the terms of any treaty or surrender, this section confers upon the governor-in-council the discretion to determine whether any purpose for which lands in a reserve are used or are to be used is for the use and benefit of the band. Le Dain concluded that the discretionary authority conferred by section 18 indicated that

> it is for the Government and not the courts to determine what is for the use and benefit of the Band. That provision is incompatible, in my opinion, with an intention to impose an equitable obligation, enforceable in the courts, to deal with the land in a reserve in a certain manner, and particularly, an obligation to develop or exploit the reserve so as to realize its potential as a source of revenue for the Band, which is in essence the obligation that is involved in the present case.[159]

Other provisions of the *Indian Act* supported him in that view:

> All of this, it seems to me, clearly excludes an intention to make the Crown a trustee in a private law sense of the land in a reserve. How the Government chooses to discharge its political responsibility for the welfare of the Indians is, of course, another thing. The extent to which the Government assumes an administrative or management responsibility for the reserve of some positive scope is a matter of governmental discretion, not legal or equitable obligation.[160]

An analysis of the surrender document led to the same conclusion. That document conferred a discretion upon the government to lease the lands to such person or persons and upon such terms as the government deemed most conducive to the welfare of the band. The surrender was construed to confer an authority to lease but not a duty to do so. Reference was also made to the use of the words "in trust," which had appeared in surrenders for well over one hundred years, and also in the *Terms of Union* upon which British Columbia was admitted into Canada and the provincial Order-in-Council that conveyed the reserve from the province to the Dominion of Canada.[161] Concluding this analysis, Le Dain said:

> Within this context of statute and intergovernmental agreement it is
> my opinion that the words "in trust" in the surrender document were
> intended to do no more than indicate that the surrender was for the
> benefit of the Indians and conferred an authority to deal with the land
> in a certain manner for their benefit. They were not intended to impose
> an equitable obligation or duty to deal with the land in a certain manner.
> For these reasons I am of the opinion that the surrender did not create
> a true trust and does not, therefore, afford a basis for liability based on
> a breach of trust.[162]

Reaction

The decision of the Federal Court of Appeal was a great shock and disappointment to the members of the band and the band's legal team in view of the favourable findings of fact and law made by Justice Collier and the team's assessment of the arguments made by both parties and how the Court of Appeal had appeared to receive them. The court had not reversed any finding of fact made by Collier. In fact, the statement of the facts set out by Justice Le Dain closely followed Collier's account but is more detailed in parts. The critical finding by Collier remained: the band had voted on certain terms and the lease as signed bore little resemblance to those terms. The government officials had acted in a manner that would have been a clear breach of trust for any private trustee. How could the Crown escape liability on those facts? It was so patently unjust and unfair by any reasonable standards. How could the legal system allow the government to lease the lands on terms that were so unfavourable to the band and so favourable to the club? It was difficult to reconcile this rejection of the band's claim by the court with basic concepts of the rule of law in a democratic society as a restraint on the arbitrary exercise of governmental powers and of the equal protection of the law.[163] What other group of citizens would be effectively barred from seeking justice on the plea of political trust, which seemed to have more to do with seventeenth-century theories of the absolute powers of rulers than with a twentieth-century democratic society?[164] The decision raised serious questions about the ability of the Indigenous peoples of Canada to resolve their legitimate grievances through the legal system. In April 1982, just months before the Federal Court of Appeal decision and after years of effort by Indigenous peoples, Parliament had added a provision to the Canadian Constitution recognizing and affirming "existing aboriginal and treaty rights."[165] What value would that hard-won constitutional provision have? The recognition and affirmation of non-enforceable "rights" would be a cynical mockery of the Constitution. The Federal Court of Appeal had effectively sanctioned the inferior status of Indigenous peoples as wards without legal rights.

In his account of the *Mabo* litigation in Australia, Bryan Keon-Cohen refers to the "king-hit," or unfair blow, of the state of Queensland intended to defeat the litigation by passing discriminatory legislation extinguishing Native title to the lands at issue and to the resulting outrage felt by the plaintiffs and their lawyers.[166] The equivalent in the *Guerin* case was the political trust defence. The band had been knocked to the floor by an unfair blow delivered in breach of the ruling of the trial judge that the defence could be used only if a minister of the Crown was made available for cross-examination and a statement by the minister of justice that it was being withdrawn.[167] Despite all this, it had been reintroduced by the Crown and upheld by the Federal Court of Appeal.

Apart from these broader implications for Indigenous peoples generally, the decision was a devastating blow for the Musqueam from a practical perspective. It meant that they were fixed with a lease that still had over fifty years to run, containing restrictions that meant they would not receive a market rent as members had understood would be the case when they agreed to lease the lands. No compensation was to be paid as had been ordered by the trial judge for the unconscionable conduct of the Crown. Moreover, they even had to pay the costs of the Crown for having started the litigation. The only way for the band to get back on its feet was to hope that it could get leave to appeal from the Supreme Court of Canada and successfully overcome this defence. It was by no means a sure thing. Only about 10 percent of applications for leave to appeal to the Supreme Court are granted.

Within hours of receiving the decision, Marvin Storrow and I attended a meeting of the band council to report on this setback. Informing clients of a defeat is never easy but this was an especially sobering experience. We explained our understanding of what the Federal Court of Appeal had done, noting the limited time to review the decision and its implications for the Musqueam and other Indigenous peoples. We also gave our initial views on the chances of getting leave to appeal and of success if leave was granted, as well as the additional costs involved. The council requested us to prepare a written opinion for presentation at a general band meeting to be held within a few days for members to provide direction on whether or not to seek leave to appeal. Delbert Guerin spoke movingly and eloquently of the years spent on the case and said that in his opinion the band had no choice but to continue to fight.

We prepared an opinion on a possible appeal to the Supreme Court of Canada that recommended an appeal. It analyzed the relevant legal principles, but the basis of the recommendation was ultimately that the decision of the Federal Court of Appeal and the position of the Government of Canada on the political trust issue was so unjust and the stakes were so high that the issue had to go to the highest court in Canada for resolution. At a well-attended meeting in the old community hall just a few days before Christmas 1982, the band members voted unanimously to approve that recommendation. Anyone familiar with band meetings will know that they can often be contentious – democracy in the raw. The expression "band beatings" is often used. This was not such a meeting and I recall no dissenting voices. When the band's best interests are at stake, politics of all sorts are put aside and the members come together. So it was that December. The focus now shifted to the Supreme Court in Ottawa.[168] The decision was taken on the seventh anniversary of the filing of the writ to commence the action, and it was almost two more years before the litigation against the Crown concluded with the Supreme Court decision (although litigation over the Shaughnessy lease would continue until at least 2016, with yet another visit to the Supreme Court, as we shall see in the next chapter).

5

The Supreme Court of Canada

O N 26 JANUARY 1983, we filed a notice of application for leave to appeal the decision of the Federal Court of Appeal in the Supreme Court of Canada. It stated that the essential question of law for the Supreme Court to determine was whether the *Indian Act* and the surrender of the land for leasing imposed "an equitable obligation upon the Crown enforceable in the Courts."[1] This squarely raised the political trust issue: would the Supreme Court give a remedy for the unconscionable conduct of the Crown or, like the Federal Court of Appeal, refuse to do so? To demonstrate the importance of the question, we filed an affidavit in support of the application setting out the concerns of Indigenous leaders and of Dr. Donovan Waters, Canada's leading expert in the law of trusts, confirming that the matter was one of fundamental importance to the law of trusts.[2] The public importance of the appeal was confirmed when, a couple of weeks later, the band was requested to give evidence to the Penner Inquiry conducted by a special committee of the House of Commons, which was investigating self-government by First Nations, including the implications of the trust responsibility of the federal government.[3] On 21 February 1983, a panel consisting of Chief Justice Bora Laskin and Justices Willard Estey and Bertha Wilson granted leave to appeal.[4] The band had overcome the substantial odds against getting leave to appeal. The real work could now begin.

THE ARGUMENTS

The amount of material relevant to the appeal is indicated by the fact that the Case on Appeal (now the Record) containing the pleadings, the transcript of the trial, the exhibits, and the judgments below filled 3,651 pages bound in eighteen volumes. Twenty copies of each set of volumes had to be filed with the court. The factum, or written argument, for the band consisted of 122 single-spaced pages (not including appendices), and twenty-one copies had to be filed with the court. More than 120 cases were cited. It may be noted that a limit on the length of factums was subsequently introduced, and factums are now usually limited to 40 pages (not more than five hundred words to a page), including mandatory material. Copies of the legal authorities were collected in Books of Authorities, which were also filed with the court. The Crown's factum in reply was about the same length and cited additional cases. There was also a factum from the lawyers for the National Indian Brotherhood, the predecessor of the Assembly of First Nations, the national organization of First Nations.

The band's main argument was that the Federal Court of Appeal had erred in law in failing to find that the surrender had "imposed an equitable obligation upon the Government enforceable in the Courts."[5] It was also submitted that "a true trust" and not a political trust had been created.[6] The Federal Court of Appeal was incorrect to allow the government to argue political trust as a defence in view of its failure to specifically plead this defence as required by the ruling of the trial judge.[7] The doctrine of political trust was also attacked on its merits as being inappropriate for a government to use against its own citizens,[8] and objectionable on several policy grounds as granting immunity to the government for its misconduct.[9] The Federal Court of Appeal's analysis of the case law, and especially the *Miller* case, was criticized,[10] as was the analysis of the statutory provisions and especially section 18 of the *Indian Act*.[11] The existence of a wide discretionary power did not preclude the existence of an enforceable equitable obligation.[12] It was also submitted that technical rules ought not to be applied strictly against "Indian" people, and reference was also made to the fiduciary obligation of the United States government towards American Indians.[13] An order was sought that the band's appeal should be allowed, that the government pay pre-judgment interest, punitive damages, and post-judgment interest at a rate higher than 5 percent, and that the damages awarded by the trial judge be increased.

The band's appeal was supported by the National Indian Brotherhood, representing status Indians in Canada, which had been allowed to intervene.[14] In its factum, it stressed the special importance of reserve lands as Aboriginal people depend upon them for the planning and development of their future.[15] It argued that the desperate economic conditions that Indian people suffer is a source of anguish for most Canadians. Those bands in Canada that have shown the ability to overcome their depressed economic condition have been, by and large, those that have enjoyed the full development of reserve resources. A declaration of breach of trust and for damages against the Crown was the only significant legal recourse available to ensure fair administration of surrendered lands.

In its factum, the Crown responded to the various points made on behalf of the band. It contended that the trust alleged by the band would be void as being in conflict with various binding statutory enactments.[16] The trust found by the trial judge was void for uncertainty,[17] and in any event, the band's interest in unsurrendered reserve lands was not in law property capable of being the subject matter of a trust.[18] In order for the Crown to be bound by an express trust, the terms had to be clearly communicated to the executive and acceptance "manifested by Order in Council or other authentic testimony."[19] The American law relied upon by the band was not relevant because the United States had developed a different conceptual framework in relation to Indians.[20]

THE HEARING

The hearing took place before the nine judges of the Supreme Court of Canada on 13 and 14 June 1983; only half a day would likely be

The four chiefs on the steps of the Supreme Court of Canada during the *Guerin* hearing, June 1983. *Left to right:* Ernest Campbell, Gertrude Guerin, Ed Sparrow, and Delbert Guerin. *Courtesy of the Musqueam Indian Band Archives*

allocated for it today, reflecting the move towards much shorter hearings and written arguments.[21] The first day was hot and humid in Ottawa, and we lawyers for the band sweated as we carried heavy bags full of books up the many steps of the Supreme Court building. This led one of our clients to joke that, for once, we were doing some real work. Unfortunately, the elderly Ed Sparrow, a former Chief of the band and witness at the trial, also had trouble climbing those steps and stumbled, but, with characteristic good humour, he got up and continued on his way. The journey to this building had been long and difficult, with more than one stumble along the way, but finally the band would have a hearing before Canada's highest court despite the determined effort of the Crown to deny it a legal remedy for the wrong done to it. Chief Ernie Campbell and three former Chiefs – Ed Sparrow, Gertrude Guerin, and Delbert Guerin – and other members of the band, including Fran Guerin, Leona Sparrow, George Guerin, and Andrew Charles, accompanied the legal team to the Supreme Court. They were joined by the leaders of the neighbouring Squamish Nation, another Coast Salish group, represented by Joe Mathias, Phillip Joe, Dave Jacobs, and Dick Williams. The presence of so many Indigenous people in the courtroom could not fail to impress upon the members of the court the importance of the case to Indigenous people generally.

The Supreme Court building is an impressive monument to the European-derived legal system of Canada. It was designed by Ernest Cormier, a renowned Montreal architect, in Art Deco style and built from 1938 to 1940. Situated west of the Parliament Buildings on a bluff high above the Ottawa River, it is separated from Wellington Street by a large lawn. Two heavy bronze doors lead into the Grand Entrance Hall. The floors and walls of the hall are made of gleaming marble, and busts of former chief justices are displayed around it. Courtrooms used by the Federal Court of Appeal and the Federal Court are located at each end of the hall.

On the first floor is the Main Courtroom used by the Supreme Court of Canada. The large courtroom is lined with black walnut walls. The judges sit on a raised platform at one end. Facing them are rows of tables for the lawyers and, behind the lawyers, rows of seats for litigants and members of the public. Separating the lawyers and non-lawyers is a low bar, from which is derived the expression for newly qualified lawyers of being called to the bar. A lectern for the lawyer addressing the judges is located in the middle of the room opposite them. Judges and lawyers are in their regalia, fully robed although no wigs are worn. Hearings may be held in both English and French. All in all, it is a graphic display of European architecture and legal traditions. What is missing is anything reflecting Canada's Indigenous heritage, which must add to the sense of alienation that some Indigenous litigants feel as their rights and futures are decided by the judges, none of whom have ever been of Indigenous ancestry despite many recommendations that the prime minister appoint an Indigenous justice.

Non-lawyers may find watching a live performance at the Supreme Court of Canada or a televised hearing on CPAC on late-night television boring, with lawyers and judges arguing about arcane legal issues that seem to have little to do with the real world. But the decisions of the judges, however technical, can have very real consequences for litigants, for those in a similar position, and for potentially all Canadians. There is no further appeal from the court, and it is not bound by decisions of other courts or even its own earlier decisions. It is an unelected and unrepresentative lawmaking body, and the end of the line for the litigant. So it was for the Musqueam on those hot June days in 1983. For the lawyers, a hearing can be an ordeal as the judges may interrupt and derail their carefully constructed arguments, raising astute points or seemingly irrelevant ones that must be politely turned away with profuse praise. Sometimes the judges unleash a barrage of questions; sometimes they are unnervingly silent. Nobody can predict with confidence the direction a case may take.[22]

The complexity of the *Guerin* case was evidenced by the tall stack of eighteen appeal books, three factums, and several books of legal authorities piled high before each judge. Ian Binnie, Mitchell Taylor, and M. Freeman were counsel for the Crown, while Marvin Storrow, Lew Harvey, and I appeared for the band. Chief Justice Laskin kept things moving along as the lawyers for both parties went over their written arguments and answered the judges' questions. It became obvious that the judges had read the legal arguments and were well prepared. There were no questions that indicated doubts about the decision of Justice Collier that a trust had been created and breached by the Crown. The only resistance to the band's argument came when it was alleged that the Crown's action constituted fraud. Laskin said that was a pretty harsh designation to level against the Crown and told Binnie that he did not have to reply to the allegation or to the claim for punitive damages. This indicated that the band had lost on those points but it was not a surprise since the trial judge had rejected fraud in the sense of dishonest, as opposed to unconscionable, conduct on the part of government officials. In a humorous moment, Laskin leaned over to Justice Brian Dickson and said, not realizing that his microphone was on, "Gerry [Le Dain] got it wrong." At the end of the hearing, we felt that it had gone well and assessed the band's chances of a win at 75 percent.

THE DECISION

The Supreme Court of Canada rendered its judgment on 1 November 1984.[23] Laskin had died a few months earlier in March and was succeeded as chief justice by Dickson in April. This caused some concern that there might be an evenly split decision, allowing the decision of the Federal Court of Appeal to stand. (Gerald Le Dain was appointed to the court in May, bringing the number back to nine, but he did not, of course, participate in the appeal from his own decision at the Federal Court of Appeal.) In the event, the eight remaining judges were unanimous in their decision that the appeal should be allowed, the decision of the Federal Court of Appeal should be set aside, and the judgment of the trial judge reinstated without variation, with costs to the band in all courts. They differed, however, in their reasons for reaching this decision. Three separate judgments were delivered: Dickson delivered judgment for himself and for Justices Jean Beetz, Julien Chouinard, and Antonio Lamer; Wilson delivered judgment for herself and for Justices Roland Ritchie and William McIntyre; Estey delivered his own judgment. Since it represented the views of the greatest number of judges, Dickson's judgment is considered the leading one.

In their biography of Dickson, Robert J. Sharpe and Kent Roach describe the process by which the court reached its decision.[24] Dickson's conference notes indicate that all justices agreed that the terms of the lease were "disgraceful" and that the Musqueam appeal should be allowed. He believed that Le Dain had taken "a very technical view of things." Despite this agreement on the outcome of the appeal, Dickson's attempt to get the court to speak with one voice was unsuccessful. Sharpe and Roach say the court was badly divided over the proper approach to be applied. Wilson and Estey insisted on writing separate reasons. Wilson had written the first draft of the reasons for consideration by the other members of the court and based the decision on a breach of an express trust. Dickson agreed with his clerk that it was "entirely unnecessary to stretch and, with respect, deform the law of trusts to this extent to achieve an equitable solution." He noted: "Ultimately, I am concerned that the Court in allowing the claim of the Indian

Band would be permitting recovery on three different legal bases. So far as humanly possible, I think we should speak as one voice."

Instead, there were three: his own based on fiduciary principles as applied to the Crown and Indigenous peoples; that of Wilson, which also relied on "true trust" principles; and that of Estey, based on the obligation owed by an agent to carry out his instructions. All agreed that the Crown owed a duty to the Musqueam but differed in the technical basis for this conclusion: should it be based on general principles of fiduciary law, unique duties owed by the Crown to Indigenous peoples, trust law, or agency law? However, as Leonard Rotman has pointed out:

> Regardless of whether the relationship between the Crown and Musqueam is described as fiduciary *or* trust-like in nature, there is no difference in the nature, scope, or extent of the Crown's obligations.
>
> ... The significance of the *Guerin* case lies in its recognition of the Crown's legal duty and the obligations which emanate from it, not whether the Crown's duty is rooted in fiduciary doctrine or the law of trusts. Upon a judicial determination that an Indian band or organization is owed equitable obligations by the Crown to act in its best interests, it is ultimately immaterial to the court whether those obligations are derived from fiduciary or trust law.[25]

As discussed below, the absence of a consistent approach is still regrettable and may have been partially responsible for some of the conceptual confusion that subsequently developed in the law, as discussed in the conclusion of this book.

Although not directly mentioned in the judgment of any member of the court, the momentous developments in the Canadian Constitution that took place between the *Guerin* trial in 1979 and the decision of the Supreme Court of Canada in 1984 may well have encouraged the court to take a bolder approach than it otherwise would have.[26] This is strongly suggested by the statement made by Chief Justice Dickson and Justice Gérard La Forest in the 1990 *Sparrow* decision that "it is essential to remember that the *Guerin* case was decided after the commencement of the *Constitution Act 1982*."[27] This confirms that the constitutional developments leading to section 35 of the *Constitution Act, 1982* recognizing and affirming existing Aboriginal and treaty rights of the Aboriginal peoples of Canada were in the minds of the judges as they heard and decided *Guerin*. As we shall see in the next chapter, *Guerin* was to strengthen the constitutional protection for these rights.

Decision of Justice Wilson

Justice Wilson gave judgment for herself and for Justices Ritchie and McIntyre. Born in Scotland and the wife of a Presbyterian minister, she was the first woman to become a Supreme Court of Canada judge.[28] She was appointed in 1982 after heading a research department in a large Toronto law firm and then serving on the Ontario Court of Appeal, and she remained on the Supreme Court until 1991. During her tenure, she wrote and participated in major decisions such as *Morgentaler*, which overturned the *Criminal Code* restrictions on abortion.[29] Her colleague Justice Claire L'Heureux-Dubé wrote that Wilson's rulings helped shape not only Canada's legal landscape but indeed also our sense of who we are as Canadians.[30]

In her judgment, Wilson noted that in any breach of trust action, the facts are extremely important, and she set out the facts as found by the trial judge.[31] She then considered the contention made on behalf of the band that section 18 of the *Indian Act* imposed on the Crown a fiduciary obligation enforceable in the courts.[32] In her view, section 18 did not *per se* create a fiduciary obligation, which has its roots in the Aboriginal title of "Canada's Indians" as discussed in the *Calder* case.[33] Section 18 acknowledged a historical reality, namely, that Indian bands have a beneficial interest in their reserves and that the Crown has a responsibility to protect that interest and make sure that any purpose to which reserve land is put will not interfere with it. This is not to say that the Crown either historically or by section 18 holds the land in trust for the bands. The bands do not have the fee (in other words, the absolute ownership) in the lands; their interest is a limited one, but it is an interest that cannot be derogated from or interfered with by the Crown's utilization of the land for purposes incompatible with the Indian title unless, of course, the "Indians" agree. She continued:

> I believe that in this sense the Crown has a fiduciary obligation to the Indian Bands with respect to the uses to which reserve land may be put and that s. 18 is a statutory acknowledgment of that obligation. It is my view, therefore, that while the Crown does not hold reserve land under s. 18 of the Act in trust for the Bands because the Bands' interests are limited by the nature of Indian title, it does hold the lands subject to a fiduciary obligation to protect and preserve the Bands' interests from invasion or destruction.[34]

She next considered the Crown's submission that any obligation imposed on the Crown by section 18 was political only and unenforceable in the courts, as held by the Federal Court of Appeal.[35] In her opinion, the discretion conferred on the governor-in-council by the section was not unfettered. It had to be exercised on proper principles and not in an arbitrary fashion. The "political trust" cases were inapplicable because the band had a beneficial interest in its reserve and those cases concerned funds that were the property of, or in the possession of, the Crown.[36] The tactics of the Crown with regard to the political trust defence earned her rebuke:

> I agree with the appellant's submission that the Crown's tactics in this regard left a lot to be desired. It is quite apparent that when the trial judge indicated a willingness to permit an amendment at trial but went on to order discovery on the issue, the Crown renounced the defence both at trial and through ministerial statements made out of court. It nevertheless went ahead and sought and obtained leave to raise it in the Federal Court of Appeal. Even although, as the Court of Appeal pointed out, the defence is a strictly legal one and the Band was probably not prejudiced by the absence of discovery, the Crown's behaviour does not,

in my view, exemplify the high standard of professionalism we have come to expect in the conduct of litigation.[37]

This was a remarkably strong reprimand, especially if one bears in mind that the senior counsel for the Crown was associate deputy minister of justice for Canada and became a member of the Supreme Court of Canada.

Continuing her analysis of section 18, Wilson noted that the governor-in-council's discretion was "subject to the terms of any treaty or surrender" so that a band could pre-empt that discretion. She also considered the Crown's submission that it could rely upon the terms of the surrender document, which gave the Crown complete discretion both as to the lessee and the terms of the lease.[38] This submission was also rejected. The Crown was well aware that the terms of the lease were important to the band. It ill became the Crown to obtain a surrender of the band's interest for lease on terms voted on and approved by the band members at a meeting specially called for the purpose and then assert an overriding discretion to ignore those terms at will:

It makes a mockery of the Band's participation. The Crown well knew that the lease it made with the golf club was not the lease the Band surrendered its interest to get. Equity will not permit the Crown in such circumstances to hide behind the language of its own document.[39]

She returned to section 18 and considered the effect of the surrender of the land in trust for a lease on specific terms upon the Crown's fiduciary duty under the section:

It seems to me that s.18 presents no barrier to a finding that the Crown became a full-blown trustee by virtue of the surrender. The surrender prevails over the s.18 duty, but in this case there is no incompatibility between them. Rather, the fiduciary duty which existed at large under the section to hold the land in the reserve for the use and benefit of the band crystallized upon the surrender into an express trust of specific land for a specific purpose.[40]

In the circumstances of this case, the Crown was compelled to hold the surrendered land in trust for the purpose of the lease that the band members had approved as being for their benefit. The Crown was no longer free to decide that a lease on some other terms would do. Its hands were tied. When the golf club refused to enter into a lease on the approved terms, the Crown should have returned to the band and informed it of this:

> I think the learned trial judge was right in finding that the Crown acted in breach of trust when it barrelled ahead with a lease on terms which, according to the learned judge, were wholly unacceptable to its *cestui que trust* [the band as the beneficiary].[41]

Wilson continued by discussing the band's claim in deceit,[42] and noted that the trial judge had rejected this claim because there was no dishonesty or moral turpitude on the part of the government officials. The trial judge's findings were sufficient to dispose of this ground of appeal. Nevertheless, there was concealment amounting to equitable fraud that prevented the Crown from applying for relief from liability for breach of trust under section 98 of the *British Columbia Trustee Act.*[43]

Finally, Wilson considered in some detail the measure of damages, interest, and costs.[44] This was one of the most difficult issues. She concluded that the trial judge had not committed any error in principle in approaching the damages issue on the basis of a lost opportunity for residential development. She did not think it was the function of the Supreme Court to interfere with the quantum of damages awarded by the trial judge if no error in principle in determining the measure of damages had been demonstrated. The trial judge was entitled to treat the termination of the lease by the club as a contingency tending towards diminution of the band's damages, and it was not for the Supreme Court of Canada to substitute the value it would have put upon that contingency for his. His refusal to award punitive damages and pre-judgment interest and his award of post-judgment interest at 5 percent were also upheld.

Decision of Justice Estey

In his judgment, Justice Estey expressed his view that the action "should be disposed of on the very simple basis of the law of agency."[45] He distinguished between "surrenders" in which the Indian band severed entirely its connection with the land, which he thought would be better described as a release, and "surrenders" in which the band did not release its interest but appointed the Crown as its agent to develop and exploit its interest in the land by a lease or licence. In this case, the band had given detailed instructions to the representatives of the Government of Canada on the terms of the lease. These representatives did not carry out these instructions or keep the band apprised of the negotiations.[46] Most seriously of all, the Crown did not give the instructing band a copy of the lease or a written description of its contents for many years after the lease was executed. Estey concluded:

> The fact that the agent is prescribed by statute in no way detracts in law from the legal capacity of the agent to act as such. The further consideration that the principal (the Indian Band as holder of the personal interest in the land) is constrained by statute to act through the agency of the Crown, in no way reduces the rights of the instructing principal to call upon the agent to account for the performance of the mandate.
>
> ... For these reasons, I would, with great respect to all who hold a contrary view, hesitate to resort to the more technical and far-reaching doctrines of the law of trusts and the concomitant law attaching to the fiduciary. The result is the same but, in my respectful view, the future application of the Act and the common law to native rights is much simpler under the doctrines of the law of agency.[47]

It may be true that using doctrines of the law of agency simplifies the application of the *Indian Act* and the common law to Aboriginal rights. As Richard Bartlett has pointed out, however, this analysis of the relationship between the Crown and Indigenous peoples as being based on agency law is startling and unusual.[48] It is inconsistent with basic principles of agency law. Agents do not have title to the property of the principal, but the Crown has title to reserve lands under section 18 of the *Indian Act*. Agency is based on an agreement, but there is no agreement between the Crown and Indigenous peoples. The major role of an agent is to create contractual relationships between the principal and a third party, but the Crown does not enter into agreements on behalf of Indigenous peoples. Further, Rotman has also observed that the Crown's relationship with Indigenous peoples cannot properly be characterized as one of agency, for "unlike the relationship created by the *Indian Act* land surrender requirements, an agency relationship is a voluntary one."[49] It should also be remembered that agents are fiduciaries. Estey's judgment has not been followed in other cases.

Decision of Chief Justice Dickson

Chief Justice Dickson was the child of Irish immigrants. He grew up in Saskatchewan and practised law in Winnipeg. He was severely injured in 1944 during the Battle of Falaise Gap in Normandy, resulting in the amputation of his leg in a field hospital. Appointed to the Supreme Court of Canada in 1973, he retired as chief justice in 1990 and passed away in 1998, leaving a lasting impact, which is described by his biographers as follows in contrasting the period before and the period after his tenure:

> For the most part, the Court spent its time dealing with technical legal questions and resolving run-of-the-mill disputes. Most judges thought that their job was to apply precedents and the clear letter of the law, leaving questions of law reform and social justice to the elected legislatures. Judgments were written for a strictly legal audience; there was little scope for the consideration of the relevant historical, social, and political context. Broader issues of theory and policy were not confronted openly in judicial decision-making and the judges rarely strayed from traditional legal sources.

Yet, by the time Dickson retired as chief justice of Canada in 1990, the Supreme Court had become a major national institution, very much in the public eye and at the centre of political life in Canada ... Under the 1982 *Canadian Charter of Rights and Freedoms,* the Court confronted extraordinarily difficult issues of human rights and social policy. Debates about fundamental rights and freedoms replaced routine personal injury and property disputes on its docket. In the process, the Court's audience expanded beyond lawyers and legal academics to the Canadian public at large. Its decisions had implications for all Canadians and were the subject of intense public debate. No longer was the Court criticized for being too cautious, narrow, and legalistic. By the time of Dickson's retirement, some observers were asking whether the Court had become too willing to play an active role in Canadian political life.

Brian Dickson was the leading figure in this transformation of the Supreme Court and Canadian law.[50]

His judgment (and that of Wilson) in *Guerin* can be seen as part of this transformation.

Justice Binnie described the judgment in a speech given minutes after hearing of the death of the former chief justice. After describing how Dickson always paid attention to the arguments being presented, he said:

The second thing I want to remember about Chief Justice Dickson was an intellectual honesty that was frank and admirably confrontational. Sometimes, if you were on the losing side, it could be brutal.

I had the dubious pleasure of arguing the *Guerin* case before the Supreme Court for the Attorney General of Canada. We had, we thought, erected an impregnable fortress of legal argument around the proposition that whatever duties were owed by the Crown to aboriginal people did not amount to a trust enforceable at law. The point is not that we lost the case. The point is that he took every one of our arguments and met it head on.

... He didn't avoid our arguments. He simply ran over them. The result was that we won a few technical battles but lost the war. Nevertheless, we felt that our objections, mean-spirited as he may have considered them, had been fully addressed. He was responding to what he considered to be the higher call of justice.[51]

He added that Dickson had revolutionized Aboriginal law.[52]

In his judgment in *Guerin*, Dickson summarized the facts as found by the trial judge, and his rulings as well as those of the Federal Court of Appeal. He expressed some doubt as to the cogency of the terminology of "higher" and "lower" trust as used by Justice Le Dain following the *Kinloch* case,[53] but he agreed that the existence of an equitable obligation was an essential element for liability.[54] However, such an obligation is not limited to relationships that can be strictly defined as trusts. Indeed, in his view, the Crown's obligation vis-à-vis the "Indians" could not be defined as a trust, but this did not mean that the Crown owed no enforceable duty to the "Indians" in the way in which it deals with their land. He summarized his conclusion as follows:

> In my view, the nature of Indian title and the framework of the statutory scheme established for disposing of Indian land places upon the Crown an equitable obligation, enforceable by the courts, to deal with the land for the benefit of the Indians. This obligation does not amount to a trust in the private law sense. It is rather a fiduciary duty. If, however, the Crown breaches this fiduciary duty it will be liable to the Indians in the same way and to the same extent as if such a trust were in effect.
>
> The fiduciary relationship between the Crown and the Indians has its roots in the concept of aboriginal, native or Indian title. The fact that Indian Bands have a certain interest in lands does not, however, in itself give rise to a fiduciary relationship between the Indians and the Crown. The conclusion that the Crown is a fiduciary depends upon the further proposition that the Indian interest in the land is inalienable except upon surrender to the Crown.[55]

Dickson noted that an Indian band was prohibited from directly transferring its interest to a third party. Any sale or lease could be carried out only after a surrender had taken place, with the Crown then acting on the band's behalf. The Crown first took this responsibility upon itself in the Royal Proclamation of 1763,[56] and it was still recognized in the surrender provisions of the *Indian Act*. In Dickson's view, "the surrender requirement, and the responsibility it entails, were the source of a distinct fiduciary obligation owed by the Crown to the Indians."[57] In order to explore the character of this obligation, he first considered the basis of Aboriginal or Indian title and the nature of the interest in land that it represented.

The existence of Indian title was traced through the decisions in *Calder, St Catherine's Milling, Johnson v McIntosh, Worcester v Georgia, Amodu Tijani,* and *Star Chrome.*[58] These were decisions that we had urged upon the Federal Court of Appeal to support our argument that the band's interest in the lands could form the subject matter of a trust. Le Dain in the Federal Court of Appeal had also relied upon them to reach his decision that the "Indians" had a beneficial interest in the land, although he went on to find that it was one that was not protected by a legally enforceable obligation on the part of the Crown. Dickson stated that Indian title was an independent legal right that, although recognized by the Royal Proclamation of 1763, nonetheless predated it.[59] For this reason, *Kinloch, Tito,* and other "political trust" decisions were inapplicable to the present case.[60] Those cases concerned essentially the distribution of public funds or other property held by the government. The situation of the Indians was entirely different as their interest in their lands was a pre-existing legal right not created by the Royal Proclamation, the *Indian Act,* or any other executive order or legislative provision.[61] It did not matter that the present case was concerned with reserve lands rather than "unrecognized aboriginal title" in traditional tribal lands. The Indian interest in the land was the same in both cases.[62]

The nature of Indian title was examined next. The *St Catherine's Milling, Johnson v McIntosh, Amodu Tijani,* and *Star Chrome* cases were cited as authorities for the proposition that Indian title was "a personal and usufructuary right" (a right to use the property of another).[63] On the other hand, this characterization had sometimes been questioned, as in the *Calder, Giroux,* and *Cardinal* decisions of the Supreme Court of Canada and the *Sarcee Developments* decision of the Alberta Court of Appeal.[64] Those cases supported Le Dain's view that the Indian title in reserve lands was a beneficial interest. In *Miller v The King*, Justice Kellock seemed implicitly to adopt a similar position.[65] Dickson reconciled this apparent conflict between the cases by pointing out that in describing what constituted a unique interest in land, the courts had almost invariably found themselves applying a somewhat inappropriate terminology drawn from general property law.[66] There was a core of truth in the way that each of the two lines of authority had described Native title, but in neither case was the categorization quite accurate.

He expressed his own view of the nature of Indian title as follows:

> The nature of the Indians' interest is therefore best characterized by its general inalienability coupled with the fact that the Crown is under an obligation to deal with the land on the Indians' behalf when the interest is surrendered. Any description of Indian title which goes beyond these two features is both unnecessary and potentially misleading.[67]

He then proceeded to describe the nature of the Crown's fiduciary obligation to "Indian" people. The concept of fiduciary obligation originated long ago in the jurisdiction of the courts of Chancery.[68] In the present case, its relevance was based on the requirement of a "surrender" to the Crown before Indian land could be alienated.[69] This requirement had been continuously maintained since the Royal Proclamation of 1763 and was now found in sections 37–41 of the *Indian Act*. Its purpose was clearly to interpose the Crown between the "Indians" and the prospective purchasers or lessees of their land so as to prevent the "Indians" from being exploited.

Section 18(1) of the *Indian Act* conferred upon the Crown a discretion to decide for itself where the Indians' best interests really lay. The Crown had contended that this discretion ousted the jurisdiction of the courts to regulate the relationship between the Crown and the "Indians." Dickson thought it had quite the opposite effect and transformed the Crown's obligation into a fiduciary duty.[70] He quoted from an article by Professor Ernest Weinrib[71] and said that he agreed that where by statute, agreement or perhaps by unilateral undertaking, one party has an obligation to act for the benefit of another, and that obligation carried with it a discretionary power, the party thus empowered becomes a fiduciary. Equity will then supervise the relationship by holding him to the fiduciary's strict standard of conduct.[72]

These words may be regarded as the *ratio decidendi,* or governing principle, of his judgment, and would have an important impact on the development of fiduciary obligations generally. He continued: "The categories of fiduciary, like those of negligence, should not be considered closed."[73] The performance of public law duties did not typically give rise to a fiduciary relationship, but the Crown's obligation to the "Indians" with respect to their interest in land was not a public law duty. While it was not a private law duty in the strict sense either, it was nonetheless in the nature of a private law duty. Therefore, in this unique, or *sui generis,* relationship, it was not improper to regard the Crown as a fiduciary.[74]

The broad discretion of the Crown in dealing with surrendered land that was conferred by section 18 of the *Indian Act* and the surrender document was subject to control by virtue of the fiduciary obligation:

When, as here, an Indian Band surrenders its interest to the Crown, a fiduciary obligation takes hold to regulate the manner in which the Crown exercises its discretion in dealing with the land on the Indians' behalf.[75]

Dickson distinguished the fiduciary obligation from a trust obligation.[76] The law of trusts is a highly developed, specialized branch of the law. An express trust requires a settlor (somebody to create the trust), a beneficiary (someone to benefit from the trust), a trust corpus (trust property), words of settlement, certainty of object, and certainty of obligation (wording that shows sufficient intention by the settlor to create a trust in favour of beneficiaries who can be clearly identified). Not all of these elements were present. There was not even a trust corpus:

As the *Smith* decision, *supra,* makes clear, upon unconditional surrender the Indians' right in the land disappears. No property interest is transferred which could constitute the trust *res,* so that even if the other *indicia* of an express or implied trust could be made out, the basic requirement of a settlement of property has not been met.[77]

Dickson then held that the surrender did not give rise to a constructive trust. He quoted an earlier decision: "The principle of unjust enrichment lies at the heart of the constructive trust."[78] The Crown was not enriched by the surrender transaction, whether unjustly or otherwise. The Crown's obligation to the Indians was not a trust, but this did not prevent the obligation being trust-like in character:

> As would be the case with a trust, the Crown must hold surrendered land for the use and benefit of the surrendering Band. The obligation is thus subject to principles very similar to those which govern the law of trusts concerning, for example, the measure of damages for breach.[79]

The fiduciary relationship between the Crown and the Indians also bears a certain resemblance to agency, since the obligation can be characterized as a duty to act on behalf of the Indian bands who have surrendered lands when negotiating for the sale or lease of the land to third parties. However, he continued:

> But just as the Crown is not a trustee for the Indians, neither is it their agent; not only does the Crown's authority to act on the Band's behalf lack a basis in contract but the Band is not a party to the ultimate sale or lease, as it would be if it were the Crown's principal. I repeat, the fiduciary obligation which is owed to the Indians by the Crown is *sui generis.* Given the unique character both of the Indian's interest in land and of their historical relationship with the Crown, the fact that this is so should occasion no surprise.[80]

Having considered the nature of the fiduciary obligation, Dickson turned to a consideration of the breach of that obligation.[81] The trial judge had found that the Crown's agents promised the band to lease the land in question on certain specified terms and then, after surrender, obtained a lease on different terms. The lease obtained was much less valuable. The oral terms that the band understood would be embodied in the lease were not incorporated as conditions into the surrender, but the Crown could not ignore those terms:

> After the Crown's agents had induced the Band to surrender its land on the understanding that the land would be leased on certain terms, it would be unconscionable to permit the Crown simply to ignore those terms. When the promised lease proved impossible to obtain, the Crown instead of proceeding to lease the land on different unfavourable terms, should have returned to the Band to explain what had occurred and seek the Band's counsel on how to proceed. The existence of such unconscionability is the key to a conclusion that the Crown breached its fiduciary duty. Equity will not countenance unconscionable behaviour in a fiduciary, whose duty is that of utmost loyalty to his principal.[82]

The Crown could not promise the band that it would obtain a lease of its land on certain stated terms, thereby inducing the band to alter its legal position by surrendering the land, and then simply ignore that promise to the band's detriment. Dickson concluded: "In obtaining without consultation a much less valuable lease than that promised, the Crown breached the fiduciary obligation it owed the Band. It must make good the loss suffered in consequence."[83]

Dickson turned to a consideration of the Crown's contention that the claim was barred by the statute of limitations and by the doctrine of laches.[84] (Laches is the doctrine that a plaintiff who delays too long in bringing an equitable claim may be denied his or her day in court.) The argument based on the statute of limitations was rejected because of the concealment of the lease from the band. Dickson agreed with Collier that this amounted to equitable fraud and was unconscionable although not dishonest. The limitation period did not therefore start until the discovery of the lease in March 1970. The defence of laches was also swiftly disposed of.[85] Since the conduct of the Indian Affairs branch personnel amounted to equitable fraud, since the band did not have actual or constructive knowledge of the actual terms of the lease until March 1970, and since the Crown suffered no disadvantage in making its defence by reason of the delay between March 1970 until suit was filed in December 1975, there were no grounds for application of the equitable doctrine of laches.

Finally, Dickson considered the question of amount of damages, which in his opinion was to be determined by analogy with the principles of trust law.[86] He saw no error in principle in the judgment of the trial judge and was content to adopt the quantum of damages awarded at trial.

Review of Judgments

Reviewing the judgments in *Guerin* taken as a whole, a few comments may be made. All the judges found for the Musqueam and agreed on the remedy to be provided. All the judges also agreed that the Crown owed some form of legally binding obligation to the Musqueam and rejected the argument that only political obligations existed. This finding of legally enforceable rights and the rejection of the argument that the relationship was political only was the major and permanent legacy of the case. The judges differed on the technical grounds for reaching this common conclusion, however. Estey found the Crown to be an agent. Wilson used both trust law and general fiduciary principles to reach her conclusion. Dickson said the Crown owed unique fiduciary or trust-like duties but was not, strictly speaking, a trustee.

There was a lack of detailed discussion of the differences in their approach and of the implications of finding a fiduciary relationship. Dickson and Estey were reluctant to get involved in technical complications. As we have seen, Dickson's conference notes indicate that he thought Le Dain had taken "a very technical view of things" in his Federal Court of Appeal decision and he was concerned about supposedly stretching trust law to achieve an equitable solution.[87] Estey said he thought agency law was a simpler approach and he did not need "to resort to the more technical and far-reaching doctrines of the law of trusts and the concomitant law attaching to the fiduciary."[88] Also, as noted by Rotman, "the *Guerin* judgment did not delve into any substantial discussion of Crown-Native fiduciary relations in general."[89] The absence of a consistent approach and the failure to provide detailed guidance is regrettable and may have been partly responsible for the subsequent conceptual confusion (to be discussed in the Conclusion of this book) between fiduciary obligations and the honour of the Crown principle.

As discussed in Chapter 6, the decision also had important impacts on other aspects of fiduciary and Aboriginal law, including, in particular, Aboriginal title. It confirmed the existence of such title as an independent legal interest, although the description of it given by Dickson was inadequate and was subsequently replaced.

REACTION

The decision was warmly greeted by Chief Ernie Campbell of the Musqueam, who noted the implications for other Indigenous peoples and its importance.[90] But there was some bitterness over the refusal of the federal government to discuss settlement and for forcing the band to litigate, which had imposed severe strains on it.[91] It may be noted that a Liberal government was in office for the period after the trial in the Federal Court. A Progressive Conservative government came into office in September 1984 and there were discussions with the new government on a possible abandonment of the political trust defence, but the decision of the Supreme Court of Canada was rendered before this could be done, even assuming the new government would agree or that it was technically possible. With the benefit of hindsight, this was fortuitous for Indigenous peoples and the development of the law given the rejection of this defence by the court. However, it underlines that many factors can influence the outcome of litigation and lawmaking through the courts. There was also disappointment over the low amount of the compensation. For its part, the federal government was said to be "reeling" over the decision and holding meetings to unravel its implications.[92] The Shaughnessy golf club appeared unconcerned. Its president was quoted as saying that the ruling did not affect it: "As far as we're concerned, it's business as usual."[93] And, indeed, it was and is.

Almost ten years after commencing legal action and twenty-seven years after the surrender of its land, the Musqueam Band was successful in its claim that the Crown was in breach of its fiduciary duty. The band had also obtained a ruling from the Supreme Court of Canada that the Crown's obligation was one that could be enforced by the courts and was not merely political in nature. This was a ruling that, in addition to achieving some measure of justice for the Musqueam, would have great implication for the rights of Indigenous peoples generally. In giving its judgment, the Supreme Court had restated the requirements to demonstrate the existence of a fiduciary relationship in a manner that would also have significant impacts on the general law relating to fiduciary obligations.

FURTHER LITIGATION

Subsequent to the Supreme Court of Canada decision, there have been two further pieces of litigation reflecting the disappointment of the Musqueam over the practical result of that decision despite its importance for the development of Aboriginal law generally. The remedy awarded was compensation of $10 million without interest from the breach of fiduciary duty in 1957 to the date of the award in 1981. The lease was left in place with its provisions, including the restriction on the rent to be paid. Also, those provisions had a major impact on the property taxes that were payable by the club, which compounded the loss suffered by the band.

An action to obtain a declaration that the lease was void was dismissed on the grounds that it was seeking to relitigate the same claim. Justice Joyal of the Federal Court rejected the band's argument that special circumstances applied that should entitle it to bring the action.

> The Band has not made out a case of unfairness deserving of special considerations and which would otherwise make its new action less abusive or more deserving of favourable treatment. I should find that

in the measure possible in our adjudicative process whenever a court is called upon to deal with monetary compensation for financial grief or prejudice, the damage award appears to me, as it did to the Trial judge, and to the several judges of the Supreme Court of Canada, to be fair and reasonable.[94]

The Shaughnessy lease was considered by the Supreme Court of Canada again on a different point: the payment of property taxes by the club to the band. Property taxes are levied each year on a percentage of the assessed value of lands. The assessor appraised the value of the Shaughnessy leased lands at only $100,000 an acre, but gave a value for unimproved forested lands located immediately adjacent to them of $1,972,500 an acre – nearly twenty times as much. The band had recently acquired those lands and was liable to pay taxes to the province on them. The assessor's explanation for this enormous discount on the value of the Shaughnessy lands was that, because of the terms of the lease, the Shaughnessy lands were restricted to golf course use and so could not be used for their highest and best use – residential use – unlike the neighbouring lands.

The appeal reached the Supreme Court of Canada in 2016. The court rejected the band's argument that, like the neighbouring lands, the Shaughnessy lands ought also to be valued at their highest and best use in accordance with standard appraisal practice.[95] Justice Russell Brown gave judgment for the court. He noted that "the issue before this Court goes only to the permissible effect, if any, of a specific provision of the Bylaw on the assessment of the actual value for the purposes of taxation by Musqueam of the reserve lands leased to the Club."[96] He held that the provision granted the assessor the discretion to consider the use restriction in establishing the value of the lands for assessment purposes. The relevant provision of the bylaw allowed the assessor to reduce the value if there was a restriction placed "by the band." The band was not a party to the lease that imposed the restriction on use (and was not even aware of its terms). In Brown's view, however, the Crown's intervention was necessitated by the *Indian Act*, which provided that reserve lands could not be leased without first being surrendered to the Crown. The bylaw must be read in light of this statutorily mandated Crown role. While the surrender document made no mention of the lease or the club, the context in which the surrender occurred and the lands were leased clarified that the Musqueam intended that the lands be leased to the club. Given that context, the court held that the use restriction in the lease was placed "by the band."

This conclusion was reached despite the fact that the restrictions in the lease were never agreed to by the band (or even known to it) and were not included in the property tax provision in the lease, although included in the rent provision. Further, the court had held in *Guerin* that it was a breach of fiduciary duty for the Crown to have entered into the lease. Given these considerations, to hold that the band placed the use restriction in the lease resulting in an artificially low value for property tax purposes was a most surprising and disappointing decision.

PART 3

THE CONSEQUENCES

The current Musqueam Administration Office, which replaced an earlier office, which was a converted house. *Courtesy of the Musqueam Indian Band Archives*

6

The Impact of *Guerin*

THE IMPACT OF THE *Guerin* case has been widely recognized. It was ranked in the Canadian Bar Association journal as the tenth most important decision of the Supreme Court of Canada in the twentieth century and among the top thirty significant legal events.[1] In *Wewaykum*, Justice Ian Binnie, writing for the Supreme Court of Canada, referred to *Guerin* as a watershed decision;[2] in an address to a legal conference, he described it as "a seismic blast."[3] The Ontario Court of Appeal described it in *Authorson v Canada* as a seminal case.[4] According to Tom Berger, a leading Aboriginal rights practitioner, until the *Guerin* decision it was most unlikely that a lawyer of ordinary competence would have advised an Indian band to bring an action for a breach of a fiduciary obligation.[5] (I leave it to the reader to decide whether this implies anything about the competence of the legal team for the Musqueam!) Professor Leonard Rotman referred to *Guerin* as a landmark case that "blazed a new path in Canadian aboriginal rights jurisprudence" and resulted in "a complete overruling of the principles which had shaped judicial considerations of aboriginal rights in Canada for almost a hundred years."[6]

The leading authority on the law of trusts in Canada, Professor Donovan Waters, noted that "for the first time, certainly so far as reserve lands are concerned, the Indians now have right of access to the courts in order to determine the propriety of the Crown's administration of their affairs."[7] Writing in 2013, Aboriginal rights lawyer Senwung Luk described *Guerin* as "perhaps the single most influential decision in Aboriginal law in the modern history of the [Supreme Court of Canada]."[8] Other judges and scholars have also noted the significance of *Guerin* to Canadian law and the development of Aboriginal rights.[9]

This book is limited to the impact of *Guerin* on Aboriginal law, but it may be noted that the case led to significant development of fiduciary law in Canada outside of the Indigenous context. Professor W.F. Flanagan commented that "the development of modern Canadian law dealing with new fiduciary relationships can be traced to the Supreme Court of Canada's decision in *Guerin v. The Queen* in 1984," and that the case "opened the door to the extension of fiduciary obligations in relationships not traditionally recognized as fiduciary."[10] In *Authorson*, the Ontario Court of Appeal referred to *Guerin* as "the foundation of this line of general jurisprudence."[11] The Supreme Court of Canada said in the *Elder Advocates of Alberta Society* case that *Guerin* (together with two other cases) outlined "fundamental principles ... which identify the existence of a fiduciary duty in cases not covered by an existing category in which fiduciary duties have been recognized."[12]

Guerin has been cited in over seven hundred cases in Canada, involving both Indigenous and non-Indigenous people, and continues to influence the development of the law.[13]

IMPACT ON ABORIGINAL LAW

Guerin was a landmark decision in the development of modern Aboriginal law that had commenced a decade earlier with the *Calder* decision in 1973.[14] The following discussion considers:

- the subsequent development of fiduciary obligations owed by the Crown to Indigenous peoples
- how fiduciary principles have been applied to the Crown's duty to consult Indigenous peoples

- how fiduciary principles have been applied to provide protection for existing Aboriginal and treaty rights by being adopted as a guiding principle for section 35 of the *Constitution Act, 1982* and incorporated into that section as part of the test that governments must satisfy to justify infringements of such rights,
- the impact of *Guerin* on Aboriginal title.

Fiduciary Obligations and Indigenous Peoples

Restatements of the law by the Supreme Court of Canada since the *Guerin* decision have resulted in the Crown's automatically owing fiduciary obligations to an Indigenous group so long as both of these conditions are met:

- There is "a specific or cognizable Aboriginal interest."
- There is an undertaking by the Crown of discretionary control over that interest.[15]

These two requirements are all that need to be shown for fiduciary duties to arise.

If an Indigenous group cannot meet these requirements, it may still be able to rely on fiduciary obligations being owed by the Crown by showing that the following three conditions have been met:

- There is an undertaking by the Crown to act in the best interests of the group.
- The group is vulnerable to the control of the Crown.
- A legal or substantial practical interest of the group could be adversely affected by the Crown's exercise of discretion or control.

This additional test broadens the scope of fiduciary duties beyond the original facts of cases like *Guerin* involving discretionary control of "cognizable Aboriginal interests" such as reserve lands.

Over the last thirty or so years, courts, government officials, and Indigenous groups have applied fiduciary principles in hundreds of cases between the Crown and Indigenous groups, either as part of litigation or in settlements or to resolve claims out of court, such as under the specific claims process.[16] These cases often arose out of mismanagement by the Crown of reserve lands or monies. Fiduciary obligations are an important part of the day-to-day practice of lawyers involved in Aboriginal law.

The influence of *Guerin* on the fiduciary obligations of governments to Indigenous peoples has extended to New Zealand. The Supreme Court of New Zealand declined to make a ruling in a 2014 decision on whether such obligations were owed.[17] However, this reluctance was reversed in 2017 by the court's decision in *Wakatu v Attorney General*,[18] which relied heavily upon *Guerin*. Lower court decisions had applied the "political trust" doctrine rejected in *Guerin* and held that certain colonial agreements were unenforceable in law. The Supreme Court of New Zealand reversed the lower courts in a four-to-one decision. The majority declared that a fiduciary duty was owed by the Crown to the ancestors of the appellants. The case was remitted to the High Court for further consideration. New Zealand law professor Carwyn Jones has described the case as "one of the most important decisions from a New Zealand court in the last 25 years."[19] He describes the outcome as "a very different pathway for dealing with Māori claims of historical land loss than the systematised and politically negotiated settlements that have predominated since the mid-1990s."

The state of the law in Australia is unclear on whether the government has a fiduciary relationship with the Indigenous peoples of that country. One of the counsel for the Indigenous group that brought the successful *Mabo* case seeking a declaration of Native or Aboriginal title notes in his account of the case that the group amended its statement of claim to allege the existence and breach of a fiduciary duty owed by the Crown based on *Guerin* when the decision was announced.[20] In his words, "from our perspective, the most important development during the 1980s was *Guerin*, an Indian rights case handed down by the Canadian Supreme Court in 1984."[21] He suggests that the developments in Canadian law on Indigenous rights, including *Guerin*, influenced the Australian High Court in coming to its decision in *Mabo* on Native title.[22] However, the existence of a fiduciary duty on the Crown towards Indigenous peoples was described as "an open question" by one judge of the High Court in 1997.[23] In an article published in 1994, Chief Justice Anthony Mason commented: "As yet, we in Australia have no counterpart to *Guerin v. The Queen*. The decision has been relied upon in aboriginal land claim cases but so far it has not formed the basis of a decision."[24] This remains the case.[25]

The Duty of the Crown to Consult and Accommodate

The duty of the Crown to consult and, if appropriate, accommodate the established and asserted rights of Indigenous groups is a key part of modern Aboriginal law and has tended to overshadow other areas of the law in recent years.[26] As we have seen, the duty first arose in the Aboriginal law context in *Guerin*. Recall from the last chapter that the Supreme Court of Canada found that after the Crown's agents had induced the Musqueam Band to surrender its land on the understanding that the land would be leased on certain terms, it was unconscionable for the Crown to ignore those terms and the Crown should have consulted the band on the changes. "When the promised lease proved impossible to obtain, the Crown, instead of proceeding to lease the land on different, unfavourable terms, should have returned to the Band to explain what had occurred and seek the Band's counsel on how to proceed."[27] The failure to do so constituted a breach of fiduciary obligation. In some situations, therefore, the duty to consult is part of a broader fiduciary obligation.

In *Little Salmon*, Justice Marie Deschamps summarized the way in which the duty to consult had developed over the last thirty or so years since the *Guerin* case:

> The Crown's constitutional duty to specifically consult Aboriginal peoples was initially recognized as a factor going to the determination of whether an Aboriginal right was infringed (*Guerin*), and was later established as one component of the test for determining whether infringements of

Aboriginal rights by the Crown were justified: *R. v. Sparrow*. The [Supreme] Court was subsequently asked in *Haida,* and *Taku,* whether such a duty to consult could apply even before an Aboriginal or treaty right is proven to exist.[28]

In the *Haida* decision, the court said that the duty arises from "the honour of the Crown" rather than as a fiduciary obligation in the case of asserted but not yet proven Aboriginal rights.[29] This was because the Aboriginal interest had not been proven to exist and was insufficiently defined. We shall review the somewhat confusing relationship between the honour of the Crown and fiduciary obligations in the concluding chapter.

Section 35(1) of the Constitution Act, 1982

The fiduciary relationship between the Crown and Indigenous peoples recognized in *Guerin* has played a key role in the interpretation and application of section 35(1) of the *Constitution Act, 1982,* which states that "the existing aboriginal and treaty rights of the aboriginal peoples of Canada are hereby recognized and affirmed."[30] The background to section 35(1) was summarized in Chapter 4. The scope of this vaguely worded provision was the subject of considerable debate.[31] It was often referred to as "an empty box." Section 35 was not contained in Part I of the *Act* setting out the *Canadian Charter of Rights and Freedoms.* Section 1 expressly guaranteed the rights and freedoms set out in the *Charter* subject only to such reasonable limits prescribed by law as can be demonstrably justified in a free and democratic society. Since they were outside the *Charter,* there was no such guarantee for existing Aboriginal and treaty rights recognized and affirmed by section 35, nor was there any other mechanism to provide substantive protection for such rights. This raised the concern that these rights were not guaranteed by the Constitution and could be extinguished or arbitrarily infringed by government. Arguably, the section merely recognized and affirmed those rights that had been legally acknowledged at the time of the passage of the act, and at most created a rule of statutory interpretation that there was a presumption against future extinguishment or infringement. There was obviously the potential for it to receive a conservative, restrictive interpretation that would have severely limited the protection provided. One leading academic specializing in Aboriginal law went so far as to say that "it may properly be asserted that [section 35 of the *Constitution Act, 1982*], far from protecting or guaranteeing the rights of the aboriginal peoples of Canada, provides for the diminution and abrogation of such rights without their consent."[32]

Fortunately for Indigenous peoples, the Supreme Court of Canada held that section 35 should be interpreted to incorporate the fiduciary relationship recognized in *Guerin*. This means that the powers of the government are to be restrained by imposing an obligation to justify any infringement of rights recognized by section 35 by showing it is consistent with the fiduciary duty. If the government fails to do so, the infringement will not be valid. This judicial incorporation of the fiduciary relationship provided the substantive protection for Aboriginal and treaty rights that the politicians had failed to provide. In *Wewaykum*, Binnie explained that "the *Guerin* concept of a *sui generis* fiduciary duty was expanded in *R. v. Sparrow* ... to include protection of the aboriginal peoples' pre-existing and still existing aboriginal and treaty rights within s. 35 of the *Constitution Act, 1982*."[33]

Sparrow, like *Guerin*, was another landmark case on the development of Aboriginal rights in Canada involving the Musqueam Band.[34] It involved charges under the federal *Fisheries Act* and whether an Aboriginal right to fish was a valid defence under section 35. The Supreme Court of Canada held that the section might provide a defence. It first noted:

Section 35(1) at the least provides a solid constitutional base upon which subsequent negotiations can take place. It also affords aboriginal peoples constitutional protection against provincial legislative power. We are, of course, aware that this would, in any event, flow from the *Guerin* case, *supra*, but for a proper understanding of the situation, it is essential to remember that the *Guerin* case was decided after the commencement of the *Constitution Act, 1982*.[35]

The court later observed:

> In our opinion, *Guerin,* together with *R. v. Taylor and Williams* (1981), 62 C.C.C. (2d) 227, 34 O.R. (2d) 360 ground a general guiding principle for s.35(1). That is, the Government has the responsibility to act in a fiduciary capacity with respect to aboriginal peoples. The relationship between the Government and aboriginals is trust-like, rather than adversarial, and contemporary recognition and affirmation of aboriginal rights must be defined in light of this historic relationship.[36]

This "guiding principle" of the "trust-like" or fiduciary relationship was relied upon as the basis for importing into section 35 some restraint on the exercise of the sovereign power to restrict Aboriginal rights:

> There is no explicit language in the provision that authorizes this Court or any court to assess the legitimacy of any governmental legislation that restricts aboriginal rights. Yet, we find that the words "recognition and affirmation" incorporate the fiduciary relationship referred to earlier and so import some restraint on the exercise of sovereign power ... federal power must be reconciled with federal duty and the best way to achieve that reconciliation is to demand the justification of any government regulation that infringes upon or denies aboriginal rights. Such scrutiny is in keeping with the liberal interpretive principle enunciated in *Nowegijick, supra,* and the concept of holding the Crown to a high standard of honourable dealing with respect to the aboriginal peoples of Canada as suggested by *Guerin v. The Queen, supra.*[37]

The court later explained how the fiduciary relationship, including the duty of consultation, could be applied as the basis for a test of justification to determine the validity of governmental restrictions on an Aboriginal right. As noted by J. Timothy McCabe, in *Sparrow* "the fiduciary concept was invoked and employed by the Court, abandoning any dependence on the *Indian Act* and expanding the idea from a source of civil liability in particular circumstances to a central tool of constitutional interpretation with practical application in more varied circumstances."[38] The fiduciary relationship "became in *Sparrow* the foundation for a key doctrine of Canadian constitutional law."[39]

After the enactment of section 35(1), governments may not extinguish Aboriginal rights but they may still infringe upon such rights if they can satisfy the test of justification set out in *Sparrow*, which was summarized as follows by the Supreme Court of Canada in *Tsilhqot'in*:

> To justify overriding the Aboriginal title-holding group's wishes on the basis of the broader public good, the government must show: (1) that it discharged its procedural duty to consult and accommodate; (2) that its actions were backed by a compelling and substantial objective; and (3) that the governmental action is consistent with the Crown's fiduciary obligation to the group: *Sparrow*.[40]

In *Delgamuukw*, Chief Justice Antonio Lamer cited *Guerin* as support for the proposition that whether the Aboriginal group has been consulted is relevant to determining whether the infringement of Aboriginal title is justified.[41] The *Tsilhqot'in* decision underlined the importance of the Crown's fiduciary obligation to the protection of Aboriginal title as part of the duty to justify infringement.[42] It impacted the justification process in two ways. First, the Crown had to act in a way that respected the fact that such title is a group interest that inheres in present and future generations. This means that incursions on Aboriginal title cannot be justified if they would substantially deprive future generations of the benefit of the land. Second, the Crown's fiduciary duty infuses an obligation of proportionality into the justification process.

As indicated above, section 35(1) of the *Constitution Act, 1982* recognizes and affirms existing treaty rights as well as existing Aboriginal rights. Prior to the enactment of that section, there was little protection for treaty rights, which could be unrestrictedly extinguished or infringed by legislation.[43] After its enactment, the courts extended to treaties the protection of the fiduciary principle. The application of the *Sparrow* test to treaty rights was expressly upheld by the Supreme Court of Canada in *R v Badger*.[44] Justice Peter Cory noted that "in *Sparrow*, certain criteria were set out pertaining to justification ... While that case dealt with infringement of aboriginal rights, I am of the view that those criteria should, in most cases, apply equally to the infringement of treaty rights."[45]

Aboriginal Title

The Supreme Court of Canada's 1973 decision in *Calder* was mentioned in Chapter 4 as the case that kicked off the developments that have led to modern Aboriginal law. In particular, it raised the possibility that Aboriginal title was a legal interest in land that had survived the assertion of British and Canadian sovereignty. However, the Nisga'a failed to get a declaration that they enjoyed such title, and the court was evenly divided on whether such title still existed in British Columbia. Little was said about the legal nature of Aboriginal title, assuming it still existed. It was another forty-one years before the court upheld a claim to title in the *Tsilhqot'in* decision, although the *Delgamuukw* decision in 1997 largely set out the current law.

Following *Calder, Guerin* was the next stepping stone on the path to judicial recognition of Aboriginal title by the Supreme Court of Canada.[46] Chief Justice Beverley McLachlin noted in *Tsilhqot'in* that "the starting point in characterizing the legal nature of Aboriginal title is Dickson J.'s concurring judgment in *Guerin.*"[47] Although the case concerned reserve lands, the court held that the interest of the Musqueam in the lands was the same as that in Aboriginal title lands. Dickson noted that "the reserve in question here was created out of the ancient tribal territory of the Musqueam Band."[48] As explained by McLachlin in *Tsilhqot'in,* "the Court confirmed the potential for Aboriginal title in ancestral lands."[49] In *Delgamuukw,* Chief Justice Antonio Lamer relied upon *Guerin* as confirming that the source of Aboriginal title was the prior occupation of the land by Aboriginal peoples and not the Royal Proclamation of 1763, and as permitting a broad variety of uses of the land, and not only traditional uses.[50] However, that case significantly modified the description in *Guerin* of the content of such title by providing a more comprehensive description, and this modified description was subsequently followed in *Tsilhqot'in.*[51]

In his opinion in *Guerin,* Dickson addressed the theory behind Aboriginal title as part of his analysis of the government's fiduciary duty. He held that the Crown had underlying and ultimate title. However, this title was burdened by the "pre-existing legal right" of Aboriginal people based on their use and occupation of the land prior to European arrival.[52] He characterized this Aboriginal interest in the land as "an independent legal interest."[53] The recognition by the court that Aboriginal title was a legal interest that pre-dated British sovereignty and was not dependent on a grant by the Crown was important to the future development of the law. It resolved the uncertainty left by the divided opinions in *Calder* on whether Aboriginal title was a legal property right in the land that continued unless it had been extinguished.[54]

Justice Binnie explained the significance of the decision to the law of Aboriginal title in a speech on the contributions made by Chief Justice Dickson to the development of the law:

> At one stroke he transformed the aboriginal interest in land, which had been considered merely a possessory interest held at the pleasure of the Crown (as characterized by Lord Watson in the *St. Catherine's Milling Company* case[55]) into a legal interest enforceable against the Crown. That skilful piece of footwork, which is the source of all of the subsequent case law dealing with the aboriginal interest in land, is buried inconspicuously in the rolling majesty of his decision on an altogether different (albeit related) topic.[56]

Michael Doherty, an Aboriginal law practitioner, provided this summary of the impact of *Guerin* on Aboriginal land claims:

> The combined effect of the reasons of Dickson J and Wilson J was to have a "profound significance for Aboriginal land claims" ... prior to the decision in *Guerin,* it might have been possible to interpret the split decision in *Calder* as leaving open the question of whether or not Aboriginal rights and title had ceased to exist everywhere, as opposed

to where it could be shown to have been extinguished by lawful authority. Dickson J, however, in referring to *Calder,* said that in that case:

> ... this Court recognized Aboriginal title as a legal right derived from the Indians' historic occupation and possession of their tribal lands.

... As one academic later put it, "Pre-existing Aboriginal title as a legal right was suddenly established in Canadian law." For academic commentators, this formed a hook upon which it was possible to hang an entire theory of Aboriginal rights.[57]

Conclusion

THERE CAN BE LITTLE dispute that *Guerin* was a landmark decision that had a major and permanent impact on Canadian law, politics, and society. Its major contribution was that it established an enforceable fiduciary relationship between the Crown and Indigenous peoples and rejected the view that any obligation owed to the latter was political only. This represented a change in the relationship between the Indigenous peoples of Canada and non-Indigenous governments from one of wardship based on the theory of a political trust that had prevailed for over a century to one based on legal rights. *Guerin* has also led directly or indirectly to some improvement in the economic conditions of Indigenous peoples and has given them greater negotiating power with governments and so improved their political position. Politically, it also spurred moves towards greater self-government for Indigenous peoples.

PROTECTION OF
ABORIGINAL AND TREATY RIGHTS

Before discussing the impact of *Guerin* on legal protection for Aboriginal and treaty rights, it is necessary to observe the lack of legal definition of such rights for most of Canada's history. A report prepared for the Indian-Eskimo Association of Canada in 1970 stated:

> The Indians have been very dependent upon the Federal Government, for Indians have, generally speaking, not gone to court to test or enforce their rights. Unfortunately, this has meant that their legal rights and

aboriginal claims are very poorly defined in our law. Being poorly defined they could easily be disregarded by the government when the frame of reference changed, and that has happened.[1]

Guerin was an important step in providing the required definition and legal protection of Aboriginal and treaty rights.

It is also important to ask what the current state of Canadian law would be if the fiduciary principle did not exist as a key principle of Canadian Aboriginal law. What protection would exist for the Indigenous peoples of Canada if there had been no appeal of the Federal Court of Appeal decision holding that the government's duty to the Musqueam Band was not legally enforceable, or if the Supreme Court of Canada had rejected the appeal? An answer to these questions may be found in the experience of Indigenous peoples in Australia, which has still to recognize that the federal and state governments have a fiduciary relationship with Indigenous peoples. Professor Larissa Behrendt has suggested some lessons for Canada from the Australian experience:

> Another reflection from the Australian experience is the implication for the failure to prove a fiduciary duty. In Australia, the lack of a clear court finding that the fiduciary relationship arises has meant that ... Indigenous peoples ... are captive to the whim of the legislature ... Australia offers sobering reflection of what can happen if there is no recognition of the doctrine.[2]

Reflecting on how Australian governments have squandered opportunities to deliver justice to traditional owners of the land, one of the counsel for the plaintiffs in the *Mabo* case said that it was tempting to go back to the common law and seek to establish the existence of a free-standing fiduciary duty.[3] It is important, of course, to recognize the different constitutional framework in Australia and the lack of constitutional protection for Aboriginal rights.

It is equally important to note that, without the application of the fiduciary doctrine to the bald recognition and affirmation of existing Aboriginal and treaty rights in section 35(1) of the *Constitution Act,*

1982, recognition and affirmation may have amounted to little more than empty words. This has been the fate of the recognition of the principle of the supremacy of God enshrined in the preamble to the *Canadian Charter of Rights and Freedoms.* Courts have said that this is not an enforceable "right" that, if breached, would permit a challenge to legislation.[4] Likewise, the commitment to promote equal opportunity in section 36 of the *Constitution Act, 1982* has been held to be not actionable by an individual or municipality.[5] The vaguely worded section 35 might have suffered a similar fate. On its face, it provided no substantive protection for the rights that it "recognized and affirmed." Unlike the rights and freedoms recognized by the *Charter,* there was no "guarantee" of existing Aboriginal and treaty rights. Indeed, as we saw in Chapter 6, in the view of one leading Aboriginal law scholar, "far from protecting or guaranteeing the rights of the aboriginal peoples of Canada, [section 35] provides for the diminution and abrogation of such rights without their consent."[6] How much weaker would this recognition and affirmation have been if the Crown had been successful in its argument that Indigenous peoples could not legally enforce their rights against the Crown? If existing Aboriginal and treaty "rights" could not be enforced by a court, what would there be to acknowledge and affirm within section 35? The constitutional protection would have been as hollow as the protection provided by the doctrine of political trust that was rejected in *Guerin.*

As noted by Professor Brian Slattery, section 35 required courts to confront many of the unresolved issues concerning Aboriginal rights.[7] Writing in 1987, three years after the Supreme Court of Canada's *Guerin* decision, he said that in that case "the Supreme Court has signalled that it is ready for the task. While not dealing directly with the new constitutional provisions,[8] the judgment provides the stimulus and much essential material for reflection on the fundamental nature and origins of aboriginal rights."[9] The decision had "a profound significance for aboriginal land claims."[10] As discussed in Chapter 6, the jurisprudence on Aboriginal title had been unclear, as the 1973 *Calder* case left room for argument over whether the Canadian law recognized the concept of Aboriginal title.[11] In Slattery's view, "the *Guerin* decision ends this aspect of the controversy, with seven of the eight judges holding that aboriginal title is a legal right that can be extinguished only by native consent or by legislation."[12] However, he saw the greatest importance of the case in "the fact that in *Guerin* the Supreme Court shows a willingness to consider the topic of aboriginal rights afresh and to initiate a dialogue concerning the broad principles that alone can make sense of the subject."[13] Subsequent decisions of the court show that this prediction was accurate. In the 1990 *Sparrow* case, the Supreme Court of Canada used the existence of the fiduciary relationship to give substance to the weak recognition of existing Aboriginal and treaty rights in section 35(1) of the *Constitution Act, 1982*.[14] The law relating to Indigenous peoples in Canada was fundamentally rewritten through the *Calder, Guerin,* and *Sparrow* decisions and the other "breakthrough" cases.[15]

We saw some key aspects of the Supreme Court's rewriting of Aboriginal law in Chapter 6 because *Guerin* has been central to that process. *Guerin* itself banished the monster of political trust to the margins of the law, and with it the repulsive proposition that any obligations owed by the Crown to Indigenous peoples could not be legally enforced. Leonard Rotman notes that *Guerin* laid to rest the Canadian courts' working conception of the relationship as one existing at the pleasure of the Crown. This characterization had been the foundation of decisions in Aboriginal rights jurisprudence for well over a hundred years.[16]

Looking to the future, *Guerin* may provide an approach to give substance to the rights of Indigenous peoples as set out in the *United Nations Declaration on the Rights of Indigenous Peoples*.[17] The declaration does not have direct force under Canadian law but federal legislation has been proposed that would affirm it as "a universal international human rights instrument with application in Canada."[18] Article 26 requires states to "give legal recognition and protection to [traditional] lands, territories and resources." The fiduciary duty of "utmost loyalty" imposed as the result of the fiduciary relationship could provide a standard of conduct equally applicable to this article.[19] The Supreme Court explained in *Wewaykum* that the fiduciary relationship meant that the Crown owed "basic obligations of loyalty, good faith in the discharge of its mandate, providing full disclosure appropriate to the subject matter, and acting with ordinary prudence with a view to the best interest of the aboriginal beneficiaries."[20] *Guerin* and other cases on the compensation payable for breach of fiduciary duty are likewise relevant to claims under Article 28.[21] This article states that just, fair, and equitable compensation must be paid if it is not possible to return lands taken, occupied, used, or damaged without the free, prior, and informed consent of Indigenous peoples.

ECONOMIC IMPACTS

In their factum, or written argument, to the Supreme Court of Canada in *Guerin,* the National Indian Brotherhood submitted that the "desperate economic conditions that Indian people suffer is a source of anguish for most Canadians."[22] By and large, those bands that have overcome their economic condition have been those that have enjoyed the full development of reserve resources. In their view, if the court failed to find an enforceable fiduciary duty, there would be a disincentive for "Indian" peoples to develop their land and so alter their economic circumstances. To the extent that the court's decision that the Crown owed legally enforceable fiduciary obligations has caused the government to manage Indigenous assets under its control in a prudent manner and obtain the return that a prudent trustee in the circumstances would have obtained, it will have improved the economic situation of Indigenous peoples dependent on such assets. For example, in the *Blueberry River* case, the Supreme Court of Canada held that a prudent trustee would not have surrendered oil rights but preserved them for the band members.[23] Likewise, to the extent that an Indigenous group receives compensation for a breach of this duty, its economic situation will be improved. As noted by Chief Justice Antonio Lamer in *Delgamuukw,* "compensation for breaches of fiduciary duty are a well-established part of the landscape of aboriginal rights: *Guerin.*"[24] Since the *Guerin* case, the amount of compensation received by Indigenous peoples for breaches of fiduciary obligations awarded by courts or negotiated in settlement of litigation or under the specific claims process must now amount to billions of dollars.[25]

It must also be said, however, that despite the broad and liberal rules for determining remedies for breach of fiduciary obligations,[26] the remedies awarded may not overcome the injustice suffered by the Indigenous group. *Guerin* and the subsequent decision of the Supreme Court of Canada in the property tax case discussed in Chapter 5 illustrate the limitations of the law.[27] The compensation awarded in *Guerin* was only $10 million, a very small fraction of the loss of income suffered and to be suffered by the Musqueam as a result of the seventy-five-year lease that the Crown entered into with the exclusive golf club to the detriment of the impoverished band. If the future negotiation of rent had been based on the highest and best use principle as understood by the government's appraisal and band members,[28] it would have dramatically increased the rent payable. Alternatively, if no lease had been signed, some other arrangement could have been concluded to reflect the true value of the land. The band's loss was compounded by the property tax case, which effectively incorporated the use restriction into the property tax provision, although there was no wording in the lease permitting this. This resulted in an assessed value one-twentieth that of immediately adjacent lands and consequently lower property taxes payable to the band by the club. Despite years of litigation and two trips to Canada's highest court, the band is still "fixed with a lease which is worth substantially less than the one they surrendered their land to receive," to quote Justice Bertha Wilson.[29]

POLITICAL IMPACTS

Guerin and the legal developments to which it contributed have strengthened the political power of Indigenous peoples.[30] The existence of legally enforceable obligations owed to them means that when they negotiate with governments, they do so with the potential of being able to commence litigation if their concerns are not given a proper reception. They are not merely supplicants dependent on the whims of the government of the day. The availability of judicial remedies also reduces the risk of the use of more confrontational approaches, such as road blockades or taking physical possession of land to which they assert rights. The existence of potential liability on the part of the Crown for mismanagement of the assets of Indigenous peoples is also a powerful incentive for the Crown to transfer some of its powers to them. Although self-government has been slow in coming and is still very limited, there has been a marked increase in the pace of the delegation of power to Indigenous peoples since the *Guerin* decision.

The *Guerin* litigation played a role in the recommendations of the Penner Inquiry on Aboriginal self-government, conducted by a special committee of the House of Commons, which reported in October 1983 and marked a key development in the movement towards greater self-government in Canada. The Musqueam were invited to give evidence and appeared before the committee on 5 February 1983. This was the week prior to the hearing of the application before the Supreme Court of Canada to obtain leave to appeal from the rejection of the claim by the Federal Court of Appeal. Members of the band and their lawyers described the case and its history and their views on the need for greater self-government powers. The committee showed great interest and one member remarked, "I want you to know that this is the very important part of the committee's work, the whole definition and enforcement of the trust relationship."[31] Another commented that "this is an excellent case to demonstrate the selectivity with which the various ministers over the years have exercised their trust responsibility." He added that "if it were a political trust, it would be meaningless, because in today's context, Indian people have no political power."[32]

In its report, the committee included a chapter on the trust relationship.[33] It summarized its most important recommendation after describing the Musqueam litigation:

> The legal aspects of the situation remain ambiguous at best. Recent attempts by Indian people to obtain redress in the courts have failed, though the legal questions are not fully settled. Recently the federal government argued that it would not compensate the Musqueam Band for losses arising from the rental of band land at well below market

value. The government asserted that it had no legal duty – it was subject only to a "'higher,'" but unenforceable, "political trust."

For all these reasons, the Committee has called throughout this report for a new approach to the special relationship ...

Old, distorted, paternalistic notions about the "protection" of Indian people and nations must be discarded. The elements of the new relationship would be as follows:

• recognition of Indian First Nation governments, with powers and jurisdiction appropriate to a distinct order of government within the Canadian federation.[34]

Although never implemented, this recommendation for a new, distinct level of government to represent Indigenous peoples, in addition to the federal and provincial levels, would have been a major constitutional development. The report did, however, play an important role in the subsequent constitutional discussions that took place between the federal and provincial governments and Indigenous leaders on greater self-government.

FIDUCIARY OBLIGATIONS AND SOVEREIGNTY

At a more fundamental level, the fiduciary relationship between the Crown and Indigenous peoples raises questions regarding their respective sovereignties. There is no doubt that the relationship, and indeed the Anglo-Canadian legal system, assumes the sovereignty of the British/Canadian state over Indigenous peoples.[35] It is this sovereignty that led to the introduction of English law, including fiduciary law, although existing Indigenous laws would continue to apply unless and until they were replaced by English law. This was explained by Justice Beverley McLachlin in *Mitchell v MNR*:

English law, which ultimately came to govern aboriginal rights, accepted that the aboriginal peoples possessed pre-existing laws and interests, and recognized their continuance in the absence of extinguishment, by cession, conquest, or legislation. At the same time, however, the Crown asserted that sovereignty over the land, and ownership of its underlying title, vested in the Crown. With this assertion arose an obligation to treat aboriginal peoples fairly and honourably, and to protect them from exploitation, a duty characterized as "fiduciary" in *Guerin v. The Queen.*[36]

In the context of the Crown and Indigenous peoples, the role of the fiduciary relationship is "to import some restraint on the exercise of sovereign power"[37] but not to deny the legitimacy of or displace Crown sovereignty. Evan Fox-Decent has explained: "By positing the Crown as fiduciary, the Court precludes the Crown from setting unilaterally the terms of its interaction with First Nations, and supplies to Crown-Native relations a measure of legitimacy that would be lacking were the Crown able to set the terms of those relations at its sole discretion."[38] However, he says it is highly debatable how much legitimacy has been conferred, and observes that "for Aboriginal peoples who reject Crown sovereignty and insist on their own, it is far from clear that the fiduciary principle, as understood and applied today, can fully legitimize the Crown's claim to authority over them."[39]

In short, the fiduciary relationship (and indeed Aboriginal law generally) is reformist, not revolutionary. Indigenous peoples now have enforceable rights recognized within the context of a legal system based on the sovereignty of the Canadian state.

Felix Hoehn has interpreted some recent Supreme Court of Canada cases as providing the basis to challenge the legitimacy of Crown sovereignty over the territory of an Indigenous nation and to recognize the sovereignty of that nation.[40] To guide the necessary negotiations to reconcile Crown and Aboriginal sovereignties, he sees a role for fiduciary duties and specifically duties similar to those that apply between equal partners. It should also be noted that, although the fiduciary principles applied in *Guerin* and subsequent cases derive from English law introduced into Canada with Crown sovereignty, similar principles may exist under Indigenous laws, and these could also guide the reconciliation process.[41] For example, Homer G. Barnett writes in his study of the Coast Salish (the larger Indigenous group to which the Musqueam belong): "Although in certain instances title to the places and instruments of exploitation might nominally be vested in [the head of an extended family], he was more a trustee of communal property than a dictatorial owner of it."[42] In some Indigenous groups, a subgroup might act as caretakers for the Nation of part of its territory.[43]

SOME CRITICISMS

Some commentators find the description of the relationship between the Crown and Indigenous peoples as fiduciary to be troubling because to them it suggests a relationship that is not between equals.[44] In his book on fiduciary obligations and the honour of the Crown, Jamie Dickson went so far as to describe the fiduciary relationship as "one of the disasters of Canada's colonial history" because it reinforces "a paternalistic and constitutionally immoral power structure."[45]

These concerns are misplaced. Inequality between the parties is not a necessary requirement for a fiduciary relationship. As Leonard Rotman points out, "nothing in fiduciary relations inherently necessitates that they exist only between dominant and subordinate parties."[46] A beneficiary may be equal in power to, or even more powerful than, the fiduciary but still, in the particular circumstances, be vulnerable to the actions of the fiduciary. An employer may be both wealthy and powerful, but he is still owed a fiduciary obligation of loyalty and honesty by his low-paid employees. Partnerships are an example of a fiduciary relationship where, far from being unequal, the parties are presumptively equal. The charge of paternalism was rejected by the Supreme Court of Canada in the *Manitoba Metis* case by quoting Brian Slattery: "The sources of the general fiduciary duty do not lie, then, in a paternalistic concern to protect a 'weaker' or 'primitive' people, as has sometimes been suggested, but rather in the necessity of persuading native peoples, at a time when they still had considerable military capacities, that their rights would be better protected by reliance on the Crown than by self-help."[47]

The cause of the concern appears to be a view of fiduciary obligations based on the guardian/ward relationship, which is certainly the analogy employed historically, as we saw in Chapter 3. However, a better analogy would be that of equal partners, which respects the autonomy of Indigenous peoples but acknowledges, as the Supreme Court of Canada did in *Guerin,* that their property is still under the control of non-Indigenous governments. The fact that fiduciary language like "a sacred trust for civilization" has been used historically as a justification for colonialism and a cloak for dispossession is no reason to deny the legal enforceability of the obligations of governments when they have taken control of the property of Indigenous peoples.[48]

Fox-Decent disputes the claim that the fiduciary relationship is paternalistic. He observes: "The fiduciary principle, however, does not condone the *Indian Act's* paternalism, nor does it imply that Aboriginal peoples need the Crown to administer their affairs because they lack capacity."[49] In his view:

> The Crown's present fiduciary obligations in no way preclude First Nations from seeking greater autonomy and recognition of their own legal institutions. Properly understood, the Crown's fiduciary obligations include a pluralist duty to accommodate Aboriginal self-determination through recognition of the legitimacy of Aboriginal legal institutions. Hence, the Crown-Native fiduciary relationship does not entail either paternalism or colonialism; on the contrary, it calls for emancipation.[50]

Criticism of the supposed paternalism of the fiduciary relationship is misdirected. Fiduciary principles are a restraint on Crown power and do not reinforce it or prevent greater powers from being recognized for Indigenous peoples.

Another criticism of *Guerin* is based on the significant development in the Aboriginal law context, since the 2004 *Haida* decision, of the principle of the honour of the Crown.[51] This principle can be traced back centuries in the general law and to early cases in Aboriginal law but has been given new application in recent Supreme Court of Canada decisions. References to the honour of the Crown can be found as early as 1608 in cases that held that the honour of the King prevented courts from interpreting grants of land or other favours from him in a manner that invalidated the grant – in other words, the courts assume that the King or the Crown will always act honourably and would never make an invalid grant.[52] The concept has been referenced in Aboriginal law from at least 1895 in the context of the performance of treaty obligations in accordance with "a trust graciously assumed by the Crown to the fulfillment of which with the Indians the faith and honour of the Crown is pledged."[53]

A link between the Crown's trust or fiduciary obligations and the honour of the Crown has remained consistent, and until the *Haida* case in 2004, the honour of the Crown was often used synonymously with the Crown's fiduciary obligations to Indigenous peoples. In *Sparrow,* the Supreme Court of Canada referred to "the concept of holding the Crown to a high standard of honourable dealing with respect to the aboriginal peoples of Canada as suggested by *Guerin v. The Queen.*"[54] In *Mitchell,* it said: "With this assertion of [sovereignty by the Crown] arose an obligation to treat aboriginal peoples fairly and honourably, and to protect them from exploitation, a duty characterized as 'fiduciary' in *Guerin.*"[55]

The first case in which the Supreme Court of Canada clearly discussed the honour of the Crown as being distinct from the Crown's trust-like or fiduciary relationship with Indigenous peoples was *Haida* in 2004.[56] The court rejected a duty to consult based on fiduciary obligations as held in *Guerin* because the asserted interest was unproven and not specific enough to trigger such obligations. However, a duty was upheld based on the honour of the Crown: "The government's duty to consult with Aboriginal peoples and accommodate their interests is grounded in the honour of the Crown. The honour of the Crown is always at stake in its dealings with Aboriginal peoples ... It is not a mere incantation, but rather a core precept that finds its application in concrete practices."[57] The court went on to observe that the honour of the Crown gives rise to different duties in different circumstances. Where the Crown has assumed discretionary control over specific Aboriginal interests, it gives rise to a fiduciary duty. It also infuses the processes of treaty making and treaty interpretation. Where treaties remain to be concluded, it requires negotiations leading to a just settlement of Aboriginal claims. It also requires that Aboriginal rights be "determined, recognized and respected."[58]

The exact relationship between the honour of the Crown and fiduciary obligations is a bit like the old question of which came first, the chicken or the egg. In *Van der Peet,* the court indicated that the fiduciary obligation is the fundamental principle from which the duty of honourable dealings is derived: "The Crown has a fiduciary obligation to aboriginal peoples with the result that in dealings between the government and aboriginals the honour of the Crown is at stake."[59] It continued: "Because of this fiduciary relationship, and its implication of the honour of the Crown, treaties, s.35(1) and other statutory and constitutional provisions protecting the interests of Aboriginal peoples must be given a generous and liberal interpretation." A few years later, in *Haida,* the court reversed this order, saying: "Where the Crown has assumed discretionary control over specific Aboriginal interests, the honour of the Crown gives rise to a fiduciary duty."[60] This sequence has generally been followed in subsequent cases. In the 2018 decision in *Mikisew Cree,* however, three of the justices reverted to the original order: "The honour of the Crown arises from the fiduciary duty that Canada owes to Indigenous peoples following the assertion of sovereignty."[61] Other justices quoted passages from earlier cases that make no distinction between the honour of the Crown, "the special trust relationship," and "the fiduciary relationship."[62]

This conceptual confusion brings to mind the inconsistent approaches taken by the court in *Guerin* on whether trust law, agency law, and special or general fiduciary principles applied, although it made no difference to the Crown's liability.[63] It may well be that this doctrinal inconsistency and the lack of detailed discussion by the justices of the differences between their approaches sowed the seeds for the subsequent confusion between fiduciary obligations and the honour of the Crown. We now have a spectrum of "trust-like duties" to Indigenous peoples: the honour of the Crown, fiduciary duties, and trust law. The court has failed to provide clear differentiation, resulting in confusion. As Peter Birks, a leading authority on fiduciary law, has pointed out, "things are ... not understood unless they are articulately differentiated from others which they closely resemble." If they are not, legal concepts will simply "spin in space, unintelligibly and unrelatedly."[64] There is a risk that this confusion will result in a dilution of the protection provided by the "trust-like duties" owed by the Crown to Indigenous peoples.

The Supreme Court of Canada has often repeated that "the honour of the Crown is always at stake in its dealings with Indian people."[65] The honour of the Crown has not been regarded as a distinct legal doctrine or body of law giving rise to a cause of action, but a fundamental, overarching principle to be applied to the Crown in all its dealings with Indigenous peoples. It might be viewed as "upstream" of, or the common foundation for, such distinct doctrines and should not be seen as replacing or competing with them.

In practice, the duty of consultation has tended to overshadow other areas of Aboriginal law since it was extended in *Haida* to asserted rights from its origins in *Guerin,* where the breach of fiduciary duty consisted in not consulting the Musqueam with respect to reserve lands in which they had established rights. Ryan Beaton has suggested that an important legacy of *Haida* would seem to be a gradual displacement of the Crown's fiduciary duty by the duty to consult and accommodate.[66] It is difficult to gauge the extent of any displacement. Certainly, *Haida* opened up an alternative and less expensive process of judicial review of Crown decisions based on failure to consult instead of costly legal actions to establish breaches of fiduciary duty or the existence of Aboriginal and treaty rights and title. However, claims of fiduciary duty are still very common, including claims brought under the specific claims process to facilitate settlement of claims outside of the normal court system.

Writing in 2015, Jamie Dickson saw recent developments in the law relating to the honour of the Crown as very positive and close to totally eclipsing the fiduciary obligation developed by the Supreme Court of Canada in the Crown/Aboriginal context, which he thought was "a good thing."[67] This view misunderstands the connection between the honour of the Crown principle and the Crown's fiduciary obligations. As we have seen, the court has said that the latter is either the same as, or an application of the former (or vice versa, depending on which justice is speaking), and not in competition with it. As far as an "eclipse" is concerned, the court reaffirmed in 2016 that the fiduciary relationship is "settled law";[68] in 2017, the New Zealand Supreme Court applied *Guerin* and the fiduciary principles to the relationship between the government and the Maori,[69] and in 2018 the Supreme Court of Canada again applied the law.[70] Although the expansion of the honour of the Crown principle in recent years has opened up additional grounds for holding the Crown liable, it has not eclipsed or displaced fiduciary obligations as one of the cornerstones of Aboriginal law.

GUERIN'S CONTRIBUTION

In my opinion, the contribution of the Supreme Court of Canada resulting from the *Guerin* decision to this area of the law is to be applauded despite some shortcomings.

As we have seen, the court can be fairly criticized for a lack of clarity and some inconsistency on occasion, and, as in *Guerin* itself, the law may not achieve a full measure of justice. The court has also pulled back from applying the case to the maximum possible extent and the full potential of *Guerin* has not been realized. The *Wewaykum* decision narrowed its potential scope in the context of the relationship between Indigenous peoples and the Crown by denying that it applied to all aspects of the relationship and limiting it to situations where a specific Aboriginal interest is involved.[71] The *Elder Advocates of Alberta Society* case narrowed its potential use in the context of the Crown generally.[72] However, this failure to allow the case to have greater scope does not diminish the role *Guerin* has played and continues to play in holding government liable for breaches of fiduciary obligations and in bringing about the changes in Aboriginal law discussed in Chapter 6.

It must be acknowledged that the role of law has been to support the colonization of Canada, including the dispossession of Indigenous peoples, disruption of their cultures and legal systems, and limitation of their powers to govern. We saw this in the case of the Musqueam in

Chapter 2. The Truth and Reconciliation Commission described Canadian law as "a tool for the dispossession and dismantling of Aboriginal societies."[73] As stated by Justice Ian Binnie in the *God's Lake* case, "the history of Indian peoples in North America has generally been one of dispossession, including dispossession of their pre-European sovereignty, of their traditional lands, and of distinctive elements of their cultures."[74] Law played a prominent part in this colonial process and continues to support its legacy by legitimizing it.

Despite the general role played by the law in the process of colonization of the Indigenous peoples of Canada, it should also be acknowledged that the role of law in society is complex and contradictory. It can and has been used by Indigenous peoples to ameliorate some of the injustices of the colonial system imposed on them and to obtain some measure of justice.[75] I have argued elsewhere that the fundamental changes necessary to resolve historical claims, restructure the political relationship, and improve living conditions for Indigenous peoples must come from political action and not through the case-by-case approach of litigation and negotiation.[76] But this is not to deny that some Indigenous groups have benefited from developments in Aboriginal law such as the *Guerin* decision.

Although some have criticized the *Guerin* decision, it is an outstanding example of the use of the law to bring about some measure of justice to people who have historically been denied their day in court. It may be seen as a tribute to the Canadian legal system and its highest court. Above all, it is a tribute to the determination of Delbert Guerin and the Musqueam people to achieve some measure of justice for the wrong done to them.

Notes

PREFACE

1 Terry Glavin and Glenn Bohn, "Musqueam Hails Court Verdict," *Vancouver Sun* (2 November 1984).

2 John Ralston Saul, *The Comeback* (Toronto: Penguin Canada, 2014) at 35.

INTRODUCTION

1 [1984] 2 SCR 335.

2 *R v Sparrow*, [1990] 1 SCR 1075.

3 Ian Binnie, "Closing Address" (Address delivered at the Canadian Institute for the Administration of Justice Annual Conference, "Justice to Order: Adjustment to Changing Demands and Co-ordination Issues in the Justice System in Canada," Saskatoon, 1998) at 451.

4 Thomas King, *The Inconvenient Indian* (Toronto: Anchor Canada, 2012) at 241–44.

5 John Ralston Saul, *The Comeback* (Toronto: Penguin Canada, 2014) at 35–36.

6 *Wakatu v Attorney-General*, [2017] NZLR 17.

7 B.A. Keon-Cohen, "The *Mabo* Litigation: A Personal and Procedural Account" (2000) 24 Melbourne UL Rev 893; see also Bryan Keon-Cohen, *A Mabo Memoir: Islan Kustom to Native Title* (Melbourne: Zemvic Press, 2013).

8 See Thomas R. Berger, *One Man's Justice: A Life in the Law* (Toronto: Douglas and McIntyre, 2002) at 4.

9 James I. Reynolds, *A Breach of Duty: Fiduciary Obligations and Aboriginal Peoples* (Saskatoon: Purich, 2005).

10 Leonard I. Rotman, *Fiduciary Law* (Toronto: Thomson Carswell, 2005) at 569.

11 See also Leonard I. Rotman, "Understanding Fiduciary Duties and Relationship Fiduciarity" (2017) 62 McGill LJ 975, which has a list of legal literature on fiduciary law.

12 Leonard Ian Rotman, *Parallel Paths: Fiduciary Doctrine and the Crown-Native Relationship in Canada* (Toronto: University of Toronto Press, 1996); J. Timothy S. McCabe, *The Honour of the Crown and Its Fiduciary Duties to Aboriginal Peoples* (Toronto: LexisNexis, 2008).

13 *Brown v Board of Education,* 347 US 483 (1954); D. Geoffrey Cowper, "Fiduciary Obligations and Aboriginal Peoples: The Candid Account of an Insider" (2006) 64 The Advocate 523 at 523.

14 John Seymour, "Parens Patriae and Wardship Powers: Their Nature and Origins" (1994) 14 Oxford J Leg Stud 159.

CHAPTER 1: THE COLONIAL CONTEXT

1 The colonies of Vancouver Island and British Columbia were united in 1866.

2 Vicki Cummings, "Hunting and Gathering in a Farmers' World" in Vicki Cummings, Peter Jordan, and Marek Zvelebil, eds, *The Oxford Handbook of the Archaeology and Anthropology of Hunter-Gatherers* (Oxford: Oxford University Press, 2014); David Reich, *Who We Are and How We Got Here: Ancient DNA and the New Science of the Human Past* (New York: Pantheon, 2018).

3 Michael Kew, *Coast Salish Ceremonial Life: Status and Identity in a Modern Village* (PhD Thesis, University of Washington, 1970) [unpublished] at 312.

4 On the process of encapsulation of hunter-gatherer societies, see Richard Borshay Lee, "Power and Property in Twenty-First Century Foragers: A Critical Examination" in Thomas Widlok and Wolde Gossa Tadesse, eds, *Property and Equality, Vol. II, Encapsulation, Commercialisation and Discrimination* (Oxford: Berghahn, 2005).

5 See generally, Cole Harris, "How Did Colonialism Dispossess? Comments from an Edge of Empire" (2004) 94 Annals of the Association of American Geographers 165.

6 London International Exhibition, *Catalogue of the Vancouver Contributions with a Short Account of Vancouver Island and British Columbia* (London, 1862) at 6.

7 For an account of pre-emption in British Columbia, see Brenna Bhandar, *Resisting the Reproduction of the Proper Subject of Rights: Recognition, Property Relations and the Movement towards Post-Colonialism in Canada* (PhD Thesis, University of London, Birkbeck College, 2007) [unpublished] at 101–57; Brenna Bhandar, *Colonial Lives of Property: Law, Land and Racial Regimes of Ownership* (Durham, NC: Duke University Press, 2018) at 33–76. For a comparative account of how European colonialism used property systems to dispossess Indigenous peoples in North America, see Allan Greer, *Property and Dispossession: Natives, Empires and Land in Early Modern North America* (Cambridge: Cambridge University Press,

2018). For essays on the history of property law in several British colonies, see John McLaren, A.R. Buck, and Nancy Wright, eds, *Despotic Dominion: Property Rights in British Settler Societies* (Vancouver: UBC Press, 2005).

8 Jim Reynolds, *Aboriginal Peoples and the Law: A Critical Introduction* (Vancouver: UBC Press/Purich, 2018) at 6–8, 94–113.

9 W. Parker Snow, *British Columbia: Emigration and Our Colonies* (London: Piper, Stephenson and Spencer, 1858) at 1. For a comprehensive study of migration around the British Empire, see Marjory Harper and Stephen Constantine, *Migration and Empire* (Oxford: Oxford University Press, 2010).

10 *Ibid* at 63.

11 Cole Harris, *The Resettlement of British Columbia: Essays on Colonialism and Geographical Change* (Vancouver: UBC Press, 1997) at xvii [*Resettlement*]. The depopulation was due to smallpox, introduced by Europeans (*ibid* at 3–30).

12 English translation from Latin by Ralphe Robinson (1551): Early English Books Online image 72 <http://name.umdl.umich.edu/A07706.0001.001>; see also John Locke, *The Second Treatise of Government* (Indianapolis: Hackett, 1980) at ch 5. For a detailed account of the theory of occupation, see Andrew Fitzmaurice, *Sovereignty, Property and Empire, 1500–2000* (Cambridge: Cambridge University Press, 2014); for the views of European writers on hunters and gatherers, see Alan Barnard, "Images of Hunters and Gatherers in European Social Thought" in Richard B. Lee and Richard Daly, eds, *The Cambridge Encyclopedia of Hunters and Gatherers* (Cambridge: Cambridge University Press, 1999).

13 Gilbert Sproat, *Scenes and Studies of Savage Life* (London: Smith, Elder, 1868) at 3–9.

14 *Haida Nation v British Columbia (Minister of Forests)*, 2004 SCC 73 at para 25.

15 For a summary of the role of violence behind the British Empire, see John Darwin, *Unfinished Empire: The Global Expansion of Britain* (London: Penguin, 2013) at 117–49 [*Unfinished Empire*]. For an account of revolts in the British Empire and their suppression, see Richard Gott, *Britain's Empire: Resistance, Repression and Revolt* (London: Verso, 2011).

16 Winston Churchill, *The River War*, vol 1 (London: Longmans, Green, 1899) at 18.

17 Eleanor Leacock and Richard Lee, *Politics and History in Band Societies* (Cambridge: Cambridge University Press, 1982) at 5.

18 Edward B. Tylor, *Primitive Culture: Researches into the Development of Mythology, Philosophy, Religion, Art and Custom*, vol 1 (London: John Murray, 1871) at 28–29; see also Lewis H. Morgan, *Ancient Society or Researches in the Lines of Human Progress from Savagery through Barbarism to Civilization* (Chicago: Kerr, 1877). For a detailed discussion, see J.W. Burrows, *Evolution and Society: A Study*

in Victorian Social Theory (Cambridge: Cambridge University Press, 1966). For a summary of evolutionary thinking in anthropology, see Peter Jordan and Vicki Cummings, "New Approaches in the Study of Hunter-Gatherers" in Cummings, Jordan, and Zvelebil, *supra* note 2 at 1098–100. Kent McNeil explores the impact of evolutionary theory on Indigenous peoples in Canada in *Flawed Precedent: The St. Catherine's Case and Aboriginal Title* (Vancouver: UBC Press, 2019) at 13–18.

19 Churchill, *supra* note 16 at 19. For an overview of the impact of European colonialism on hunter-gatherers, see John H. Bodley, "Hunter-Gatherers and the Colonial Encounter" in Lee and Daly, *supra* note 12.

20 Klaus Knorr, *British Colonial Theories 1570–1850* (Toronto: University of Toronto Press, 1944) at 246–48, 366–71, 376–88.

21 Herman Merivale, *Lectures on Colonization and Colonies. Delivered before the University of Oxford in 1839, 1840 & 1841* (London: Longman, Brown, Green and Longman, 1842), vol 2, at 155, 157 [*Lectures (1842)*].

22 John Stuart Mill, "On Liberty" (1859) in *Utilitarianism, Liberty and Representative Government* (London: Allen & Unwin, 1968) at 73.

23 Knorr, *supra* note 20 at 247, 386–87.

24 Merivale, *Lectures (1842), supra* note 21 at 158.

25 *Report of the Parliamentary Select Committee on Aboriginal Tribes (British Settlements), Reprinted with Comments by the Aborigines Protection Society* (London: William Bell, 1837) at 117.

26 Merivale, *Lectures on Colonization and Colonies,* new ed (London: Longman, 1861) at 495 [*Lectures (1861)*].

27 Mill, "Representative Government" in *Utilitarianism, supra* note 22 at 386.

28 *Ibid* at 387.

29 Merivale, *Lectures (1842), supra* note 21 at 179. For the views of another government official, the first attorney-general of New South Wales, see S. Bannister, *Humane Policy or Justice to the Aborigines of New Settlements* (London: Thomas and Underwood, 1830), and *British Colonization and Coloured Tribes* (London: William Ball, 1838).

30 Merivale, *Lectures (1842), supra* note 21 at 180.

31 Merivale, *Lectures (1861), supra* note 26 at 522.

32 Merivale, *Lectures (1842), supra* note 21 at 160.

33 Cole Harris, *Making Native Space* (Vancouver: UBC Press, 2002) especially at 136–66; Sarah P. Pike, *Gilbert Malcolm Sproat: British Columbia Indian Reserve Commissioner (1876–1880) and the "Humanitarian Civilizing" of Indigenous Peoples* (LLM Thesis, University of British Columbia, 2018) [unpublished].

34 Sproat, *supra* note 13 at 279.

35 *Ibid* at 284. For a more contemporary account of the role played by anomie – the absence of societal norms – resulting from colonialism, see Wolfgang G.

Jilek, *Indian Healing – Shamanic Ceremonialism in the Pacific Northwest Today* (Surrey, BC: Hancock House, 1982).

36 Sproat, *supra* note 13 at 287.

37 *Ibid* at 290.

38 F.D. Lugard, *The Dual Mandate in British Tropical Africa* (Edinburgh: William Blackwood, 1922) at 617. For a critical analysis of his philosophy, see Olufemi Taiwo, "Reading the Colonizer's Mind: Lord Lugard and the Philosophical Foundations of British Colonialism" in Susan E. Babbit and Sue Campbell, eds, *Racism and Philosophy* (Ithaca, NY: Cornell University Press, 1999).

39 Alan Burns, *In Defence of Colonies* (London: George Allen & Unwin, 1957) at 303.

40 George Orwell, *Burmese Days* (London: Martin, Secker and Warburg, 1976) at 94; Gordon Bowker, *George Orwell* (London: Abacus, 2004) at 75–95.

41 Lugard, *supra* note 38 at 617. For one example, see E.K. Lumley, *Forgotten Mandate: A British District Officer in Tanganyika* (London: Hurst, 1976).

42 A general account of Britain's imperial administration is provided in Anthony Kirk-Greene, *Britain's Imperial Administrators, 1858–1966* (London: Palgrave Macmillan, 2000) [*Britain's Imperial Administrators*]. For a collection of papers from former colonial administrators and academics, see John Smith, ed, *Administering Empire: The British Colonial Service in Retrospect* (London: London University Press, 1999). For comparative accounts, see J.S. Furnivall, *Colonial Policy and Practice: A Comparative Study of Burma and Netherlands India* (Cambridge: Cambridge University Press, 1948); A. Lawrence Lowell, *Colonial Civil Service: The Selection and Training of Colonial Officials in England, Holland and France* (New York: Macmillan, 1900). For a bibliography of materials on the colonial service, see Anthony Kirk-Greene, *On Crown Service: A History of HM Colonial and Overseas Civil Services 1837–1997* (London: Tauris, 1999) at 125 [*On Crown Service*].

43 Philip Mason, *The Men Who Ruled India* (London: Jonathan Cape, 1985) provides a detailed account. For Haileybury, see H. Morse Stephens, "An Account of the East India College at Haileybury (1806–1857)" in Lowell, *supra* note 42.

44 For the situation in the decades leading up to the independence of India in 1947, see Charles Allen, *Plain Tales from the Raj: Images of British India in the 20th Century* (London: Futura, 1976) especially at 42. See also David Gilmour, *The British in India* (London: Penguin, 2019) at 161–78, 193–98.

45 James (Jan) Morris, *Pax Britannica: The Climax of an Empire* (Harmondsworth, UK: Penguin, 1979) at 186–87. Strictly, Colonial Services as each colony had its own administration until they were unified starting in 1930: Charles Jeffries, *The Colonial Empire and Its Civil Service* (Cambridge: Cambridge University Press, 1938).

46 Alan Burns, *Colonial Civil Servant* (London: George Allen & Unwin, 1949) at 294–95 [*Colonial Civil Servant*] (emphasis in original).

47 This was often code for being of the right social class – colonial administrators were overwhelmingly from private schools and ancient universities: Robert Heussler, *Yesterday's Rulers: The Making of the British Colonial Service* (New York: Syracuse University Press, 1963); Morris, *supra* note 45 at 187–88. For a contrary view, see Nile Taro Gardiner, *Sentinels of Empire: The British Colonial Administrative Service, 1919–1954* (PhD Thesis, Yale University, 1998).

48 For the district officer in Africa, see Anthony Kirk-Greene, *Symbol of Authority: The British District Officer in Africa* (London: Tauris, 2006) [*Symbol of Authority*]; Christopher Prior, *Exporting Empire: Africa, Colonial Officials and the Construction of the Imperial State, c. 1900–39* (Manchester: Manchester University Press, 2015). A classic account that inspired some recruits to the colonial service was Kenneth Bradley, *The Diary of a District Officer* (London: Thomas Nelson, 1947). The 1935 movie *Sanders of the River* was one fictitious account subsequently denounced by its star, Paul Robeson, as imperialist propaganda: Martin Bauml Duberman, *Paul Robeson: A Biography* (New York: Ballantine, 1989) at 178–81. It was based on the short stories written by Edgar Wallace. Some of William Somerset Maugham's short stories were based on the lives of district officers and commissioners in Malaya: W. Somerset Maugham, *Collected Short Stories*, vol 4 (London: Pan, 1976) especially "The Back of Beyond" and "The Outstation." The novelist Joyce Cary was a former district officer and he included them as characters in some of his novels, such as *Mister Johnson* (Harmondsworth, UK: Penguin, 1962). See generally, Anthony Kirk-Greene, "The Colonial Service in the Novel" in Smith, *supra* note 42.

49 Lugard, *supra* note 38 at 59.

50 Charles Allen, *Tales from the South China Seas: Images of the British in South East Asia in the Twentieth Century* (London: Futura, 1983) at 162.

51 Kirk-Greene, *Symbol of Authority, supra* note 48 at 42.

52 For detailed accounts, see Furnivall, *supra* note 42 at 484–512; Heussler, *supra* note 47. See also Margery Perham, *The Colonial Reckoning* (London: Collins, 1962) at 120–29.

53 Charles Jeffries, *The Colonial Office* (London: George Allen & Unwin, 1956) at 38–46, 150–59.

54 Memorandum by Sir R. Furse, Feb. 27, 1943, partially reproduced in S.R. Ashton and S.E. Stockwell, eds, *British Documents on the End of Empire,* Series A, vol 1 (London: HMSO, 1996) at 27–39; Kirk-Greene, *On Crown Service, supra* note 42 at 43.

55 Burns, *Colonial Civil Servant, supra* note 46 at 321; see also Furnivall, *supra* note 42 at 428.

56 Charles Allen, *Tales from the Dark Continent: Images of British Colonial Africa in the Twentieth Century* (London: Futura, 1980) at xvii.

57 Kirk-Greene, *Symbol of Authority, supra* note 48 at 12; Chris Jeppeson, "Sanders of the River: Still the Best Job for a British Boy – Recruitment to the Colonial Administrative Service at the End of Empire" (2016) 59 Historical Journal 469.

58 Kirk-Greene, *Symbol of Authority, supra* note 48 at 36–41.

59 *Ibid* at 17, 42–56; Prior, *supra* note 48 at 35–43.

60 Kirk-Greene, *On Crown Service, supra* note 42 at 42–47, 198–209; Sarah Stockwell, *The British End of the British Empire* (Cambridge: Cambridge University Press, 2018) at 26–38, 93–130.

61 Burns, *Colonial Civil Servant, supra* note 46 at 302.

62 For a discussion of ruling methods used in the British Empire, see Darwin, *Unfinished Empire, supra* note 15 at 189–222.

63 Margery Perham, *Lugard: The Years of Authority 1898–1945* (London: Collins, 1960) at 138. For a detailed discussion, see Lugard, *supra* note 38 at 193–229; see also C.L. Temple, *Native Races and Their Rulers* (Cape Town: Argus, 1918). For a somewhat critical review of indirect rule, see Lord Hailey, *An African Survey: A Study of Problems Arising in Africa South of the Sahara* (London: Oxford University Press, 1938) at 527–45.

64 Furnivall, *supra* note 42 at 276–77.

65 *Ibid* at 428.

66 Frank Swettenham, *British Malaya* (London: John Lane, 1906) at 221; N.J. Ryan, *The Making of Modern Malaya* (Kuala Lumpur: Oxford University Press, 1963) at 130; Philip Loh Fook Seng, *The Malay States 1877–1895: Political Change and Social Policy* (Singapore: Oxford University Press, 1969).

67 Swettenham, *supra* note 66 at 176–77.

68 Martin Chanock, *Law, Custom and Social Order: The Colonial Experience in Malawi and Zambia* (Cambridge: Cambridge University Press, 1985) at 145; Terence Ranger, "The Invention of Tradition in Colonial Africa" in Eric Hobsbawm and Terence Ranger, eds, *The Invention of Tradition* (Cambridge: Cambridge University Press, 1983) at 211, 247–51.

69 Mason, *supra* note 43 at 271–335.

70 Burns, *Colonial Civil Servant, supra* note 46 at 323–24.

71 *Ibid* at 318.

72 C.E. Carrington, *The Liquidation of the British Empire* (Toronto: Clarke, Irwin, 1961) at 71.

73 A.P. Thornton, *The Imperial Idea and Its Enemies: A Study in British Power,* 2d ed (Basingstoke: Macmillan, 1985) at xv.

74 Hong Kong was the last to go in 1997, and Her Majesty's Overseas Civil Service was then terminated. There are currently fourteen former colonies, a collection of islands and rocks with a total population of about 250,000, still claimed as under British sovereignty: *British Overseas Territories Act* (UK), 2002, c 8. A detailed account of the end of the British Empire is given in Judith M. Brown and Wm. Roger Louis, eds, *The Oxford History of the British Empire. Volume 4: The Twentieth Century* (Oxford: Oxford University Press, 1999); see also John Darwin, *Britain and Decolonization: The Retreat from Empire in the Post-war World* (Basingstoke: Macmillan, 1988). For summaries, see Eric Hobsbawm, *Age of Extremes: The Short Twentieth Century 1914–1991* (London: Abacus, 1995) at 199–222; Tony Judt, *Postwar: A History of Europe since 1945* (London: Penguin, 2005) at 278–302.

75 Kirk-Greene, *On Crown Service, supra* note 42 at 62.

76 *Ibid* at 75.

77 Furnivall, *supra* note 42 at 312–18, 484–512. See also Ronald Hyam, "Bureaucracy and 'Trusteeship' in the Colonial Empire" in Brown and Louis, *supra* note 74.

78 Alan Cairns, *First Nations and the Canadian State: In Search of Coexistence* (Kingston, ON: Institute of Intergovernmental Relations, Queen's University, 2005) at 8 [*First Nations*].

79 Cole Harris, *Resettlement, supra* note 11 at xvii.

80 Lorenzo Veracini, "Introduction: Settler Colonization as a Distinct Mode of Domination" in Edward Cavanagh and Lorenzo Veracini, eds, *The Routledge Handbook of the History of Settler Colonialism* (Abingdon, UK: Routledge, 2017) at 5.

81 For a summary of settlement in the British Empire, see Darwin, *Unfinished Empire, supra* note 15 at 89–116.

82 Douglas C. Harris, *Fish, Law and Colonialism: The Legal Capture of Salmon in British Columbia* (Toronto: University of Toronto Press, 2001) at 198. On the general amnesia about Canada's role in the Empire, see Phillip Buckner, "Presidential Address: Whatever Happened to the British Empire?" (1993) 4 Journal of the Canadian Historical Association 3. For a detailed account that expresses the relationship between the law applying to Indigenous groups in North America and that applying to colonial peoples generally, see Alpheus Henry Snow, *The Question of Aborigines in the Law and Practice of Nations* (New York: Putnam's, 1921). For studies linking colonial history in British Columbia to that of other parts of the British Empire, see Renisa Mawani, *Colonial Proximities: Crossracial Encounters and Juridical Truths in British Columbia, 1871–1921* (Vancouver: UBC Press, 2009) [*Colonial Proximities*]; Renisa Mawani, *Across Oceans of Law: The Komagata Maru and Jurisdiction in the Time of Empire* (Durham, NC: Duke University Press, 2018).

83 Harsha Walia, "Really, Harper: Canada Has No History of Colonialism?" *Vancouver Sun* (27 September 2009).

84 Phillip Buckner and R. Douglas Francis, *Canada and the British World: Culture, Migration and Identity* (Vancouver: UBC Press, 2006); Phillip Buckner, ed, *Canada and the British Empire* (Oxford: Oxford University Press, 2010).

85 Darwin, *Unfinished Empire, supra* note 15 at 96.

86 Harper and Constantine, *supra* note 9 at 3.

87 Stephen Leacock, *Our British Empire: Its Structure, Its History, Its Strength* (London: John Lane, 1940) at 218. For a review of Canadian attitudes to the Empire in 1938, see Norman MacKenzie, "A Canadian Looks at the Empire" (1938) 9 Political Quarterly 551.

88 Darwin, *Unfinished Empire, supra* note 15 at 202, 387. For an account of correspondence between 1858 and 1914 from settlers in BC to their relatives in Britain showing their continued identification as British, see Laura Ishiguro, *Nothing to Write Home About: British Family Correspondence and the Settler Colonial Everyday in British Columbia* (Vancouver: UBC Press, 2019).

89 Rudyard Kipling, *Recessional* (1897).

90 Kirk-Greene, *On Crown Service, supra* note 42 at 29–30. For a memoir by a Canadian district officer in Tanganyika, see J.C. Cairns, *Bush and Boma* (London: John Murray, 1959). A Canadian serving in the police force of an African colony was the leading character in Elspeth Huxley's novel *Murder at Government House* (New York: Harper, 1937).

91 Phillip Buckner, ed, *Canada and the End of Empire* (Vancouver: UBC Press, 2005) at 3 [*Canada and the End of Empire*]. For a recent examination of Canadian participation in imperial wars, see Steve Marti and William Pratt, *Fighting with the Empire: Canada, Britain and Global Conflict, 1867–1947* (Vancouver: UBC Press, 2019).

92 Phillip Buckner, "Was There a 'British' Empire? *The Oxford History of the British Empire* from a Canadian Perspective" (2002) 32 Acadiensis 110 at 128.

93 E. Brian Titley, *A Narrow Vision: Duncan Campbell Scott and the Administration of Indian Affairs in Canada* (Vancouver: UBC Press, 1986) at 25. See also Mark Abley, *Conversations with a Dead Man: The Legacy of Duncan Campbell Scott* (Madeira Park, BC: Douglas and McIntyre, 2012); Wendy Wickwire, *At the Bridge: James Teit and an Anthropology of Belonging* (Vancouver: UBC Press, 2019) at 214–47.

94 John Seeley, *Expansion of England: Two Courses of Lectures* (London: Macmillan, 1883).

95 See generally, Duncan Bell, *The Idea of Greater Britain: Empire and the Future of World Order, 1860-1900* (Princeton: Princeton University Press, 2007).

96 Viscount Milner, *Questions of the Hour* (London: Hodder and Stoughton, 1923) at 146–47, 153.

97 Carl Berger, *The Sense of Power: Studies in the Ideas of Canadian Imperialism 1867–1914* (Toronto: University of Toronto Press, 1970).

98 Cairns, *First Nations, supra* note 78 at 5.

99 *Ibid;* see also Alan Cairns, *Citizens Plus: Aboriginal Peoples and the Canadian State* (Vancouver: UBC Press, 2001) at 19–28 [*Citizens Plus*].

100 Cairns, *First Nations, supra* note 78 at 9.

101 *Ibid* at 6.

102 Albert Memmi, *The Colonizer and the Colonized* (New York: Orion Press, 1965). In 1961, Frantz Fanon wrote his condemnation of colonialism, which also enjoyed wide influence: *The Wretched of the Earth* (New York: Grove Press, 2004).

103 Bryan D. Palmer, *Canada's 1960s: The Ironies of Identity in a Rebellious Age* (Toronto: University of Toronto Press, 2009) at 4–5.

104 *Ibid* at 19.

105 James (Jan) Morris, *Farewell the Trumpets: An Imperial Retreat* (London: Penguin, 1979) at 63n.

106 Jośe E. Igartua, *The Other Quiet Revolution: National Identities in English Canada, 1945–71* (Vancouver: UBC Press, 2006).

107 *Ibid* at 72. See also George Richardson, "Nostalgia and National Identity: The History and Social Studies Curricula of Alberta and Ontario at the End of Empire" in Buckner, *Canada and the End of Empire, supra* note 91.

108 Quoted in Richardson, *supra* note 107 at 184.

109 Igartua, *supra* note 106 at 95. The reference to the constitution is to s 7(1) of the *Statute of Westminster, 1931* (UK), 22 & 23 Geo V, c 4, which left changes to the Canadian Constitution (then the *British North America Act*) to the British Parliament.

110 Igartua, *supra* note 106 at 129.

111 Buckner and Francis, *supra* note 84 at 3.

112 Igartua, *supra* note 106 at 173. See also C.P. Champion, *The Strange Demise of British Canada: The Liberals and Canadian Nationalism, 1964–1968* (Montreal and Kingston: McGill-Queen's University Press, 2010).

113 Chad Reimer, *Writing British Columbia History, 1784–1958* (Vancouver: UBC Press, 2010) especially at 44–60, 146–47. The percentages of the British Columbia population with British origins were 70 percent in 1941, 66 percent in 1951, and 60 percent in 1961: see Jean Barman, *The West beyond the West: A History of British Columbia* (Toronto: University of Toronto Press, 1991) at Table 5, 138–41.

114 For a study of international legal literature, see Chris Tennant, "Indigenous Peoples, International Institutions, and the International Legal Literature from

1945–1993" (1994) 16 Hum Rts Q 1. For both official and popular attitudes in Canada in the 1930s and 1940s, see R. Scott Sheffield, *The Red Man's on the Warpath: The Image of the "Indian" and the Second World War* (Vancouver: UBC Press, 2005).

115 Igartua, *supra* note 106 at 66. See also Patricia V. Ofner, *The Indian in Textbooks: A Content Analysis of History Books Authorized for Use in Ontario Schools* (MA Thesis, Lakehead University, 1982) [unpublished].

116 Margaret Ormsby, *British Columbia: A History* (Toronto: Macmillan, 1958); see Reimer, *supra* note 113 at 125–48 for an account of Ormsby's work. Reimer's book also provides an account of historians' generally dismissive and negative attitude towards Indigenous peoples for the period until 1958. See also Bruce Trigger, "The Historians' Indian: Native Americans in Canadian Historical Writing from Charlevoix to the Present" (1986) 67 Canadian Historical Review 315.

117 Ormsby, *supra* note 116 at 494.

118 *Ibid* at 37, 127.

119 *Ibid* at 113.

120 *Ibid* at 168.

121 Julian Park, ed, *The Culture of Contemporary Canada* (Ithaca, NY: Cornell University Press, 1957).

122 Mia Reimers, *"BC at Its Most Sparkling, Colourful Best": Post-war Province Building through Centennial Celebrations* (PhD Thesis, University of Victoria, 2007) [unpublished]. For accounts of Musqueam participation in the 1936 celebration of Vancouver's fiftieth anniversary, see Alexander Sanya Pleshakov, *"We Do Not Talk about Our History Here": The Department of Indian Affairs, Musqueam-Settler Relations and Memory of a Vancouver Neighbourhood* (MA Thesis, University of British Columbia, 2010) [unpublished] at 3–5; for the Musqueam role in the 1966 celebrations of the centennial of the uniting of the colonies of Vancouver Island and British Columbia, see Susan Roy, "Performing Musqueam Culture and History at British Columbia's 1966 Centennial Celebrations" (2002) 135 BC Studies 55.

123 Reimers, *supra* note 122 at 213.

124 Phillip Buckner, "The Last Great Royal Tour: Queen Elizabeth's 1959 Tour to Canada" in Buckner, *Canada and the End of Empire, supra* note 91 at 76–77.

125 Forrest E. La Violette, *The Struggle for Survival: Indian Cultures and the Protestant Ethic in British Columbia* (Toronto: University of Toronto Press, 1961) at 6–11.

126 Reimer, *supra* note 113 at 20, 66.

127 Celia Haig-Brown and David A. Nock, *With Good Intentions: Euro-Canadian and Aboriginal Relations in Colonial Canada* (Vancouver: UBC Press, 2006) at 9–20.

128 App 8 in Ronald St. John Macdonald, *Native Rights in Canada* (Toronto: Indian-Eskimo Association, 1970).

129 Cole Harris, *Making Native Space: Colonialism, Resistance and Reserves in British Columbia* (Vancouver: UBC Press, 2002) at 7, 15, 30, 45 (Colonial Office), 71, 98, 119, 164–65, 167, 192, 193, 196, and, especially, 203 (Ottawa).

130 *Ibid* at 45.

131 Noel Dyck, *What Is the Indian "Problem": Tutelage and Resistance in Canadian Indian Administration* (St. John's: Institute of Social and Economic Research, 1991) at 74–75; examples are given at 85.

132 Titley, *supra* note 93 at 20.

133 *Ibid* at 21.

134 *Ibid.*

135 *Ibid* at 47.

136 John Giokas, "The Indian Act – Evolution, Overview and Options for Amendment and Transition" (Research report prepared for the Royal Commission on Aboriginal Peoples, 22 March 1995) at 19; see also John Leslie, "Commissions of Inquiry into Indian Affairs in the Canadas, 1828–1858" (Report prepared for Indian and Northern Affairs Canada, 1985) at 21–25.

137 T. MacInnes, "History of Indian Administration in Canada" (1946) 12 Canadian Journal of Economics and Political Science 387 at 393.

138 Quoted in Cairns, *Citizens Plus, supra* note 99 at 17.

139 *Ibid.*

140 Sean Fine, "Chief Justice Says Canada Attempted 'Cultural Genocide' on Aboriginals," *Globe and Mail* (28 May 2015).

141 Diamond Jenness, *The Indians of Canada,* 2d ed, (Ottawa: National Museum of Canada, 1935) at 350.

142 *Constitution Act, 1867* (UK), 30 & 31 Vict, c 3, reprinted in RSC 1985, Appendix II, No 5, s 91(24).

143 John Leslie, *Assimilation, Integration or Termination? The Development of Canadian Indian Policy, 1943–1963* (PhD Thesis, Carleton University, 1999) [unpublished] at 73–74.

144 H. Hawthorn, ed, *A Survey of the Contemporary Indians of Canada: Economic, Political, Educational Needs and Policies* (Ottawa: Indian Affairs Branch, 1966), vol 1 at 368–70 [*Hawthorn Report 1966*].

145 Leslie, *supra* note 143. See also R.W. Dunning, "Some Aspects of Government Indian Policy and Administration" (1962) 4 Anthropologica 209.

146 Leslie, *supra* note 143 at 117.

147 *Ibid* at 126.

148 *Ibid* at 185.

149 *Ibid* at 238.

150 Dyck, *supra* note 131 at 96–97.

151 Leslie, *supra* note 143 at 246–47.

152 *Ibid* at 406.

153 See Dyck, *supra* note 131 at 104–18 for those changes.

154 H.B. Hawthorn, C.S. Belshaw, and S.M. Jamieson, *The Indians of British Columbia: A Study of Contemporary Social Adjustment* (Berkeley: University of California Press, 1958). [Hawthorn, Belshaw, and Jamieson]. For the background to the report, see Byron King Plant, "A Relationship and Exchange of Experience" (2009) 165 BC Studies 5. It should be distinguished from the *Hawthorn Report 1966, supra* note 144, which was a comprehensive review of the condition of Indians in Canada and which recommended special status as "Citizens-Plus."

155 Leslie, *supra* note 143 at 277. The published version has fewer pages and some edits.

156 *Ibid* at 278; Plant, *supra* note 154 at 24–25.

157 It was mentioned at a January 1956 conference of Indian agents: *Indian Superintendent's Conference, British Columbia & Yukon Regions, January 16 to 20, 1956* (Ottawa: Department of Citizenship and Immigration, Indian Affairs Branch, 1956) at 84.

158 Hawthorn, Belshaw, and Jamieson, *supra* note 154 at 242, 431 and *passim*. It should be noted that there was no meaningful Indigenous participation in the commissioning or recommendations of the report.

159 *Ibid* at 455.

160 *Ibid* at 458.

161 *Ibid* at 460.

162 *Ibid* at 451.

163 *Ibid* at 489.

164 *Ibid* at 490.

165 *Ibid* at 490–92.

166 *Ibid* at 493.

167 For studies of the role of Indian agents, see Robin Jarvis Brownlie, *A Father's Eye: Indian Agents, Government Power, and Aboriginal Resistance in Ontario, 1918–1939* (Oxford: Oxford University Press, 2003); Vic Satzewich and Linda Mahood, "Indian Agents and the Residential School System in Canada, 1946–1970" (1995) 7 Historical Studies in Education 45; Victor Satzewich, "Indian Agents and the 'Indian Problem' in Canada in 1946: Reconsidering the Theory of Coercive Tutelage" (1997) 17 Canadian Journal of Native Studies 227; John L. Steckley, *Indian Agents: Rulers of the Reserves* (New York: Peter Lang, 2016). For a memoir by an Indian agent, see W.M. Halliday, *Potlatch and Totem: And the Recollections*

of an Indian Agent (London: J.M. Dent, 1935); for a semi-autobiographical novel, see Alan Fry, *How a People Die* (Madeira Park, BC: Harbour Publishing, 1994).

168 Brownlie, *supra* note 167 at ix.

169 *Ibid* at 32.

170 J.E.M. Kew, *A Synopsis of Musqueam Culture and History* (14 August 1979) [unpublished] at 17.

171 *Ibid* at 16.

172 Rolf Knight, *Indians at Work* (Vancouver: New Star Books, 1978) at 266.

173 Satzewich and Mahood, *supra* note 167 at 68.

174 Brownlie, *supra* note 167 at 35.

175 Pleshakov, *supra* note 122 at 17–27.

176 Kew, *supra* note 170 at 21–22. For other descriptions of the powers of Indian agents, see Dyck, *supra* note 131 at 83–84; Fry, *supra* note 167 at 79; Hawthorn, Belshaw, and Jamieson, *supra* note 154 at 486; Titley, *supra* note 93 at 13–14.

177 Brownlie, *supra* note 167, epigraph quoting John Daly, Indian agent, 1930. On the attitudes of Indian agents towards "Indians" in the 1930s and 1940s, see Sheffield, *supra* note 114.

178 Halliday, *supra* note 167 at 226–27. For the different views of Indian agents on people with both Indigenous and non-Indigenous ancestry, see Mawani, *Colonial Proximities, supra* note 82 at 163–200.

179 Halliday, *supra* note 167 at 134–35.

180 *Ibid* at 189–90.

181 Brownlie, *supra* note 167 at x, xii.

182 *Ibid* at 58; see also Dyck, *supra* note 131 at 88.

183 Dyck, *supra* note 131 at 88.

184 Pleshakov, *supra* note 122 at 23.

185 Brownlie, *supra* note 167 at 124–49, 154.

186 *Ibid* at 154.

187 Fry, *supra* note 167 at 78.

188 *Ibid* at 81–82.

189 Brownlie, *supra* note 167 at 33–34.

190 *Ibid* at 32.

191 Knight, *supra* note 172 at 266.

192 See Brownlie, *supra* note 167 at 56–79. For an account of band councils in British Columbia in 1955, see Hawthorn, Belshaw, and Jamieson, *supra* note 154 at 445–68.

193 Brownlie, *supra* note 167 at 35.

194 Fry, *supra* note 167 at 88–89.

195 Steckley, *supra* note 167 at 149–50.

CHAPTER 2: THE MUSQUEAM AND THEIR LAND

1 For accounts of the pre-contact period, see Homer G. Barnett, *The Coast Salish of British Columbia* (Eugene: University of Oregon Press, 1955); Cole Harris, *The Resettlement of British Columbia* (Vancouver: UBC Press, 1997) at 68–76 [*Resettlement*] (especially on seasonal movements and resource use); J.E.M. Kew, *Coast Salish Ceremonial Life: Status and Identity in a Modern Village* (PhD Thesis, University of Washington, 1970) [unpublished] [*Coast Salish Ceremonial Life*]; J.E.M. Kew, *A Synopsis of Musqueam Culture and History* (14 August 1979) [unpublished] [*Synopsis*], entered at trial of *Guerin v The Queen,* [1982] 2 FC 385; Ralph Maud, ed, *The Salish People: The Local Contribution of Charles Hill-Tout* (Vancouver: Talonbooks, 1978); Susan Roy, *These Mysterious People: History and Archaeology in a Northwest Coast Community,* 2d ed (Montreal and Kingston: McGill-Queen's University Press, 2016); William C. Sturtevant and Wayne Suttles, eds, *Handbook of North American Indians, Vol 7: Northwest Coast* (Washington, DC: Smithsonian Institution, 1990), especially Wayne Suttles, "Central Coast Salish" at 453–75; Wayne Suttles, *Coast Salish Essays* (Vancouver: Talonbooks, 1987); Wayne Suttles, *Musqueam Reference Grammar* (Vancouver: UBC Press, 2004).

2 For a discussion of claims that the Coast Salish displaced an earlier population, see Maud, *supra* note 1 at 22–23, 83–88, 93, and Suttles, *Coast Salish Essays, supra* note 1 at 256–64.

3 *Guerin v The Queen,* [1984] 2 SCR 335 at 379 [*Guerin*].

4 Roy, *supra* note 1 at 103.

5 Suttles, *Coast Salish Essays, supra* note 1 at 15–25, 209–21.

6 Kew, *Synopsis, supra* note 1 at 1.

7 W. Kaye Lamb, ed, *The Letters and Journals of Simon Fraser, 1806–1808* (Toronto: Macmillan, 1960) at 106.

8 Harris, *Resettlement, supra* note 1 at 69.

9 See generally Robert Kelly, *The Lifeways of Hunter-Gatherers – The Foraging Spectrum,* 2d ed (Cambridge: Cambridge University Press, 2013) [*Lifeways*].

10 Suttles, *Coast Salish Essays, supra* note 1 at 3–4. For a discussion of communal ownership among hunter-gatherers generally, see R.B. Lee, "Reflections on Primitive Communism" in T. Ingold, D. Riches, and J. Woodburn, eds, *Hunters and Gatherers, Vol 1: History, Evolution and Social Change* (Oxford: Berg, 1988). For an account of communal ownership in Indigenous communities in America generally, see Lewis H. Morgan, *Houses and House-Life of the American Aborigines* (Washington, DC: US Government Printing Office, 1881).

11 Kelly, *Lifeways, supra* note 9 at 261–66; Kent Flannery and Joyce Marcus, *The Creation of Inequality: How Our Prehistoric Ancestors Set the Stage for Monarchy, Slavery and Empire* (Cambridge, MA: Harvard University Press, 2012) at 71–88.

12 For a comparison, see Gary Coupland, Terence Clark, and Amanda Palmer, "Hierarchy, Communalism, and the Spatial Order of Northwest Coast Plank Houses: A Comparative Study" (2009) 74 *American Antiquity* 77.

13 For a discussion of the differing meanings of "egalitarian" by ethnographers and archaeologists, see Brian Hayden, "Social Complexity" in Vicki Cummings, Peter Jordan, and Marek Zvelebil, eds, *The Oxford Handbook of the Archaeology and Anthropology of Hunter-Gatherers* (Oxford: Oxford University Press, 2014) at 643. Hayden uses "trans-egalitarian" to describe societies that are neither egalitarian nor stratified.

14 Leslie A. White, *The Evolution of Culture: The Development of Civilization to the Fall of Rome* (New York: McGraw-Hill, 1959) at 199–203; Aaron Glass, Book Review of *Aboriginal Slavery on the Northwest Coast of North America* by Leland Donald (1999) 23 *American Indian Quarterly* 191.

15 Suttles, *Coast Salish Essays, supra* note 1 at 4–14. See also Brian Thom, *The Dead and the Living: Burial Mounds and Cairns and the Development of Social Class in the Gulf of Georgia Region* (MA Thesis, University of British Columbia, 1995) [unpublished].

16 Wayne Suttles, "They Recognize No Superior Chief: The Strait of Juan de Fuca in the 1790s" in José Luis Peset, ed, *Culturas de la Costa Noroeste de América* (Spain: Turner, 1989). It has been suggested that the theory of anarchism is a useful approach to understanding Coast Salish communities: Bill Angelbeck and Colin Grier, "Anarchism and the Archaeology of Anarchic Societies: Resistance to Centralization in the Coast Salish Region of the Pacific Northwest Coast" (2012) 53 *Current Anthropology* 547.

17 See Max Gluckman, *Politics, Law and Ritual in Tribal Society* (Oxford: Blackwell, 1965) at 15–17.

18 Keith Thor Carlson, "Towards an Indigenous Historiography: Events, Migrations, and the Formation of 'Post-Contact' Coast Salish Collective Identities" in Bruce Granville Miller, ed, *Be of Good Mind: Essays on the Coast Salish* (Vancouver: UBC Press, 2007) at 157–64 [*Be of Good Mind*].

19 Barnett, *supra* note 1 at 252; see Naxaxalhts'i, "We Have to Take Care of Everything That Belongs to Us" in Miller, *Be of Good Mind, supra* note 18 at 99. On free access to resources in hunter-gatherer societies, see generally White, *supra* note 14 at 252; Marshall Sahlins, *Stone Age Economics* (New York: Routledge, 2017) at 83–85. There were, of course, divergences from this generalization: see Kelly, *Lifeways, supra* note 9 for a discussion.

20 Barnett, *supra* note 1 at 244.

21 See Colin Grier, "Expanding Notions of Hunter-Gatherer Diversity: Identifying Core Organisational Principles and Practices in Coast Salish Societies of

the Northwest Coast of North America" in Bill Finlayson and Graeme Warren, eds, *The Diversity of Hunter-Gatherer Pasts* (Oxford: Oxbow, 2017).

22 For accounts of the post-contact period, see Wilson Duff, *The Indian History of British Columbia: The Impact of the White Man* (Victoria: Provincial Museum, 1964) [*Indian History*]; Robin Fisher, *Contact and Conflict*, 2d ed (Vancouver: UBC Press, 1992); Miller, *Be of Good Mind, supra* note 18; Bruce Granville Miller and Darby C. Stapp, *The Contemporary Coast Salish: Essays by Bruce Granville Miller*, Memoir 12 (Richland, WA: Journal of Northwest Anthropology, 2016). For accounts of the history of Aboriginal title in British Columbia, see *Papers Connected with the Indian Land Question 1850–1875* (Victoria: Government Printing Office, 1875; reprinted 1987) [*Papers*]; House of Commons and Senate, *Report and Evidence of the Special Committees of the Senate and House of Commons Appointed to Inquire into the Claims of the Allied Tribes of British Columbia* (11 April 1927) [*Special Joint Committees Report*]; George Edgar Shankel, *The Development of Indian Policy in British Columbia* (PhD Thesis, University of Washington, 1945) [unpublished]; Paul Tennant, *Aboriginal Peoples and Politics: The Indian Land Question in British Columbia 1849–1989* (Vancouver: UBC Press, 1990).

23 Henry R. Wagner, *Spanish Explorations in the Strait of Juan de Fuca* (Santa Ana, CA: Fine Arts Press, 1933); Tomas Bartroli, *Genesis of Vancouver City: Explorations of Its Site 1791, 1792 and 1808* (Vancouver: Tomas Bartroli, 1997); Jim McDowell, *Uncharted Waters: The Explorations of José Narváez* (Vancouver: Ronsdale Press, 2015).

24 Jose Espinosa y Tello, *Relacion del Viage Hecho par las Goletas "Suti" y "Mexicana" en el Ano 1792* (Madrid, 1802), translated in Wagner, *supra* note 23 at 260. See Bartroli, *supra* note 23 at 87–92; McDowell, *supra* note 23 at 136–39.

25 George Vancouver, *A Voyage of Discovery to the North Pacific Ocean and Round the World, 1791–1795*, ed by W. Kaye Lamb, vol 2 (London: Hakluyt Society, 1984) at 581.

26 Lamb, *supra* note 7 at 106.

27 Barnett, *supra* note 1 at 1–2. They are mentioned in the journals kept by the Hudson's Bay Company: see Morag Maclachlan, *The Fort Langley Journals 1827–1830* (Vancouver: UBC Press, 1998).

28 For the impact of colonialism on one Coast Salish group, see Wayne Suttles, "Post-Contact Culture Changes among the Lummi Indians" (1954) 18 British Columbia Historical Quarterly 29.

29 See generally Robert T. Boyd, "Demographic History, 1774–1874" in Sturtevant and Suttles, *Handbook, supra* note 1 at 135.

30 For a case that illustrates the pre-emption process, see *Williams Lake Indian Band v Canada,* 2018 SCC 4.

31 *R v Van der Peet,* [1996] 2 SCR 507 at paras 272, 275 [*Van der Peet*].

32 Allan Greer, *Property and Dispossession: Natives, Empires and Land in Early Modern North America* (Cambridge: Cambridge University Press, 2018) at 10.

33 Cole Harris, "How Did Colonialism Dispossess? Comments from an Edge of Empire" (2004) 94 Annals of the Association of American Geographers 165 at 169 ["Colonialism"].

34 See especially Fisher, *supra* note 22 at 102–6, 162–67, 175–205; Cole Harris, *Making Native Space: Colonialism, Resistance and Reserves in British Columbia* (Vancouver: UBC Press, 2002) [*Making Native Space*]; Harris, *Resettlement, supra* note 1 at 85–92.

35 Harris, "Colonialism," *supra* note 33 at 167.

36 "Petition of the Chiefs of the Fraser River to the Superintendent of Indian Affairs" (14 July 1874) in *Papers, supra* note 22 at 137; Robert E. Cail, *Land, Man, and the Law: The Disposal of Crown Lands in British Columbia, 1871–1913* (Vancouver: UBC Press, 1974) at 205–6.

37 Harris, *Resettlement, supra* note 1 at 86–88; for details of pre-emption during the 1860s, see Bruce Macdonald, *Vancouver: A Visual History* (Vancouver: Talonbooks, 1992) at 14–15.

38 Roy, *supra* note 1 at 103.

39 Fitzgerald McCleery, *Diary, Fitzgerald McCleery, Earliest Settler (North Arm, Fraser River)* (Vancouver: City Archives, 1940) at 65–66.

40 Fisher, *supra* note 22 at 196. For a discussion of Musqueam-settler relations generally, see Alexander Sanya Pleshakov, "*We Do Not Talk about Our History Here": The Department of Indian Affairs, Musqueam-Settler Relations and Memory of a Vancouver Neighbourhood* (MA Thesis, University of British Columbia, 2010) [unpublished].

41 See Barnett, *supra* note 1 at 244, 250–51; Suttles, *Coast Salish Essays, supra* note 1 at 20–21; Russel Barsh, "Coast Salish Property Law: An Alternative Paradigm for Environmental Relationships" (2005) 12 Hastings W-Nw J Envtl L & Pol'y 1.

42 Harris, *Resettlement, supra* note 1 at 101.

43 *Ibid* at 171; Harris, *Making Native Space, supra* note 34 at 17–69; *Papers, supra* note 22 at 5–11; Cail, *supra* note 36 at 161–243.

44 Harris, *Making Native Space, supra* note 34 at 75, 351, n 13. The original size of the reserve is unclear. Harris suggests 342 acres but notes that there is uncertainty. The schedule to Dr. Powell's report of 1872 shows a reserve of 342 acres: *Report of the Superintendent of Indian Affairs for British Columbia for 1872 & 1873* (Ottawa, 1873) at 20.

45 *Papers, supra* note 22 at 41–43.

46 See Harris, *Making Native Space, supra* note 34 at 75.

47 *Constitution Act, 1867* (UK), 30 & 31 Vict, c 3, reprinted in RSC 1985, App II, No 5, s 91(24).

48 *British Columbia Terms of Union* (UK), 1871, reprinted in RSC 1985, App II, No 10.

49 Fisher, *supra* note 22 at 182–83; *Papers, supra* note 22 at 116–43.

50 Fisher, *supra* note 22 at 182–83; *Papers, supra* note 22 at 119.

51 *Papers, supra* note 22 at 134.

52 *Ibid;* Harris, *Making Native Space, supra* note 34 at 75; Cail, *supra* note 36 at 201.

53 *Papers, supra* note 22 at 139 [emphasis in original].

54 *Ibid* at 143.

55 Margaret Ormsby, *British Columbia: A History* (Toronto: Macmillan, 1958) at 284.

56 *Papers, supra* note 22 at 152; see Harris, *Making Native Space, supra* note 34 at 91–98 for the federal position.

57 *Papers, supra* note 22 at 152–54.

58 *Ibid* at 161–63, 169–70.

59 Shankel, *supra* note 22 at 108.

60 Fisher, *supra* note 22 at 190; Harris, *Making Native Space, supra* note 34 at 104–66.

61 Fisher, *supra* note 22 at 190; Harris, *Making Native Space, supra* note 34 at 111. The reserve was shown in the 1913 Schedule of Indian Reserves as having 392.5 acres. The McKenna-McBride Commission, which visited the reserve on 24 June 1913, had it resurveyed and confirmed it at 416.82 acres: *Report of the Royal Commission on Indian Affairs for the Province of British Columbia,* vol 3 (Victoria: Province of British Columbia, 1916) at 632, 658, 671, 685 [*McKenna-McBride Report*]. There was another reserve of 60.75 acres confirmed on neighbouring Sea Island, and one in Langley of 5.16 acres used with other bands as a fishing station.

62 Harris, *Resettlement, supra* note 1 at 91. For an account of the hearing, see Roy, *supra* note 1 at 71–81.

63 Harris, *Resettlement, supra* note 1 at 92.

64 *McKenna-McBride Report, supra* note 61 at 632.

65 *Ibid* at 623.

66 See Harris, *Making Native Space, supra* note 34 at xxv.

67 Dianne Newell, *Tangled Webs of History: Indians and the Law in Canada's Pacific Coast Fisheries* (Toronto: University of Toronto Press, 1993) at 56; Douglas C. Harris, *Fish, Law and Colonialism: The Legal Capture of Salmon in British*

Columbia (Toronto: University of Toronto Press, 2001) at 44–45 [*Fish, Law and Colonialism*]; Douglas C. Harris, *Landing Native Fisheries: Indian Reserves and Fishing Rights in British Columbia 1849–1925* (Vancouver: UBC Press, 2008) [*Landing Native Fisheries*].

68   *Papers, supra* note 22 at 134.

69   *McKenna-McBride Report, supra* note 61 at 643.

70   Kew, *Synopsis, supra* note 1 at 7. For a map of Musqueam territory with names of places, see Suttles, *Musqueam Reference Grammar, supra* note 1 at 566–74.

71   Fisher, *supra* note 22 at 165; *Papers, supra* note 22 at 25, 147; Harris, *Making Native Space, supra* note 34 at 35–36, 68, 87–88. Brenna Bhandar, *Colonial Lives of Property: Law, Land and Racial Regimes of Ownership* (Durham, NC: Duke University Press, 2018) at 33–76 gives an account of pre-emption in British Columbia.

72   Fisher, *supra* note 22 at 165. Trutch was appointed as the first lieutenant-governor of the province of British Columbia in 1871.

73   Fisher, *supra* note 22 at 165.

74   British Columbia, *The Pre-Emption Ordinance,* Ordinance No 13 (31 March 1866), s 1. This provision was subsequently re-enacted in provincial *Land Acts,* including s 12 of the 1948 *Land Act* , RSBC 1948, c 175, and was not repealed until 1953: *Land Act Amendment Act,* SBC 1953, c 23, s 3.

75   Fisher, *supra* note 22 at 165.

76   *Report of the Government of British Columbia on the Subject of Indian Reserves* (18 August 1875) in *Papers, supra* note 22 at 4.

77   British Columbia, *Land Ordinance (British Columbia) 1865,* Ordinance No 27 (11 April 1865), s 20.

78   Harris, *Fish, Law and Colonialism, supra* note 67 at 78.

79   *Ibid* at 75–76.

80   Harris, *Landing Native Fisheries, supra* note 67 at 138.

81   Barnett, *supra* note 1 at 2. In the same year, Phillip Drucker gave an equally gloomy assessment of the almost complete disappearance of the Northwest Coast culture: Phillip Drucker, "Preface" in *Indians of the Northwest Coast* (New York: McGraw-Hill, 1955).

82   Kew, *Coast Salish Ceremonial Life, supra* note 1 at 212–13. It may be noted that attempts were made in the 1950s to salvage something of the past through Musqueam authorization and participation in archaeological digs at the reserve: Roy, *supra* note 1 at 119–45.

83   For an autobiographical essay, see J.E.M. Kew, "Reflections on Anthropology at the University of British Columbia" (2017) 193 BC Studies 163.

84   Kew, *Synopsis, supra* note 1 at 7.

85 *Fisheries Regulations for the Province of British Columbia,* OIC (26 November 1888) 22 C Gaz 956.

86 Kew, *Synopsis, supra* note 1 at 8–11.

87 *Ibid* at 10–11.

88 *Ibid* at 11.

89 *Ibid* at 11–12.

90 Duff, *supra* note 22 at 105; for a comprehensive discussion of ethnic relations in British Columbia in 1958, see H.B. Hawthorn, C.S. Belshaw, and S.M. Jamieson, *The Indians of British Columbia: A Study of Contemporary Social Adjustment* (Berkeley: University of California Press, 1958) at 58–71.

91 *The Province* (5 June 1941) at 4. There was a proposal in the 1930s to sell all of the main reserve and relocate the population across the Fraser River to a smaller reserve: Roy, *supra* note 1 at 93. There were also plans by the City of Vancouver to acquire the reserve for park use: Jordan Stranger-Ross, "Municipal Colonialism in Vancouver: City Planning and the Conflict over Indian Reserves 1928–1950s" (2008) 89 Canadian Historical Review 541.

92 For Musqueam ceremonies in the 1960s, see Part 2 of Kew, *Coast Salish Ceremonial Life, supra* note 1. On winter ceremonies, see generally Pamela Amoss, *Coast Salish Spirit Dancing: The Survival of an Ancestral Religion* (Seattle: University of Washington Press, 1978); Suttles, *Coast Salish Essays, supra* note 1 at 199–208, 223–27; Barnett, *supra* note 1 at 272–310. For the potlatch and attempts to suppress it, see Douglas Cole and Ira Chaikin, *An Iron Hand upon the People* (Vancouver: Douglas and McIntyre, 1990).

93 Miller and Stapp, *supra* note 22 at 11.

94 Hawthorn, Belshaw, and Jamieson, *supra* note 90 at 7.

95 Kew, *Synopsis, supra* note 1 at 16. For detailed discussion, see Kew, *Coast Salish Ceremonial Life, supra* note 1 at 311–51; Wolfgang G. Jilek, *Indian Healing: Shamanic Ceremonialism in the Pacific Northwest Today* (Surrey, BC: Hancock House, 1982.)

96 Kew, *Coast Salish Ceremonial Life, supra* note 1 at 2.

97 The following account is based on the transcript of the *Guerin* trial.

98 Vera J. Kirkness, ed, *Khot-La-Cha: The Autobiography of Chief Simon Baker* (Vancouver: Douglas and McIntyre, 1994) at 41.

99 J.R. Miller, *Shingwauk's Vision: A History of Native Residential Schools* (Toronto: University of Toronto Press, 1996) at 205–6 [*Shingwauk's Vision*]. See also J.R. Miller, *Reflections on Native-Newcomer Relations: Selected Essays* (Toronto: University of Toronto Press, 2004) at 206.

100 Miller, *Shingwauk's Vision, supra* note 99 at 427.

101 Sarah de Leeuw, *Artful Places: Creativity and Colonialism in British Columbia's Indian Residential School* (PhD Thesis, Queen's University, 2007) at 284–85.

102 Hughina Harold, *Totem Poles and Tea* (Surrey, BC: Heritage House, 1996) at 218.

103 de Leeuw, *supra* note 101 at 176. She notes that the school had some significant shortcomings (at 178).

104 Victor Satzewich, "Indian Agents and the 'Indian Problem' in Canada in 1946: Reconsidering the Theory of Coercive Tutelage" (1997) 17 Canadian Journal of Native Studies 227 at 240.

105 Brendan Frederick R. Edwards, *Paper Talk: A History of Libraries, Print Culture, and Aboriginal Peoples in Canada before 1960* (Lanham, MD: Scarecrow Press, 2005) at 134–35.

106 Helen Raptis, "Exploring the Factors Prompting British Columbia's First Integration Initiative: The Case of Port Essington's Indian Day School" (2011) 51 History of Education Quarterly 519. For integrated schooling in postwar British Columbia, see Byron King Plant, *A Revisonist History of Intrastate Relations in Mid-Twentieth Century British Columbia* (PhD Thesis, University of Saskatchewan, 2009) [unpublished] at 96–151.

107 de Leeuw, *supra* note 101 at 178. In 1954, he challenged the young Indigenous people of Alert Bay to get a higher education so they could become missionaries, teachers, and nurses: "Historic Event Commemorated," *Native Voice* (May 1954).

108 Cole and Chaikin, *supra* note 92 at 152.

109 Margaret Whitehead, "'A Useful Christian Woman': First Nations' Women and Protestant Missionary Work in British Columbia" (1992) 18 Atlantis 142 at 156.

110 Truth and Reconciliation Commission, *Canada's Residential Schools: The History, Part 2 1939 to 2000, The Final Report of the Truth and Reconciliation Commission of Canada,* vol 1 (Montreal and Kingston: McGill-Queen's University Press, 2015) at 128.

111 Satzewich, *supra* note 104 at 236–37. Compare the discussion of "inferiority complex" as a factor in claims of discrimination by Alan Burns, former colonial administrator, in his book *Colour Prejudice* (London: Allen & Unwin, 1948) at 137–44.

112 Quoted by the trial judge, Justice Collier, *Guerin v The Queen,* [1982] 2 FC 385 at 390 (FCTD) [*Guerin* FCTD].

113 R. Scott Sheffield, *The Red Man's on the Warpath: The Image of the "Indian" and the Second World War* (Vancouver: UBC Press, 2005) at 118 [underlining in original].

114 *Indian Superintendent's Conference, British Columbia & Yukon Regions, January 16 to 20, 1956* (Ottawa: Department of Citizenship and Immigration, Indian Affairs Branch, 1956) at 27–28, 107.

115 *Guerin* FCTD, *supra* note 112 at 400–1.

116 *Ibid* at 392, 395.

117 See Chapter 3.

118 *Guerin v The Queen*, [1984] 2 SCR 335, Case on Appeal, vol 6 at 1156, vol 18 at 3590 [Case on Appeal].

119 *Guerin* FCTD, *supra* note 112 at 425.

120 Case on Appeal, *supra* note 118, vol 10 at 1816.

121 *Report of the House of Commons Special Committee on Indian Self-Government*, Minutes of Proceedings, Issue No 6 (15 February 1983) at 52–53 (Frank Oberle, MP).

122 *Guerin* FCTD, *supra* note 112 at 408–9, 425.

123 Case on Appeal, *supra* note 118, vol 9 at 1640.

124 *Ibid*, vol 13 at 2457–59.

125 Decision of Federal Court of Appeal, *The Queen v Guerin* [1983] 2 FC 656 at 666.

126 *Guerin* FCTD, *supra* note 112 at 397.

127 Kew, *Synopsis*, *supra* note 1 at 20.

128 *Ibid*.

129 Pleshakov, *supra* note 40 at 21.

130 Jan Morris, *The Spectacle of Empire* (New York: Doubleday, 1982) at 199–200.

131 Betty Walsh, "Shaughnessy and Adjacent Areas" in Chuck Davis, ed, *The Vancouver Book* (Vancouver: J.J. Douglas, 1976) at 102–3.

132 Shaughnessy Golf and Country Club, "The 1960s," online: <https://www.shaughnessy.org/About/History.aspx>.

133 Case on Appeal, *supra* note 118, vol 8 at 1590–91.

134 Given the evidence in the case on this point, it is somewhat ironic that Justice Ian Binnie, who was counsel for the Crown during the appeals, should refer to the case as involving the lease of land in "suburban Vancouver" rather than the west side of the city in *Wewaykum Indian Band v Canada*, 2002 SCC 79 at para 76. The difference in land values was significant.

135 BC Golf House Society, "Quilchena Golf Course 1925–1957," online: <http://www.bcgolfhouse.com/quilchena-golf-course-1925-1954>.

136 Case on Appeal, *supra* note 118, vol 9 at 1638.

137 *Ibid*, vol 9 at 1638.

138 *Ibid*, vol 2 at 390.

139 *Ibid*, vol 9 at 1641.

140 *Ibid*, vol 2 at 326, 389.

141 E.M. Forster, *A Passage to India* (Harmondsworth, UK: Penguin, 1985) at 60.

142 Case on Appeal, *supra* note 118, vol 7 at 1795.

143 *Ibid*, vol 7 at 1285.

144 See Duff, *supra* note 22 at 69–70; Harris, *Making Native Space, supra* note 34 at 217–61.

145 *Special Joint Committees Report, supra* note 22.

146 For more information about this remarkable man, see Mary Haig-Brown, "Arthur Eugene O'Meara: Servant, Advocate, Seeker of Justice" in Celia Haig-Brown and David A. Nock, eds, *With Good Intentions: Euro-Canadians and Aboriginal Relations in Colonial Canada* (Vancouver: UBC Press, 2006); Hamar Foster, "We Are Not O'Meara's Children: Law, Lawyers and the First Campaign for Aboriginal Title in British Columbia" in Hamar Foster, Heather Raven, and Jeremy Webber, eds, *Let Right Be Done: Aboriginal Title, The Calder Case, and the Future of Indigenous Rights* (Vancouver: UBC Press, 2007).

147 *Special Joint Committees Report, supra* note 22 at vii–x.

148 Hawthorn, Belshaw, and Jamieson, *supra* note 90 at 49, 56.

149 For an account of some of these experiences, see Tennant, *supra* note 22, *passim*.

150 See *Final Report of the Truth and Reconciliation Commission of Canada* (Montreal and Kingston: McGill-Queen's University Press, 2015). For an account of the education of Indian people in British Columbia in the 1950s, see Hawthorn, Belshaw, and Jamieson, *supra* note 90 at 291–322.

151 For an account of economic and social conditions at Musqueam from the 1860s to the 1960s, see Kew, *Coast Salish Ceremonial Life, supra* note 1 at 28–62.

152 *The Native Voice* (January 1958) at 4–5.

153 Leona Marie Sparrow, *Work Histories of a Coast Salish Couple* (MA Thesis, University of British Columbia, 1976) at 20.

154 "Sordid Living Conditions on Musqueam Indian Reserve Scored by Alderman," *Vancouver Sun* (21 February 1962). See also "Indian Reserve: Musqueam Indian Reserve Is Inside Vancouver," *Vancouver Sun* (10 July 1954); "Have You Heard? Indian Shame," *Vancouver Sun* (23 June 1960).

155 For accounts of economic activity by Indian peoples in British Columbia in the 1950s, see Hawthorn, Belshaw, and Jamieson, *supra* note 90 at 72–273.

156 The Chief of the band in 1962, Mrs. Gertrude Guerin, was quoted as saying that only 10 of the 250 band members had regular employment: "Musqueam Reserve Squalor Attacked by Ald. Rathie," *Vancouver Sun* (21 February 1962) at 29.

157 Case on Appeal, *supra* note 118, vol 10 at 1814.

158 See Chapter 4.

159 *Vancouver v Chow Chee*, [1942] 1 WWR 72.

160 *Vancouver Sun* (15 June 1967).

161 For his autobiography, see Harry Rankin, *Rankin's Law: Recollections of a Radical* (Vancouver: November House, 1975).

162 For details of the band's negotiations with the city over taxes and services, see articles in the *Vancouver Sun* of 13 and 22 February 1969; 7 and 19 March 1969; and 23 June 1970.

CHAPTER 3: THE GOVERNMENT AS FIDUCIARY

1 Plato, *The Republic*, translated by H. Spens (London: J.M. Dent, 1906) at 107.

2 Evan Criddle et al, ed, *Fiduciary Government* (Cambridge: Cambridge University Press, 2018) at 2.

3 John Adams, "A Dissertation on the Canon and Feudal Law" in John Patrick Diggins, ed, *The Portable John Adams* (New York: Penguin, 2004) at 219. For the role of fiduciary principles in the debates that led to the US Constitution, see D. Theodore Rave, "Politicians as Fiduciaries" (2013) 126 Harv L Rev 671 at 708–11.

4 Edmund Burke, *The Modern Orator: The Speeches of the Right Hon. Edmund Burke* (London: Aylott and Jones, 1847) at 671. For a history of the power of the Crown and Chancery courts to protect the vulnerable, see John Seymour, "Parens Patriae and Wardship Powers: Their Nature and Origins" (1994) 14 Oxford J Leg Stud 159.

5 *R v Bembridge* (1783), 22 State Trials 1 at 155.

6 Criddle et al, *supra* note 2 at 1. For detailed denials of theories used to apply fiduciary principles to governments, see Seth Davis, "The False Promise of Fiduciary Government" (2014) 89 Notre Dame L Rev 1145; Robert Flannigan, "Contesting Public Service Fiduciary Accountability" (2017) 36 UQLJ 7.

7 Ethan J. Leib and Stephen R. Galoob, "Fiduciary Political Theory: A Critique" (2016) 125 Yale LJ 1820 at 1877.

8 Evan Fox-Decent, *Sovereignty's Promise: The State as Fiduciary* (Oxford: Oxford University Press, 2011) at 3.

9 *Ibid* at 5.

10 *Ibid* at 39.

11 *Ibid* at 48.

12 *Ibid* at 153.

13 Evan J. Criddle and Evan Fox-Decent, *Fiduciaries of Humanity: How International Law Constitutes Authority* (Oxford: Oxford University Press, 2016) at 2.

14 *Ibid* at 3.

15 *Ibid* at 4.

16 *Ibid* at 3.

17 *Ibid* at 30.

18 Charles G. Fenwick, *Wardship in International Law* (Washington, DC: Government Printing Office, 1919); Alpheus Henry Snow, *The Question of Aborigines in the Law and Practice of Nations* (New York: Putnam's, 1921). For a history from British India to the present, see William Bain, *Between Anarchy and Society: Trusteeship and the Obligations of Power* (Oxford: Oxford University Press, 2003). For a history going back to Spanish conquests in the Americas, see Andrew Fitzmaurice, "Sovereign Trusteeship and Empire" (2015) 16 Theor Inq L 447.

19 John Darwin, *Unfinished Empire: The Global Expansion of Britain* (London: Penguin, 2013) at 26–27; see also Klaus Knorr, *British Colonial Theories 1570–1850* (Toronto: University of Toronto Press, 1944) at 246–48.

20 Knorr, *supra* note 19 at 388. For a detailed discussion of the impact of the humanitarian movement on the British Empire, see G.R. Mellor, *British Imperial Trusteeship 1783–1850* (London: Faber & Faber, 1951).

21 Quoted on the title page of F.D. Lugard, *The Dual Mandate in British Tropical Africa* (Edinburgh: William Blackwood, 1922).

22 James C. Hales, "The Reform and Extension of the Mandate System" (1940) 26 Transactions of the Grotius Society 153 at 155. See Kenneth Robinson, *The Dilemmas of Trusteeship: Aspects of British Colonial Policy between the Wars* (London: Oxford University Press, 1965); Ronald Hyam, "Bureaucracy and 'Trusteeship' in the Colonial Empire" in Judith M. Brown and Wm. Roger Louis, eds, *The Oxford History of the British Empire, Vol 4: The Twentieth Century* (Oxford: Oxford University Press, 1999).

23 Quoted in James (Jan) Morris, *Farewell the Trumpets: An Imperial Retreat* (London: Penguin, 1979) at 485.

24 Reproduced in S.R. Ashton and S.E. Stockwell, eds, *British Documents on the End of Empire,* Series A, vol 1 (London: HMSO, 1996) at 200.

25 *Covenant of the League of Nations,* 28 June 1919 (entered into force 10 January 1920), online: Avalon Project <http://avalon.law.yale.edu/20th_century/leagcov.asp>. For a detailed discussion, see H. Duncan Hall, *Mandates, Dependencies and Trusteeship* (London: Stevens, 1948). For a discussion of the impact of the mandate system on international law, see Antony Anghie, *Imperialism, Sovereignty and the Making of International Law* (Cambridge: Cambridge University Press, 2005) at 115–95.

26 *Covenant of the League of Nations,* art 22. Article 22 was replaced by Chapters XII and XIII of the United Nations Charter in 1945, which states that promotion of self-government or independence is a basic objective of the trusteeship system. These chapters have been inoperative since 1994 when Palau, the last remaining trust territory, became independent. For the argument that modern international

territorial administration is similar to colonial trusteeship, see Bain, *supra* note 18; Ralph Wilde, *International Territorial Administration: How Trusteeship and the Civilizing Mission Never Went Away* (Oxford: Oxford University Press, 2008).

27 Morris, *supra* note 23 at 208.

28 H.A.L. Fisher, *A History of Europe* (London: Edward Arnold, 1936) at 1174.

29 Lugard, *supra* note 21 at 17. For some of the legal problems associated with the historical Canadian treaties, see Jim Reynolds, *Aboriginal Peoples and the Law: A Critical Introduction* (Vancouver: UBC Press/Purich, 2018) at 130–39.

30 Lugard, *supra* note 21 at 18.

31 *Ibid* at 50.

32 Harold Laski, "The Colonial Civil Service" (1938) 9 Political Quarterly 541 at 541. See also J.A. Hobson, *Imperialism: A Study* (London: Allen & Unwin, 1902) at 237–46.

33 B.R. Tomlinson, "Imperialism and After: The Economy of the Empire on the Periphery" in Brown and Louis, *supra* note 22 at 375. For more sympathetic assessments of colonialism, see Alan Burns, *In Defence of Colonies* (London: Allen & Unwin, 1957); Anthony Kirk-Greene, *On Crown Service: A History of HM Colonial and Overseas Civil Services, 1837–1997* (London: Taurus, 1999) at 109–24; Niall Ferguson, *Empire: How Britain Made the Modern World* (London: Allen Lane, 2003).

34 Gilbert Sproat, *Scenes and Studies of Savage Life* (London: Smith, Elder, 1868) at 290.

35 Quoted in Robert E. Cail, *Land, Man, and the Law: The Disposal of Crown Lands in British Columbia, 1871–1913* (Vancouver: UBC Press, 1974) at 183.

36 As confirmed by Prime Minister Trudeau's defence of his White Paper of that year: "They are wards of the federal government," quoted in app 8 in Ronald St. John Macdonald, *Native Rights in Canada* (Toronto: Indian-Eskimo Association, 1970).

37 Jordan Stranger-Ross, "Municipal Colonialism in Vancouver: City Planning and the Conflict over Indian Reserves, 1928–1950s" (2008) 89 Canadian Historical Review 541 at 575.

38 *Report of the House of Commons Special Committee on Indian Self-Government,* Minutes of Proceedings, Issue No 6 (15 February 1983) at 59 (Warren Allmand, MP).

39 Leonard Barnes, "The Empire as Sacred Trust: The Problem of Africa" (1938) 9 Political Quarterly 503 at 503.

40 This was also true for British Columbia, the province from which *Guerin v The Queen,* [1984] 2 SCR 335 [*Guerin*] came: see *Calder v Attorney-General for British Columbia,* [1973] SCR 313 at 328, Judson J.

41 See generally J.R. Miller, *Skyscrapers Hide the Heavens: A History of Indian-White Relations in Canada* (Toronto: University of Toronto Press, 1991) at 23–80.

42 *R v Sioui*, [1990] 1 SCR 1025 at 1054, per Lamer J. for the Court.

43 See the Royal Proclamation of 1763: George R, Proclamation, 7 October 1763 (3 Geo III), reprinted in RSC 1985, App II, No 1 [Royal Proclamation].

44 For more details, see Reynolds, *supra* note 29 at 32–35.

45 [1990] 2 SCR 85 at 108. See also *R v Sparrow*, [1990] 1 SCR 1075 at 1108.

46 Brian Slattery, "Understanding Aboriginal Rights" (1987) 66 Can Bar Rev 727.

47 *Wewaykum Indian Band v Canada*, 2002 SCC 79 at para 79.

48 Slattery, *supra* note 46 at 753.

49 Royal Proclamation, *supra* note 43.

50 *Guerin, supra* note 40 at 383.

51 See Chapter 2.

52 See, for example, the decisions in *Delgamuukw v British Columbia*, [1997] 3 SCR 1010 and *Tsilhqot'in Nation v British Columbia*, 2014 SCC 44.

53 Wilson Duff, *The Indian History of British Columbia: The Impact of the White Man* (Victoria: Provincial Museum of Natural History and Anthropology, 1965) at 43; Robin Fisher, *Contact and Conflict*, 2d ed (Vancouver: UBC Press, 1992) at 12–17, 98–100, 106–9. For examples of conflict, see B.A. McKelvie, *Tales of Conflict* (Vancouver: Daily Province, 1949); Chris Arnett, *The Terror of the Coast* (Burnaby, BC: Talon, 1999).

54 M. Gautreau, "Demystifying the Fiduciary Mystique" (1989) 68 Can Bar Rev 1 at 1–2.

55 See generally Leonard I. Rotman, *Fiduciary Law* (Toronto: Thomson-Carswell, 2005) [*Fiduciary Law*]; Leonard I. Rotman, "Understanding Fiduciary Duties and Relationship Fiduciarity" (2017) 62 McGill LJ 975.

56 [1994] 3 SCR 377.

57 *Ibid* at 406.

58 *Ibid* at 422.

59 [2002] 3 SCR 631 at para 16.

60 L.C. Green, "North America's Indians and the Trusteeship Concept" (1975) 4 Anglo-Am L Rev 137 at 149. See also his article "Trusteeship and Canada's Indians" (1976) 3 Dal LJ 104 at 118. Other discussions of the pre-*Guerin* law are: unpublished paper by Doug Sanders, "The Friendly Care and Directing Hand of the Government Trusteeship of Indians in Canada" (1977), partially reproduced in Bradford Morse, ed, *Aboriginal Peoples and the Law: Indian, Metis and Inuit Rights in Canada* (Ottawa: Carleton University Press, 1985) at 508–12; J. Timothy

S. McCabe, *The Honour of the Crown and Its Fiduciary Duties to Aboriginal Peoples* (Markham, ON: LexisNexis, 2008) at 2–34; Leonard Ian Rotman, *Parallel Paths: Fiduciary Doctrine and the Crown-Native Relationship in Canada* (Toronto: University of Toronto Press, 1996) at 66–87; Rotman, *Fiduciary Law, supra* note 55 at 557–65.

61 *An Act for the Protection of the Lands of the Crown in this Province from Trespass and Injury and to Make Further Provision for that Purpose*, 1849 (12 Vict), c 9.

62 1850 (13–14 Vict), c 42, s 1; see also *An Act Respecting Management of the Indian Lands and Property*, 1860 (23 Vict), c 151, s 8.

63 *British Columbia Terms of Union* (UK), 1871, reprinted in RSC 1985, App II, No 10.

64 *Indian Act*, SC 1876, c 18, s 4.

65 *Ontario Boundary Act*, SC 1912, c 40, s 2; *Quebec Boundaries Extension Act*, SC 1912, c 45.

66 Early cases contain non-binding or "obiter" statements that the trust was not a "true" trust: see, for example, *Church v Fenton* (1878), 28 UCCP 384 at 388.

67 (1916), 53 SCR 172 [*Giroux*]; see also *Henry v The King*, (1905) 9 Ex CR 417, which referred to a trust being created by a surrender of lands.

68 *Giroux, supra* note 67 at 196 [emphasis added].

69 [1921] 1 AC 401 at 411 [*Star Chrome*].

70 (1935), 5 CNLC 92.

71 [1940] 1 DLR 390 (NS Co Ct).

72 *Ibid* at 397.

73 [1948] 3 DLR 797 (Exch).

74 [1950] SCR 168.

75 *Ibid* at 174.

76 1979 CanLII 2598 (FC) [*Pawis*].

77 See Chapter 4. For a discussion of the political trust doctrine, see Lorne Sossin, "Public Fiduciary Obligations, Political Trusts and the Equitable Duty of Reasonableness in Administrative Law" (2003) 66 Sask L Rev 129 at 159–69; Paul Finn, "Public Trusts, Public Fiduciaries" (2010) 38 Fed L Rev 335; Lindsay Breach, "Fiducia in Public Law" (2017) 48 VUWLR 413.

78 (1881–82), 7 AC 619 (HL).

79 *Ibid* at 625–26.

80 (1876) 1 QBD 487.

81 *Ibid* at 492–93, Cockburn CJ.

82 [1977] 3 All ER 129 (CH) [*Tito*]; see Michael Chapman, "*Tito v Waddell* (No. 2): A Colonial Relic" 2013 Lawasia J 91.

83 *Tito, supra* note 82 at 216–17.

84 [1978] AC 359 (HL).

85 *Ibid* at 397.

86 [1925] All ER 24 (HL) [*Roberts*]. For a discussion of fiduciary obligations and English administrative law, see Fox-Decent, *supra* note 8 at 159–64.

87 *Roberts, supra* note 86 at 33.

88 [1982] 1 All ER 129 (HL).

89 *Ibid* at 154.

90 *Ibid* at 172.

91 J.A.G. Griffith, *The Politics of the Judiciary,* 4th ed (London: Fontana, 1991) at 131.

92 (1894), 24 SCR 1.

93 (1908), 39 SCR 657 [*MacIllreith*]. See also *Bowes v City of Toronto* (1858), 14 ER 770 (PC).

94 *MacIllreith, supra* note 93 at 670.

95 (1914), 50 SCR 283.

96 (1913), 13 DLR 463 at 465–66, Meredith CJO.

97 *Ibid.*

98 It was also applied by the Privy Council in the 1902 New Zealand case of *Te Teira Te Paea v Te Roera Tareha,* [1902] AC 56, involving a title allotted to a Maori chief in trust.

99 (1887), 13 SCR 577 at 649.

100 [1950] SCR 211.

101 *Ibid* at 219.

102 See generally: Reid Peyton Chambers, "Judicial Enforcement of the Federal Trust Responsibility to Indians" (1975) 27 Stan L Rev 1213; Felix Cohen, *Handbook of Federal Indian Law* (Newark, NJ: LexisNexis, 2012) at ss 5.04–05; William C. Canby, *American Indian Law in a Nutshell,* 6th ed (St Paul, MN: West, 2015) at 35–62; Stephen L. Pevar, *The Rights of Indians and Tribes* (New York: Oxford University Press, 2012) at 29–44.

103 Cohen, *supra* note 102 at s 5.04[4][a].

104 Canby, *supra* note 102 at 35.

105 Pevar, *supra* note 102 at 44.

106 30 US 1 (1831) at 17.

107 118 US 375 (1886) at 383–84 [emphasis added].

108 187 US 553 (1903).

109 Chambers, *supra* note 102 at 1230–34.

110 299 US 476 (1937).

111 316 US 286 (1942) [*Seminole*]; applied in *Morton v Ruiz,* 415 US 199 (1974); see also *United States v Sioux Nation,* 448 US 371 (1980); *Nevada v United States,* 463 US 110 (1983).

112 *Seminole, supra* note 111 at 296–97 [citations omitted].

113 *Pawis, supra* note 76.

114 *Ibid* at para 6.

115 Douglas Sanders, *First Nations and Canadian Law – Supplementary Materials* (2 October 2000) [unpublished, archived at University of British Columbia Faculty of Law] at 1.

116 Richard H. Bartlett, *Indian Reserves and Aboriginal Lands in Canada: A Homeland* (Saskatoon: University of Saskatchewan Native Law Centre, 1990) at 189.

117 Richard H. Bartlett, "Reserve Lands" in Bradford W. Morse, ed, *Aboriginal Peoples and the Law: Indian, Metis and Inuit Rights in Canada* (Ottawa: Carleton University Press, 1985) at 576.

CHAPTER 4: THE TRIAL
AND FEDERAL COURT OF APPEAL

1 This chapter is based in part on the transcript of the trial as contained within the Case on Appeal filed in the Supreme Court of Canada in *Guerin v The Queen*, [1984] 2 SCR 335 [Case on Appeal], the factums of the parties filed in the Federal Court of Appeal and the Supreme Court of Canada, the reported decisions, and the recollections of Delbert Guerin, other members of the Musqueam, and members of their legal team, including the author.

2 Jim Reynolds, *Aboriginal Peoples and the Law: A Critical Introduction* (Vancouver: UBC Press/Purich, 2018) at 17–19.

3 *Statement of the Government of Canada on Indian Policy* (Ottawa: Indian Affairs Branch, 1969).

4 For statements from Indigenous leaders voicing their opposition, see Harold Cardinal, *The Unjust Society* (Edmonton: M.G. Hurtig, 1969); Indian Association of Alberta, *Citizens Plus* (Edmonton: Indian Association of Alberta, 1970). For a contrary position, see William Wuttunee, *Ruffled Feathers: Indians in Canadian Society* (Calgary: Bell, 1971).

5 For an account of the "breakthrough" cases in Canada, Australia, and New Zealand, see ch 2 in P.G. McHugh, *Aboriginal Title: The Modern Jurisprudence of Tribal Land Rights* (Oxford: Oxford University Press, 2011).

6 *Calder v Attorney-General for British Columbia*, [1973] SCR 313 [*Calder*]; see K.M. Lysyk, "The Indian Title Question in Canada: An Appraisal in the Light of Calder" (1973) 51 Can Bar Rev 450; David Elliott, *Baker Lake* and the Concept of Aboriginal Title," (1980) 18 Osgoode Hall LJ 653 at 655; Thomas Berger, *One Man's Justice: A Life in the Law* (Toronto: Douglas and McIntyre, 2002) at 107–39; Hamar Foster, Heather Raven, and Jeremy Webber, *Let Right Be Done: Aboriginal*

Title, the Calder Case and the Future of Indigenous Rights (Vancouver: UBC Press, 2007).

7 *Delgamuukw v British Columbia*, [1997] 3 SCR 1010; *Tsilhqot'in Nation v British Columbia*, 2014 SCC 44.

8 John Kirkwood, "Hidden Report – Raw Deal for Indians," *The Province* (1 April 1972) at 5.

9 Case on Appeal, *supra* note 1, Exhibit 86.

10 Information provided by Delbert Guerin to the author.

11 Bob Chamberlain, "Ex-Indian Affairs Official Raps Musqueam Lease," *The Province* (12 October 1979) ["Ex-Indian Affairs Official"].

12 Bob Chamberlain, "'Bitter Surprise' Leads Indians to Court," *The Province* (16 September 1979).

13 Case on Appeal, *supra* note 1, vol 10 at 1814 (evidence of William Grant, witness for the Crown).

14 See Chapter 3 for the cases.

15 George Bernard Shaw, "Appendix: Maxims for Revolutionists" in *Man and Superman* (Harmondsworth, UK: Penguin, 1946) at 281–82.

16 Joanne Lysyk and Maria Morelatto, "Marvin R.V. Storrow, Q.C." (2006) 64 The Advocate 481.

17 For a history of the firm from 1892 to 1985, see Christine Mullins, *Damarell: A History of Davis & Company 1892–1985* (1 January 1986) [unpublished]. The firm merged in 2015 with the international firm of DLA Piper and the name disappeared.

18 Mullins, *supra* note 17 at 75–82. For the litigation, see *Reference to the Validity of Orders in Council in Relation to Persons of Japanese Race*, [1946] SCR 248 (badly divided court upholding some of the proposed deportations); *The Co-operative Committee on Japanese Canadians v Attorney-General of Canada*, [1946] UKPC 48.

19 Ron Caston, "The Mabo Case" (Paper delivered on 23 May 1992), quoted in Bryan Keon-Cohen, *A Mabo Memoir: Islan Kustom to Native Title* (Melbourne: Zemvic Press, 2013) at ch 18.1 n 103.

20 (1999) 57 Advocate (BC) 760.

21 Bob Chamberlain, "Band Hikes Insurance on Trial Judge's Life," *Vancouver Sun* (22 May 1981).

22 "The Honourable Frank U. Collier" (1996) 54 Advocate (BC) 947; see also "New Judge: Frank U. Collier" (1971) 29 Advocate (BC) 292.

23 Bob Chamberlain, "Musqueam Case Proving Lengthy, Costly," *The Province* (24 September 1979) ["Musqueam Case"].

24 *Ibid.*

25 Case on Appeal, *supra* note 1, vol 1 at 27–33; Larry Still, "Band Seeks $40 Million Damages," *Vancouver Sun* (19 September 1979). See Chapter 3 for the case law as it stood at the time of the trial.

26 Case on Appeal, *supra* note 1, vol 1 at 36–38.

27 Chamberlain, "Musqueam Case," *supra* note 23.

28 Case on Appeal, *supra* note 1, vol 1 at 40–67.

29 J.E. Michael Kew, "Reflections on Anthropology at the University of British Columbia" (2017) 193 BC Studies 163 at 178.

30 Case on Appeal, *supra* note 1, vol 1 at 79–111.

31 *Ibid*, vol 1 at 111–200; *ibid*, vol 2 at 201–311; Larry Still, "Indians 'Denied Lease Details,'" *Vancouver Sun* (20 September 1979).

32 Chamberlain, "Musqueam Case," *supra* note 23.

33 Case on Appeal, *supra* note 1, vol 1 at 120.

34 *Ibid*, vol 1 at 143.

35 *Ibid; ibid*, vol 2 at 311–400; *ibid*, vol 3 at 401–507.

36 Leona Sparrow, *Work Histories of a Coast Salish Couple* (MA Thesis, University of British Columbia, 1976). He died in August 1998 at the age of ninety-nine: for his obituary, see *Vancouver Sun* (6 August 1998) at B7.

37 See Chapter 2.

38 Case on Appeal, *supra* note 1, vol 6 at 1147–1206.

39 *Ibid*, vol 6 at 1156.

40 *Ibid*, vol 7 at 1282–87.

41 *Ibid*, vol 7 at 1297–1355.

42 *Ibid*, vol 7 at 1287–97; Chamberlain, "Ex-Indian Affairs Official," *supra* note 11.

43 Case on Appeal, *supra* note 1, vol 7 at 1296.

44 *Ibid*, vol 7 at 1293–94.

45 *Ibid*, vol 7 at 1295.

46 *Ibid*, vol 7 at 1297.

47 *Ibid*, vol 5 at 906–74; Chamberlain, "Ex-Indian Affairs Official," *supra* note 11.

48 Case on Appeal, *supra* note 1, vol 5 at 938.

49 *Ibid*, vol 3 at 509–600; *ibid*, vol 4 at 601–800; *ibid*, vol 5 at 801–905.

50 *Ibid*, vol 8 at 1464–1506; *ibid*, vol 12 at 2201–35.

51 *Ibid*, Exhibit 148.

52 *Ibid*, vol 12 at 2211.

53 *Ibid*, vol 8 at 1508–40.

54 "Golfers Say Indian Agent Drove Hard Bargain," *The Province* (17 October 1979).

55   Case on Appeal, *supra* note 1, vol 9 at 1627.

56   *Ibid,* vol 9 at 1641.

57   *Ibid,* vol 9 at 1638.

58   *Ibid,* vol 9 at 1640.

59   *Ibid,* vol 9 at 1647–48.

60   *Ibid,* vol 9 at 1691–1753; "Indians Shortchanged, Says Appraiser," *The Province* (18 October 1979).

61   Case on Appeal, *supra* note 1, vol 9 at 1722.

62   *Ibid,* vol 9 at 1719.

63   *Ibid,* vol 13 at 2461.

64   *Ibid,* vol 9 at 1756–1800; *ibid,* vol 10 at 1801–39.

65   *Ibid,* vol 10 at 1816.

66   *Ibid,* vol 10 at 1814.

67   *Ibid,* vol 10 at 1819.

68   *Ibid,* vol 10 at 1826.

69   *Ibid,* vol 10 at 1820.

70   *Ibid.*

71   *Ibid,* vol 10 at 1824.

72   *Guerin v The Queen,* [1982] 2 FC 385 at 411 (FCTD) [*Guerin* FCTD].

73   *Ibid* at 419.

74   Case on Appeal, *supra* note 1, vol 10 at 1874–1921.

75   *Ibid,* vol 10 at 1898.

76   *Ibid,* Exhibit 166.

77   *Ibid,* vol 12 at 2297–BB. For the political trust doctrine, see Chapter 3.

78   *Ibid,* vol 12 at 2297–PP.

79   The Crown's reliance on the political trust defence was criticized in the press and Minister of Justice Jacques Flynn ordered its withdrawal on 20 November 1979: *Vancouver Sun* (20 and 21 November 1979).

80   Case on Appeal, *supra* note 1, vol 12 at 2298–2339.

81   *Ibid,* vol 12 at 2316.

82   *Guerin* FCTD, *supra* note 72 at 421.

83   Yorke Vickers, "Indians Win $10 Million Suit," *Vancouver Sun* (4 July 1981).

84   *Guerin* FCTD, *supra* note 72 at 393.

85   *Ibid* at 392.

86   *Ibid* at 395.

87   *Ibid* at 398.

88   *Ibid* at 399.

89   *Ibid* at 400.

90   *Ibid* at 401.

91 *Ibid* at 405–6.

92 *Ibid* at 406–7.

93 *Ibid* at 409–10.

94 *Ibid* at 413.

95 *Ibid.*

96 *Ibid* at 419.

97 *Ibid* at 425.

98 *Ibid* at 415.

99 *Ibid.*

100 *Ibid* at 416.

101 *Ibid* at 417–18.

102 *Ibid* at 418.

103 *Ibid* at 418–29.

104 *Ibid* at 425.

105 *Ibid.*

106 *Ibid* at 429–30.

107 *Ibid* at 430–43.

108 *Ibid* at 437.

109 *Ibid* at 439.

110 *Ibid.*

111 *Ibid.*

112 *Ibid* at 440–41.

113 *Ibid* at 441.

114 *Ibid* at 441–42.

115 *Ibid* at 443.

116 Bob Chamberlain, "Golf Club 'Fraud' May Cost Ottawa an Extra \$60m," *The Province* (5 July 1981) ["Golf Club 'Fraud'"].

117 Case on Appeal, *supra* note 1, vol 10 at 1814–18 (evidence of William Grant, witness for the Crown).

118 *Ibid,* vol 8 at 1590–91.

119 "B.C. Indians Lose Bid for Interest," *Vancouver Sun* (11 July 1981); Bob Chamberlain, "Indians Getting Nothing on \$10 m," *The Province* (4 August 1981).

120 Chamberlain, "Golf Club 'Fraud,'" *supra* note 116.

121 He left to become a senior partner at a large Toronto law firm, from which he was appointed directly to the Supreme Court of Canada in 1998, where he sat until he retired in 2011. His judgments include *Wewaykum Indian Band v Canada,* 2002 SCC 79, which was the first case since *Guerin* in 1984 in which the Supreme Court reviewed the fiduciary duty of the Crown to Indigenous people in any significant detail. The result was to narrow the potential scope of *Guerin*. His prior involvement in the case as an associate deputy minister raised concerns about the

appearance of bias or a conflict of interests: Leonard I. Rotman, "Let's Face It, We Are All Here to Stay" in Kerry Wilkins, ed, *Advancing Aboriginal Claims: Visions/Strategies/Directions* (Saskatoon: Purich, 2004). The Supreme Court of Canada rejected these concerns in a subsequent hearing: 2003 SCC 45.

122 *Guerin v. The Queen*, [1982] 2 FC 445 ["Supplementary Reasons"]; Bob Chamberlain, "Judge Rejects Interest Claim," *The Province* (5 August 1981); Larry Still, "Indians May Appeal 'No Interest' Decision," *Vancouver Sun* (5 August 1981).

123 "Supplementary Reasons," *supra* note 122 at 452.

124 "Musqueam Band to Appeal Upset of $10 Million Award," *Vancouver Sun* (22 December 1982) ["Musqueam Band to Appeal"].

125 Tony Wanless, "Indians' Award Appealed," *The Province* (30 September 1981).

126 See *The Queen v. Guerin* (Memorandum of fact and law, Appellant) [Appellant's Memorandum].

127 *Ibid.* at 30–37.

128 *Kinloch v Secretary of State for India* (1881–82), 7 AC 619 (HL) [*Kinloch*]; *Tito v Waddell* [1977] 3 All ER 129 (ChD) [*Tito*]; *St Ann's Island Shooting and Fishing Club v The King*, [1950] SCR 211.

129 *The Queen v. Guerin* (Memorandum of fact and law, Respondent) at 45–66 [Respondent's Memorandum].

130 *Miller v The King*, [1950] SCR 168 [*Miller*]; *Dreaver v The King* (1935), 5 CNLC 92 (Ex); *Kruger v The Queen* (1982), 125 DLR (3d) 513 (FCTD).

131 *Canada Elections Act*, RSC 1952, c 23, s 14(2)(e).

132 Respondent's Memorandum, *supra* note 129 at 42.

133 *Canadian Bill of Rights*, SC 1960, c 44, s 1; *Canadian Charter of Rights and Freedoms*, Part 1 of the *Constitution Act, 1982*, being Schedule B to the *Canada Act 1982* (UK), 1982, c 11, s 15, not in effect until 1985 (see s 32(2)).

134 Appellant's Memorandum, *supra* note 126 at 22–26.

135 One case that was relevant to this argument was *Smith v The Queen*, [1983] 1 SCR 554, in which it was held that an absolute surrender of lands for sale by Indians for whose benefit the lands were set aside leaves no retained or other interest. This case was clearly distinguishable as the surrender in the *Guerin* case was for lease, not sale, of the lands. Therefore, the band clearly retained an interest in the lands.

136 *Calder, supra* note 6.

137 Respondent's Memorandum, *supra* note 129 at 36–37.

138 Citing Judson J in *Calder, supra* note 6 at 328.

139 *Shoshone Tribe v United States*, 299 US 476 (1937) [*Shoshone Tribe*]; *United States v Sioux Nation of Indians*, 448 US 371 (1980) [*Sioux Nation*].

140 Appellant's Memorandum, *supra* note 126 at 50–52.

141 Respondent's Memorandum, *supra* note 129 at 81–83.

142 See, for example, *The Trust and Loan Company of Upper Canada v Ruttan*, [1877] 1 SCR 564.

143 *The Queen v Guerin* (1982), 143 DLR (3d) 416 (FCA) [*Guerin FCA*]; see comment by T.C. Youdan, (1983) 13 ETR 248.

144 He was subsequently elevated to the Supreme Court of Canada in 1984, the same year that the court reversed his decision in *Guerin*. He was forced to retire from that court in 1988 as the result of clinical depression, which has been the subject of criticism: CBC Radio, "'He Didn't Have a Choice': How Depression Cost Gerald Le Dain His Supreme Court Post," online: <http://www.cbc.ca/radio/thesundayedition/the-sunday-edition-january-14-2018-1.4471379/he-didn-t-have-a-choice-how-depression-cost-gerald-le-dain-his-supreme-court-post-1.4471385>. For a biography and essays describing his contributions to the law, see G. Blaine Baker and Richard Janda, eds, *Tracings of Gerald Le Dain's Life in the Law* (Montreal and Kingston: McGill-Queen's University Press, 2019).

145 *St Catherine's Milling and Lumber Co v The Queen* (1888), 14 AC 46 (PC); *Attorney-General for Quebec v Attorney-General for Canada*, [1921] 1 AC 401 (PC) [*Star Chrome*]; *Calder, supra* note 6.

146 *Shoshone Tribe, supra* note 139; *Sioux Nation, supra* note 139.

147 *Amodu Tijani v Secretary of State, Southern Nigeria*, [1921] 2 AC 399 (PC).

148 *The Queen v Devereux*, [1965] 1 Ex CR 602, [1965] SCR 567; *Joe v Findlay* (1978), 87 DLR (3d) 239 (BCSC), (1981) 122 DLR (3d) 377 (BCCA); *Brick Cartage Ltd v The Queen*, [1965] 1 Ex CR 102.

149 *Lysyk, supra* note 6.

150 *Guerin FCA, supra* note 143 at 462.

151 *Indian Act*, RSC 1970, c I-6, ss 37–41.

152 *Ibid*, s 39(1)(c).

153 (1981), 62 CCC (2d) 227.

154 *Guerin FCA, supra* note 143 at 442.

155 Citing *Rustomjee v The Queen*, [1876] 2 QBD 69 (Eng CA) at 74; *Civilian War Claimants Association Limited v The King*, [1932] AC 14 (HL) at 27; *Miller, supra* note 130 at 175; *Tito, supra* note 128.

156 *Kinloch, supra* note 128; *Hereford Railway Co v The Queen* (1894), 24 SCR 1 [*Hereford Railway*]; *Tito, supra* note 128; *Town Investments Ltd v Department of the Environment*, [1978] AC 359 (HL).

157 *Miller, supra* note 130.

158 *Guerin FCA, supra* note 143 at 467.

159 *Ibid* at 467.

160 *Ibid* at 469.

161 See Chapter 3 for the *Terms of Union: British Columbia Terms of Union* (UK), 1871, reprinted in RSC 1985, App II, No 10. The Order-in-Council was No 1036 dated 29 July 1938.

162 *Guerin* FCA, *supra* note 143 at 470.

163 In *Reference Re Language Rights under s 23 of the Manitoba Act, 1870 and s 133 of the Constitution Act, 1867*, [1985] 1 SCR 721 at 748, the Supreme Court of Canada wrote: "The rule of law, a fundamental part of our Constitution, must mean ... that the law is supreme over officials of the government as well as private individuals, and thereby preclusive of the influence of arbitrary power."

164 See *R v Hampden* (1637), 3 St Tr 825 (Exch).

165 *Constitution Act, 1982*, being Schedule B to the *Canada Act 1982* (UK), 1982, c 11, s 35(1).

166 Keon-Cohen, *supra* note 19 at pts 2 and 4; *Mabo v Queensland (No 1)* [1988] HCA 69.

167 See comment by Justice Wilson in the Supreme Court of Canada, *Guerin*, *supra* note 1 at 353.

168 "Musqueam Band to Appeal," *supra* note 124; Bob Chamberlain, "Musqueams Taking Claim to Top Court," *The Province* (22 December 1982).

CHAPTER 5: THE SUPREME COURT OF CANADA

1 *Guerin v The Queen*, [1984] 2 SCR 335 (SCC) [*Guerin*], Case on Appeal, vol 1 at 20–69 [Case on Appeal].

2 *Ibid* at 20–60 to 20–63.

3 *Report of the House of Commons Special Committee on Indian Self-Government*, Minutes of Proceedings, Issue No 6 (15 February 1983) at 40–68.

4 Case on Appeal, *supra* note 1 at 20–76.

5 *Guerin*, *supra* note 1 (Factum of the appellant at 40) [Appellants' Factum]. The factum is available online at the website of the Native Law Centre, University of Saskatchewan: <http://www.usask.ca/nativelaw/factums>.

6 *Ibid* at 49.

7 *Ibid* at 42–45.

8 *Ibid* at 58–62.

9 *Ibid* at 68–77.

10 *Ibid* at 45–52; *Miller v The King*, [1950] SCR 168 [*Miller*].

11 Appellants' Factum, *supra* note 5 at 52–54.

12 Reliance was placed on *Fales v Canada Permanent Trust Co*, [1977] 2 SCR 302; see M. Cullity, "Judicial Control of Trustees' Discretions" (1975) 25 UTLJ 99.

13 See *The Queen v Nowegijick*, [1983] 1 SCR 29 at 36, Dickson J; cf *Northern Cheyenne Tribe v Hollowbreast*, 425 US 649 (1976) at 655 n 7.

14   *Guerin, supra* note 1 (Factum of National Indian Brotherhood) [Factum of NIB]. The applications to intervene of the Union of Ontario Indians, the Union of British Columbia Indian Chiefs, the Treaty 8 Tribal Association, the Gitksan-Carrier Tribal Council, the Carrier-Sekani Tribal Council, and the Association of Iroquois and Allied Indians were dismissed on 14 April 1983. Interventions are granted more often today.

15   *Ibid* at 4–6.

16   *Guerin, supra* note 1 (Factum of the Crown at 67–72) [Factum of the Crown].

17   *Ibid* at 77–78.

18   *Ibid* at 79–82.

19   *Ibid* at 82–83, relying upon *Ontario Mining Company v Seybold,* [1903] AC 73 at 83–84, Lord Davey.

20   Factum of the Crown, *supra* note 16 at 55–64.

21   Canadian Press, "Indians Seek Fraud Ruling" (14 June 1983).

22   For a leading Aboriginal law case from Australia, the *Mabo* case, that took an unexpected turn during the hearing, see ch 16.3 in Bryan Keon-Cohen, *A Mabo Memoir: Islan Kustom to Native Title* (Melbourne: Zemvic Press, 2013).

23   "Indians Win Suit over Lease," *Globe and Mail* (2 November 1984); "Musqueam Indians Awarded $10 Million," *Vancouver Sun* (1 November 1984).

24   Robert J. Sharpe and Kent Roach, *Brian Dickson: A Judge's Journey* (Toronto: Osgoode Society for Canadian Legal History, 2003) at 446–48. It may be noted that such accounts of the inner workings of the Supreme Court are very unusual and may not be repeated: Sean Fine, "Case Closed – Canada's Top Court Will Keep Records of Its Deliberations Secret for at Least Half a Century," *Globe and Mail* (14 May 2018).

25   Leonard Ian Rotman, *Parallel Paths: Fiduciary Doctrine and the Crown-Native Relationship in Canada* (Toronto: University of Toronto Press, 1996) at 103–5 [*Parallel Paths*]. As noted by Prof. Rotman, the distinction is quite significant from an evidentiary viewpoint.

26   See Chapter 4.

27   *R v Sparrow,* [1990] 1 SCR 1075 at 1105.

28   For her biography, see Ellen Anderson, *Judging Bertha Wilson: Law as Large as Life* (Toronto: University of Toronto Press, 2001); Constance Backhouse, *Two Firsts: Bertha Wilson and Claire L'Heureux-Dubé at the Supreme Court of Canada* (Toronto: Second Story, 2019). Her contributions to the law are reviewed in a collection of essays: Kim Brooks, ed, *Justice Bertha Wilson: One Woman's Difference* (Vancouver: UBC Press, 2009).

29   *R v Morgentaler,* [1988] 1 SCR 30.

30   Brooks, *supra* note 28 at x.

31 *Guerin, supra* note 1 at 341–48.

32 *Ibid* at 348–52.

33 *Calder v Attorney-General for British Columbia,* [1973] SCR 313 [*Calder*].

34 *Guerin, supra* note 1 at 349–50.

35 *Ibid* at 350–52. See Chapter 3 for the political trust doctrine.

36 *Ibid* at 351.

37 *Ibid* at 353.

38 *Ibid* at 353–55.

39 *Ibid* at 354.

40 *Ibid* at 355.

41 *Ibid.*

42 *Ibid* at 356.

43 RSBC 1960, c 390.

44 *Guerin, supra* note 1 at 356–64.

45 *Ibid* at 391.

46 *Ibid* at 393.

47 *Ibid* at 394.

48 Richard H. Bartlett, *Indian Reserves and Aboriginal Lands in Canada: A Homeland* (Saskatoon: University of Saskatchewan Native Law Centre, 1990) at 202 [*Indian Reserves*].

49 Rotman, *Parallel Paths, supra* note 25 at 101.

50 Sharpe and Roche, *supra* note 24 at 5.

51 Ian Binnie, "Closing Address" (Address delivered at the Canadian Institute for the Administration of Justice Annual Conference, Justice to Order: Adjustment to Changing Demands and Co-ordination Issues in the Justice System in Canada, Saskatoon, 1998) at 448.

52 *Ibid* at 450.

53 *Kinloch v Secretary of State for India* (1881–82), 7 AC 619 (HL) at 625–26 [*Kinloch*].

54 *Guerin, supra* note 1 at 375.

55 *Ibid* at 376.

56 George R, Proclamation, 7 October 1763 (3 Geo III), reprinted in RSC 1985, App II, No 1 [Royal Proclamation]. See Chapter 3.

57 *Guerin, supra* note 1 at 376.

58 *Calder, supra* note 33; *St Catherine's Milling and Lumber Co v The Queen,* (1888) 14 AC 46 (PC) [*St Catherine's Milling*]; *Johnson v McIntosh,* 21 US (8 Wheat) 543 (1823); *Worcester v Georgia,* 31 US (6 Peters) 515 (1832); *Amodu Tijani v Secretary of State, Southern Nigeria,* [1921] 2 AC 399 (PC) [*Amodu Tijani*]; *Attorney-General for Quebec v Attorney-General for Canada,* [1921] 1 AC 401 [*Star Chrome*].

59 *Guerin, supra* note 1 at 378.

60 *Kinloch, supra* note 53; *Tito v. Waddell,* [1977] 3 All ER 129 (Ch).

61 *Guerin, supra* note 1 at 379. See Chapter 3 for the political trust doctrine.

62 *Ibid.*

63 In the *St Catherine's Milling* case, *supra* note 58 at 58, Lord Watson described the Indian title as "a mere burden" on the Crown's proprietary estate in the land. See Kent McNeil, *Flawed Precedent: The St. Catherine's Case and Aboriginal Title* (Vancouver: UBC Press, 2019).

64 *Calder, supra* note 33; *Attorney-General for Canada v Giroux* (1916), 53 SCR 172 [*Giroux*]; *Cardinal v Attorney General of Alberta,* [1974] SCR 695, Laskin J [*Cardinal*]; *Western International Contractors Ltd v Sarcee Development Ltd,* [1979] 3 WWR 631 [*Sarcee Development*].

65 *Miller, supra* note 10.

66 *Guerin, supra* note 1 at 382.

67 *Ibid.* The impact of *Guerin* on Aboriginal title is discussed in Chapter 6. It should be noted that this description of Aboriginal title no longer represents the law.

68 *Ibid* at 383. See Chapter 3 for the origin of fiduciary obligations.

69 *Ibid.*

70 *Ibid* at 384. See Chapter 4 for the decision of the Federal Court of Appeal on this point.

71 E. Weinrib, "The Fiduciary Obligation" (1975) 25 UTLJ 1 at 4.

72 *Guerin, supra* note 1 at 384. In *Authorson v Canada* (2000), 215 DLR (4th) 496 at para 69, the Ontario Court of Appeal referred to these words as Justice Dickson's "most famous passage."

73 *Guerin, supra* note 1 at 384.

74 *Ibid* at 385.

75 *Ibid.*

76 *Ibid* at 386.

77 *Ibid.* It may be noted that this passage overlooks the fact that the surrender in question was a conditional and not an unconditional surrender as in *Smith v The Queen,* [1983] 1 SCR 554. The surrender was for the purpose of lease, not for sale as in *Smith:* see Bartlett, *Indian Reserves, supra* note 48 at 198–99. In the view of Professor Waters, there was a sufficient interest for the purposes of a trust: Donovan Waters, "New Directions in the Employment of Equitable Doctrines: The Canadian Experience" in Timothy G. Youdan, ed, *Equity, Fiduciaries and Trusts* (Toronto: Carswell, 1989) at 423.

78 *Guerin, supra* note 1 at 386, quoting *Pettkus v Becker,* [1980] 2 SCR 834 at 847; see Leonard Rotman, *Fiduciary Law* (Toronto: Thomson Carswell, 2005) especially at 717–23, for discussion of constructive trusts.

79 *Guerin, supra* note 1 at 387.

80 *Ibid* at 387.

81 *Ibid* at 388–90.

82 *Ibid* at 388–89.

83 *Ibid* at 389.

84 *Ibid* at 389–90.

85 *Ibid* at 390.

86 *Ibid* at 390–91.

87 Sharpe and Roach, *supra* note 24 at 446–48.

88 *Guerin, supra* note 1 at 394.

89 Leonard I. Rotman, "Crown-Native Relations as Fiduciary: Reflections Almost Twenty Years after Guerin" (2003) 22 Windsor YB Access Just 363 at 366.

90 Rudy Platiel, "Indians' $10 Million Award May Lead to More Claims," *Globe and Mail* (3 November 1984).

91 "Musqueam Indian Band Wins $10 Million in Golf Club Land Suit," *Vancouver Sun* (1 November 1984); Terry Glavin and Glenn Bohn, "Musqueam Hails Court Verdict," *Vancouver Sun* (2 November 1984).

92 Craig Spence, "Officials Reeling over Major Ruling," *Vancouver Courier* (7 November 1984).

93 Glavin and Bohn, *supra* note 91.

94 *Musqueam Indian Band v Canada,* [1990] 2 FC 351 (FCTD) at 383.

95 *Musqueam Indian Band v Musqueam Indian Band (Board of Review),* 2016 SCC 36.

96 *Ibid* at para 15.

CHAPTER 6: THE IMPACT OF *GUERIN*

1 Jordan Furlong, "Our Legal Century," *National (Journal of the Canadian Bar Association)* (December 2000) at 17.

2 *Wewaykum Indian Band v Canada,* 2002 SCC 79 at para 73 [*Wewaykum*].

3 Ian Binnie, "Closing Address" (Address delivered at the Canadian Institute for the Administration of Justice Annual Conference, Justice to Order: Adjustment to Changing Demands and Co-ordination Issues in the Justice System in Canada, Saskatoon, 1998) at 451.

4 *Authorson v Canada* (2002), 215 DLR (4th) 496 (Ont CA) at para 61[*Authorson*]; rev'd [2003] 2 SCR 40 on another point.

5 *Mathias v Canada* (1998), 144 FTR 106.

6 Leonard I. Rotman, *Parallel Paths: Fiduciary Doctrine and the Crown-Native Relationship in Canada* (Toronto: University of Toronto Press, 1996) at 3, 8 [*Parallel*

Paths]. See also Leonard I. Rotman, "Crown-Native Relations as Fiduciary: Reflections Almost Twenty Years after Guerin" (2003) 22 Windsor YB Access Just 363.

7 Donovan W.M. Waters, "New Directions in the Employment of Equitable Doctrines: The Canadian Experience" in T.G. Youdan, ed, *Equity, Fiduciaries and Trusts* (Toronto: Carswell, 1989) at 414.

8 Senwung Luk, "Not So Many Hats: The Crown's Fiduciary Obligations to Aboriginal Communities since *Guerin*" (2013) 76 Sask L Rev 1.

9 Judge D. Arnot, "Treaties as a Bridge to the Future" (2001) 50 UNBLJ 57 at 66; Brian Slattery, "Understanding Aboriginal Rights" (1987) 66 Can Bar Rev 727 at 728–31; Former Chief Justice of Canada Beverley McLachlin, *Truth Be Told: My Journey Through Life and the Law* (New York: Simon & Schuster, 2019) at 287; Paul Tennant, *Aboriginal Peoples and Politics* (Vancouver: UBC Press, 1990) at 222.

10 W.F. Flanagan, "Fiduciary Duties in Commercial Relationships: When Does the Marketplace Set the Rules?" in A. Anand and W.F. Flanagan, *Selected Topics in Corporate Litigation* (Kingston, ON: Queen's Annual Business Law Symposium, 2001) at 3, 17. See also Leonard I. Rotman, "Justice Cromwell and Fiduciary Duties: Placing Law into Context" (2017) 80 SCLR (2d) 263 at 292, describing *Guerin* and *Frame v Smith*, [1987] 2 SCR 99 as "the cases that established the foundation of modern Canadian fiduciary jurisprudence."

11 *Authorson, supra* note 4 at para 70.

12 *Alberta v Elder Advocates of Alberta Society*, 2011 SCC 24 at para 29; see also *Galambos v Perez*, 2009 SCC 48.

13 Based on a search of the Canadian Legal Information Institute website, <https://canlii.org/en/>.

14 *Calder v Attorney-General for British Columbia*, [1973] SCR 313 [*Calder*].

15 For a recent summary, see *Williams Lake Indian Band v Canada*, 2018 SCC 4 at para 44 [*Williams Lake*]. For detailed accounts of the law, see Rotman, *Parallel Paths, supra* note 6; Leonard Ian Rotman, *Fiduciary Law* (Toronto: Thomson Carswell, 2005) at 524–608; James I. Reynolds, *A Breach of Duty: Fiduciary Obligations and Aboriginal peoples* (Saskatoon: Purich, 2005); J. Timothy S. McCabe, *The Honour of the Crown and Its Fiduciary Duties to Aboriginal peoples* (Markham, ON: LexisNexis, 2008). There have been numerous articles. One that stands out is by Luk, *supra* note 8.

16 See *Specific Claims Tribunal Act*, SC 2008, c 22, s 14(1)(b), (c); *Williams Lake, supra* note 15.

17 *Paki v Attorney General*, [2014] NZSC 118. For a discussion of the relevance of the Canadian law to New Zealand, see Alex Frame, "The Fiduciary Duties of

the Crown to Maori: Will the Canadian Remedy Travel?" (2005) 13 Waikato L Rev 70.

18 [2017] NZSC 17; see Special Issue, 2019 NZLR 1.

19 Carwyn Jones, "Analysis: Proprietors of Wakatū and Others v Attorney-General," online: <https://iacl-aidc-blog.org/2017/05/13/analysis-proprietors-of-wakatu-and-others-v-attorney-general-2017-nzsc-17/>. See also, Alex Frame, *The Wakatū Decision: A Landmark Moment in New Zealand Law*, Maori Law Review, April 2017, online: <http://maorilawreview.co.nz/2017/04/fiduciary-duty-a-few-remarks-on-proprietors-of-wakatu-v-attorney-general-2017-nzsc-17/>; Miriam Bookman, "A 'Legal Backstop' for Historical Maori Grievances: Proprietors of Wakatu v. Attorney-General" (2017) 23 Auckland UL Rev 348.

20 See chs 8.5 and 9.1 in Bryan Keon-Cohen, *A Mabo Memoir: Islan Kustom to Native Title* (Melbourne: Zemvic Press, 2013).

21 *Ibid*, text accompanying ch 8.5 n 27.

22 *Ibid*, text accompanying ch 16.1 n 50.

23 *Thorpe v Commonwealth of Australia (No. 3)* (1997), 144 ALR 677 at 688 per Kirby J. See *Love, Thoms v Australia* [2020] HCA 3 at para 215 per Keane J.

24 Anthony Mason, "The Place of Equity and Equitable Remedies in the Contemporary Common Law World" (1994) 110 Law Q Rev 238 at 246–47.

25 Kirsty Glover, "The Honour of the Crowns: State-Indigenous Fiduciary Relationships and Australian Exceptionalism" (2016) 38 Sydney L Rev 339.

26 Jim Reynolds, *Aboriginal Peoples and the Law: A Critical Introduction* (Vancouver: UBC Press/Purich, 2018) at 144–73 [*Aboriginal Peoples*].

27 *Guerin v The Queen*, [1984] 2 SCR 335 at 388 [*Guerin*].

28 *Beckman v Little Salmon First Nation*, 2010 SCC 53 at para 93 (full citations omitted). See also *Delgamuukw v British Columbia*, [1997] 3 SCR 1010 at para 168 [*Delgamuukw*], tracing the duty to consult to *Guerin*.

29 *Haida Nation v British Columbia (Minister of Forests)*, 2004 SCC 73 at para 18.

30 *Constitution Act, 1982*, being Schedule B to the *Canada Act 1982* (UK), 1982, c 11, s 35 (1).

31 See Reynolds, *Aboriginal Peoples, supra* note 26 at 41–44.

32 Richard H. Bartlett, "Survey of Canadian Law – Indian and Native Law" (1983) 15 Ottawa L Rev 431 at 500.

33 *Wewaykum, supra* note 2 at para 78; see also *R v Van der Peet*, [1996] 2 SCR 507.

34 *R v Sparrow*, [1990] 1 SCR 1075 [*Sparrow*].

35 *Ibid* at 1105, Dickson CJC and La Forest J.

36 *Ibid* at 1108.

37 *Sparrow, supra* note 34 at 1109.

38 McCabe, *supra* note 15 at 44.

39 *Ibid* at 163.

40 *Tsilhqot'in Nation v British Columbia,* 2014 SCC 44 at para 77 [*Tsilhqot'in*].

41 *Delgamuukw, supra* note 28 at para 168.

42 *Tsilhqot'in, supra* note 40 at paras 85–87.

43 *R v Sikyea* (1964), 43 DLR (2d) 150 (NWTCA), aff'd [1964] SCR 642.

44 *R v Badger,* [1996] 1 SCR 771.

45 *Ibid* at para 75. See also *R v Sundown,* [1999] 1 SCR 393; *R v Marshall,* [1999] 3 SCR 456, further reasons, [1999] 3 SCR 533.

46 Peter W. Hogg, "The Constitutional Basis of Aboriginal Rights" in Maria Morellato, ed, *Aboriginal Law since Delgamuukw* (Aurora, ON: Canada Law Book, 2009) at 3–4. For an important lower court decision, see *Baker Lake v Minister of Indian Affairs,* [1980] 1 FC 518 (FCTD).

47 *Tsilhqot'in, supra* note 40 at para. 69.

48 *Guerin, supra* note 27 at 379.

49 *Tsilhqot'in, supra* note 40 at para 12.

50 *Delgamuukw, supra* note 28 at paras 114, 119–22.

51 See Kent McNeil, *Flawed Precedent: The St. Catherine's Case and Aboriginal Title* (Vancouver: UBC Press, 2019) at 144–83.

52 *Guerin, supra* note 27 at 379–82.

53 *Ibid* at 385.

54 Slattery, *supra* note 9 at 731, 749.

55 *St Catherine's Milling and Lumber Co v The Queen,* (1888) 14 AC 46 (PC); see McNeil, *supra* note 51.

56 Binnie, *supra* note 3 at 448.

57 Michael Doherty, *Aboriginal Dominion in Canada* (PhD Thesis, University of Aberdeen, 2017) at 46–47. The quotations are from Slattery, *supra* note 9 at 730; *Guerin, supra* note 27 at 348; and Tennant, *supra* note 9 at 222–26.

CONCLUSION

1 Ronald St. John Macdonald, *Research Project on Treaty and Aboriginal Rights of Canadian Indians and Eskimos* (Toronto: Indian-Eskimo Association of Canada, 1970) at 201.

2 Larissa Behrendt, "Lacking Good Faith: Australia, Fiduciary Duties and the Lonely Place of Indigenous Rights" in Law Commission of Canada, *In Whom We Trust: A Forum on Fiduciary Relationships,* ed by Association of Iroquois and Allied Indians (Toronto: Irwin Law, 2002) at 264–65. For a more recent review

of the Australian law, see Kirsty Glover, "The Honour of the Crowns: State-Indigenous Fiduciary Relationships and Australian Exceptionalism" (2016) 38 Sydney L Rev 339.

3 B.A. Keon-Cohen, "The *Mabo* Litigation: A Personal and Procedural Account" (2000) 24 Melbourne UL Rev 893 at 944.

4 *Johnson v British Columbia (Securities Commission)* (1999), 67 BCLR (3d) 145 at para 25 (BCSC), Allan J.

5 *Cape Breton v Nova Scotia,* 2009 NSCA 44; leave to appeal to SCC denied, CanLII 71470, 2009.

6 Richard H. Bartlett, "Survey of Canadian Law – Indian and Native Law" (1983) 15 Ottawa L Rev 431 at 500.

7 Brian Slattery, "Understanding Aboriginal Rights" (1987) 66 Can Bar Rev 727.

8 Section 35 did not apply because the action was commenced and the trial held before it came into effect.

9 Slattery, *supra* note 7 at 728.

10 *Ibid* at 730.

11 *Calder v Attorney-General for British Columbia,* [1973] SCR 313 [*Calder*].

12 Slattery, *supra* note 7 at 731. (Justice Estey did not consider the issue.)

13 *Ibid.*

14 *R v Sparrow,* [1990] 1 SCR 1075 [*Sparrow*]. See Chapter 6.

15 See Jim Reynolds, *Aboriginal Peoples and the Law: A Critical Introduction* (Vancouver: UBC Press/Purich, 2018), list of leading cases at xiv.

16 Leonard Ian Rotman, *Parallel Paths: Fiduciary Doctrine and the Crown-Native Relationship in Canada* (Toronto: University of Toronto Press, 1996) at 88 [*Parallel Paths*].

17 GA Res 61/295, UNGAOR, UN Doc A/RES/61/295 (2007). For more details, see *Williams Lake Indian Band v Canada,* 2018 SCC 4 [*Williams Lake Indian Band*] (Factum of the Intervenor, Assembly of Manitoba Chiefs, at 5–10), online: Supreme Court of Canada <https://www.scc-csc.ca/WebDocuments -DocumentsWeb/36983/FM050_Intervener_Assembly-of-Manitoba-Chiefs.pdf>.

18 Reynolds, *Aboriginal Peoples, supra* note 15 at 187–91. The British Columbia legislature has recently passed legislation to affirm the application of the Declaration to the laws of the province: *Declaration on the Rights of Indigenous Peoples Act,* SBC 2019, c. 44, s. 2.

19 *Guerin v The Queen,* [1984] 2 SCR 335 at 389 [*Guerin*].

20 *Wewaykum Indian Band v Canada,* 2002 SCC 79 at para 86 [*Wewaykum*].

21 See Leonard I. Rotman, *Fiduciary Law* (Toronto: Thomson Carswell, 2005) at 685–757 for remedies for breach of fiduciary obligations.

22 *Guerin, supra* note 19 (Factum of National Indian Brotherhood at 4–6) [Factum of NIB].

23 *Blueberry River Indian Band v Canada (Department of Indian Affairs and Northern Development)*, [1995] 4 SCR 344 [*Blueberry River*].

24 *Delgamuukw v British Columbia*, [1997] 3 SCR 1010 at para 169 [*Delgamuukw*].

25 Michael Hudson, a lawyer for the Crown, estimated as early as 1997 that there were over three hundred actions against the Crown for breach of fiduciary obligation, with approximately $2 billion at stake: Michael Hudson, "Crown Fiduciary Duties under the *Indian Act*" in Andrea Morrison and Irwin Cotler, eds, *Justice for Natives – Searching for Common Ground* (Montreal and Kingston: McGill-Queen's University Press, 1997) at 257–58. The 2018–19 Interim Estimates from the Treasury Board included approximately $800 million to settle specific and special claims negotiated by Canada and/or awarded by the Specific Claims Tribunal: Treasury Board, *Interim Estimates 2018–19* (Ottawa: Treasury Board, 2018) at 1–8.

26 Rotman, *Fiduciary Law, supra* note 21 at 685–757.

27 Property tax case: *Musqueam Indian Band v Musqueam Indian Band (Board of Review)*, 2016 SCC 36.

28 *Guerin v The Queen*, [1982] 2 FC 385 at 400, 433 [*Guerin* FCTD]. See Chapter 4.

29 *Guerin, supra* note 19 at 357.

30 For a different perspective, see W.I.C. Binnie, "The Sparrow Doctrine: Beginning of the End or End of the Beginning?" (1990) 15 Queen's LJ 217 at 241.

31 *Report of the House of Commons Special Committee on Indian Self-Government*, Minutes of Proceedings, Issue No 6 (15 February 1983) at 58.

32 *Ibid* at 53–54.

33 *Report of the House of Commons Special Committee on Indian Self-Government*, Minutes of Proceedings, Issue No 40 (12 and 20 October 1983) ch 9.

34 Canada, Parliament, House of Commons Special Committee on Indian Self-Government, *Indian Self-Government in Canada: Report of the Special Committee* (Ottawa: Canadian Government Publishing Centre, Supply and Services Canada, 1983) at 121.

35 Reynolds, *Aboriginal Peoples, supra* note 15 at 56–72. For the view that *Guerin* can be interpreted as possible recognition of a nation-to-nation relationship and a criticism of later decisions of the Supreme Court of Canada that have moved towards a sovereign-to-subject relationship, see Ryan Beaton, "The Crown Fiduciary Duty at the Supreme Court of Canada: Reaching across Nations, or Held within

the Grip of the Crown?" (January 2018) Centre for International Governance Innovation (CIGI), Canada in International Law at 150 and Beyond, Paper No 6, online: CIGI <https://www.cigionline.org/sites/default/files/documents/Reflections%20Series%20Paper%20no.6%20Beaton_0.pdf>.

36 *Mitchell v MNR,* 2001 SCC 33 at para 9 [*Mitchell;* citations omitted].

37 *Sparrow, supra* note 14 at 1109.

38 Evan Fox-Decent, *Sovereignty's Promise: The State as Fiduciary* (Oxford: Oxford University Press, 2011) at 69.

39 *Ibid.* For a discussion of trusteeship and sovereignty in international law, see Evan Fox-Decent and Ian Dahlman, "Sovereignty and Trusteeship and Indigenous Peoples" (2015) 16 Theor Inq L 507.

40 Felix Hoehn, *Reconciling Sovereignties: Aboriginal Nations and Canada* (Saskatoon: Native Law Centre, 2012) at 114–19, 146–48.

41 For Indigenous laws in Canada, see John Borrows, *Canada's Indigenous Constitution* (Toronto: University of Toronto Press, 2012); Reynolds, *Aboriginal Peoples, supra* note 15 at 174–86.

42 Homer G. Barnett, *The Coast Salish of British Columbia* (Portland: University of Oregon Press, 1955) at 244; see also Russel Barsh, "Coast Salish Property Law: An Alternative Paradigm for Environmental Relationships" (2005) 12 Hastings W-Nw J Envtl L & Pol'y 1; Colin Grier, "Expanding Notions of Hunter-Gatherer Diversity: Identifying Core Organisational Principles and Practices in Coast Salish Societies of the Northwest Coast of North America" in Bill Finlayson and Graeme Warren, eds, *The Diversity of Hunter-Gatherer Pasts* (Oxford: Oxbow, 2017) at 22–26. See S.K.B. Asante, "Fiduciary Principles in Anglo-American Law and the Customary Law of Ghana: A Comparative Study" (1965) 14 ICLQ 1144 for a detailed account of fiduciary principles in an Indigenous legal system, and Max Gluckman, *Politics, Law and Ritual in Tribal Society* (Oxford: Blackwell, 1965) at 36–43 for a more general discussion.

43 For an example, see *William v British Columbia,* 2012 BCCA 285 at para 4 (on appeal from *Tsilhqot'in Nation v British Columbia,* 2007 BCSC 1700).

44 Mark L. Stevenson and Albert Peeling, "Probing the Parameters of Canada's Crown-Aboriginal Fiduciary Relationship" in Law Commission of Canada, *supra* note 2 at 7. See also Patrick Macklem, "First Nations Self-Government and the Borders of the Canadian Legal Imagination" (1991) 36 McGill LJ 382 at 410–14; Gordon Christie, "Considering the Future of the Crown-Aboriginal Fiduciary Relationship" in Law Commission of Canada, *supra* note 2 at 289. For a criticism of trusteeship in the international sphere, see William Bain, *Between Anarchy and Society: Trusteeship and the Obligations of Power* (Oxford: Oxford University Press, 2003) at ch 7.

45 Jamie D. Dickson, *The Honour and Dishonour of the Crown: Making Sense of Aboriginal Law in Canada* (Saskatoon: Purich, 2015) at 9.

46 Rotman, *Parallel Paths, supra* note 16 at 13.

47 *Manitoba Metis Federation v Canada*, 2013 SCC 14 at para 66 [*Manitoba Metis*], quoting from Slattery, *supra* note 7 at 753.

48 *Covenant of the League of Nations*, 28 June 1919 (entered into force 10 January 1920) at art 22, online: Avalon Project <http://avalon.law.yale.edu/20th_century/leagcov.asp>. See Chapter 3.

49 Fox-Decent, *supra* note 38 at 76.

50 *Ibid* at 78. See also Rotman, *Parallel Paths, supra* note 16 at 14.

51 *Haida Nation v British Columbia (Minister of Forests)*, 2004 SCC 73 [*Haida*].

52 *Rutland's (Earl) Case*, (1608) 77 ER 555.

53 *Province of Ontario v Dominion of Canada*, (1895) 25 SCR 434 at 512.

54 *Sparrow, supra* note 14 at 1109.

55 *Mitchell, supra* note 36 at para 9.

56 In *Wewaykum, supra* note 20 at para 80, Justice Binnie made a vague and curious comment that "the need to uphold the 'honour of the Crown'" was "somewhat associated with the ethical standards required of a fiduciary in the context of the Crown and Aboriginal peoples."

57 *Haida, supra* note 51 at paras 16–17.

58 *Ibid* at para 25.

59 *R v Van der Peet*, [1996] 2 SCR 507 at para 24 [*Van der Peet*].

60 *Haida, supra* note 51 at para 18.

61 *Mikisew Cree First Nation v Canada (Governor General in Council)*, 2018 SCC 40 at para 153 [*Mikisew Cree*]. See also the majority judgment in *Newfoundland and Labrador (Attorney General)* v *Uashaunnuat (Innu of Uashat and of Mani-Utenam)*, 2020 SCC 4 at para 35.

62 *Ibid* at paras 64–65.

63 See Chapter 5 of this book and James Reynolds, "The Spectre of Spectra" in Maria Morelatto, ed, *Aboriginal Law since Delgamuukw* (Aurora, ON: Canada Law Book, 2009) at 135–44.

64 Peter Birks, "The Content of Fiduciary Obligations" (2000) 34 Israel L Rev 3 at 7, 12.

65 For example, *R v Badger*, [1996] 1 SCR 771 at para 41.

66 Beaton, *supra* note 35 at 5.

67 Dickson, *supra* note 45 at 150.

68 *Daniels v Canada*, 2016 SCC 12 at para 53.

69 *Wakatu v Attorney General*, [2017] NZSC 17.

70 *Williams Lake Indian Band, supra* note 17.

71 *Wewaykum, supra* note 20 at para 81.

72 *Alberta v Elder Advocates of Alberta Society,* 2011 SCC 24 at paras 37–54.

73 *Canada's Residential Schools: Reconciliation, The Final Report of the Truth and Reconciliation Commission of Canada,* vol 6 (Montreal and Kingston: McGill-Queen's University Press, 2015) at 51.

74 *McDiarmid Lumber Ltd v God's Lake First Nation,* 2006 SCC 58 at para 106.

75 See Douglas C. Harris, *Fish, Law and Colonialism: The Legal Capture of Salmon in British Columbia* (Toronto: University of Toronto Press, 2001) at 186–216, and compare the discussion in E.P. Thompson, *Whigs and Hunters: The Origins of the Black Act* (New York: Pantheon, 1975) at 258–69.

76 Reynolds, *Aboriginal Peoples, supra* note 15 at 212.

Selected Bibliography

The endnotes to each chapter of this book give detailed references. The purpose of this selected bibliography is to direct the reader's attention to those sources that are especially helpful.

CHAPTER 1: THE COLONIAL CONTEXT

Brownlie, Robin Jarvis. *A Father's Eye: Indian Agents, Government Power, and Aboriginal Resistance in Ontario, 1918–1939* (Oxford: Oxford University Press, 2003).

Cairns, Alan. *First Nations and the Canadian State: In Search of Coexistence* (Kingston, ON: Institute of Intergovernmental Relations, Queen's University, 2005).

Fry, Alan. *How a People Die* (Madeira Park, BC: Harbour Publishing, 1994).

Furnivall, J.S. *Colonial Policy and Practice: A Comparative Study of Burma and Netherlands India* (Cambridge: Cambridge University Press, 1948).

Halliday, W.M. *Potlatch and Totem: And the Recollections of an Indian Agent* (London: J.M. Dent, 1935).

Harris, Cole. "How Did Colonialism Dispossess? Comments from an Edge of Empire" (2004) 94 Annals of the Association of American Geographers 165.

Igartua, José E. *The Other Quiet Revolution: National Identities in English Canada, 1945–71* (Vancouver: UBC Press, 2006).

Kirk-Greene, Anthony. *On Crown Service: A History of HM Colonial and Overseas Civil Services 1837–1997* (London: Tauris, 1999) [contains a bibliography of materials on the Colonial Service].

Leslie, John. *Assimilation, Integration or Termination? The Development of Canadian Indian Policy, 1943–1963* (PhD Thesis, Carleton University, 1999).

Lugard, F.D. *The Dual Mandate in British Tropical Africa* (Edinburgh: William Blackwood, 1922).

Merivale, Herman. *Lectures on Colonization and Colonies. Delivered before the University of Oxford in 1839, 1840 &1841* (London: Longman, Brown, Green and Longman, 1842).

Morris, James (Jan). *Farewell the Trumpets: An Imperial Retreat* (London: Penguin, 1979).

Sproat, G.M. *Scenes and Studies of Savage Life* (London: Smith, Elder, 1868).

Titley, E. Brian. *A Narrow Vision – Duncan Campbell Scott and the Administration of Indian Affairs in Canada* (Vancouver: UBC Press, 1986).

CHAPTER 2: THE MUSQUEAM AND THEIR LAND

Bhandar, Brenna. *Colonial Lives of Property: Law, Land and Racial Regimes of Ownership* (Durham, NC: Duke University Press, 2018).

Fisher, Robin. *Contact and Conflict*, 2d ed (Vancouver: UBC Press, 1992).

Harris, Cole. *Making Native Space: Colonialism, Resistance, and Reserves in British Columbia* (Vancouver: UBC Press, 2002).

–. *The Resettlement of British Columbia: Essays on Colonialism and Geographical Change* (Vancouver: UBC Press, 1992).

Harris, Douglas C. *Fish, Law and Colonialism: The Legal Capture of Salmon in British Columbia* (Toronto: University of Toronto Press, 2001).

–. *Landing Native Fisheries: Indian Reserves and Fishing Rights in British Columbia 1849–1925* (Vancouver: UBC Press, 2008).

Hawthorn, H.B., C.S. Belshaw, and S.M. Jamieson, *The Indians of British Columbia: A Study of Contemporary Social Adjustment* (Berkeley: University of California Press, 1958).

Kew, J.E.M. *Coast Salish Ceremonial Life: Status and Identity in a Modern Village* (PhD Thesis, University of Washington, 1970).

Miller, Bruce Granville. *Be of Good Mind: Essays on the Coast Salish* (Vancouver: UBC Press, 2007).

Papers Connected with the Indian Land Question 1850–1875 (Victoria: Government Printing Office, 1875; reprinted 1987).

Sparrow, Leona Marie. *Work Histories of a Coast Salish Couple* (MA Thesis, University of British Columbia, 1976).

Suttles, Wayne. *Coast Salish Essays* (Seattle: University of Washington Press, 1987).

Tennant, Paul. *Aboriginal Peoples and Politics: The Indian Land Question in British Columbia 1849–1989* (Vancouver: UBC Press, 1990).

CHAPTER 3: THE GOVERNMENT AS FIDUCIARY

Chambers, Reid Peyton. "Judicial Enforcement of the Federal Trust Responsibility to Indians" (1975) 27 Stan L Rev 1213.

Cohen, Felix. *Handbook of Federal Indian Law* (Newark, NJ: LexisNexis, 2012), sections 5.04–5.05.

Criddle, Evan, et al, eds. *Fiduciary Government* (Cambridge: Cambridge University Press, 2018).

Flannigan, Robert. "Contesting Public Service Fiduciary Accountability" (2017) 36 UQLJ 7.

Fox-Decent, Evan. *Sovereignty's Promise: The State as Fiduciary* (Oxford: Oxford University Press, 2011).

Green, L.C. "North America's Indians and the Trusteeship Concept" (1975) 4 Anglo-Am L Rev 137.

Kinloch v Secretary of State for India, (1881–82) 7 AC 619 (HL).

McCabe, J. Timothy S. *The Honour of the Crown and Its Fiduciary Duties to Aboriginal Peoples* (Toronto: LexisNexis, 2008).

Miller v The King, [1950] SCR 168.

Roberts v Hopwood, [1925] AC 578.

Rotman, Leonard I. "Understanding Fiduciary Duties and Relationship Fiduciarity" (2017) 62 McGill LJ 975 [contains a list of legal literature on fiduciary law].

–. *Fiduciary Law* (Toronto: Thomson Carswell, 2005).

–. *Parallel Paths: Fiduciary Doctrine and the Crown-Native Relationship in Canada* (Toronto: University of Toronto Press, 1996).

Royal Proclamation of 1763: George R, Proclamation, 7 October 1763 (3 Geo III), reprinted in RSC 1985, App II, No 1.

St Ann's Island Shooting and Fishing Club v The King, [1950] SCR 211.

Tito v Waddell, [1977] 3 All ER 129 (Ch).

CHAPTER 4: THE TRIAL
AND FEDERAL COURT OF APPEAL

Calder v Attorney-General for British Columbia, [1973] SCR 313.

Guerin v The Queen, [1982] 2 FC 385 (FCTD).

McHugh, P.G. *Aboriginal Title: The Modern Jurisprudence of Tribal Land Rights* (Oxford: Oxford University Press, 2011), ch 2.

The Queen v Guerin (1982), 143 DLR (3d) 416 (FCA).

CHAPTER 5: THE SUPREME COURT OF CANADA

Guerin v The Queen, [1984] 2 SCR 335 (SCC).

Musqueam Indian Band v Canada, [1990] 2 FC 351 (FCTD).

Musqueam Indian Band v Musqueam Indian Band (Board of Review), 2016 SCC 36 (SCC).

CHAPTER 6: THE IMPACT OF *GUERIN*

Alberta v Elder Advocates of Alberta Society, 2011 SCC 24.

Binnie, Ian. "Closing Address" (Address delivered at the Canadian Institute for the Administration of Justice Annual Conference, Justice to Order: Adjustment to Changing Demands and Co-ordination Issues in the Justice System in Canada, Saskatoon, 1998).

Blueberry River Indian Band v Canada (Department of Indian Affairs and Northern Development), [1995] 4 SCR 344.

Bookman, Miriam. "A 'Legal Backstop' for Historical Maori Grievances: Proprietors of Wakatu v. Attorney-General" (2017) 23 Auckland UL Rev 348.

Glover, Kirsty. "The Honour of the Crowns: State-Indigenous Fiduciary Relationships and Australian Exceptionalism" (2016) 38 Sydney L Rev 339.

Luk, Senwung. "Not So Many Hats: The Crown's Fiduciary Obligations to Aboriginal Communities since *Guerin*" (2013) 76 Sask L Rev 1.

R v Sparrow, [1990] 1 SCR 1075.

Tsilhqot'in Nation v British Columbia, 2014 SCC 44.

Wakatu v Attorney General, [2017] NZSC 17.

Wewaykum Indian Band v Canada, 2002 SCC 79.

Williams Lake Indian Band v Canada, 2018 SCC 4.

CONCLUSION

Beaton, Ryan. "The Crown Fiduciary Duty at the Supreme Court of Canada: Reaching across Nations, or Held within the Grip of the Crown?" (January 2018) Centre for International Governance Innovation (CIGI), Canada in International Law at 150 and Beyond, Paper No 6, online: CIGI <https://www.cigionline.org/sites/default/files/documents/Reflections%20Series%20Paper%20no.6%20Beaton_0.pdf>.

Behrendt, Larissa. "Lacking Good Faith: Australia, Fiduciary Duties and the Lonely Place of Indigenous Rights" in Law Commission of Canada, *In Whom We Trust: A Forum on Fiduciary Relationships*, ed by Association of Iroquois and Allied Indians (Toronto: Irwin Law, 2002).

Dickson, Jamie D. *The Honour and Dishonour of the Crown: Making Sense of Aboriginal Law in Canada* (Saskatoon: Purich, 2015).

Slattery, Brian. "Understanding Aboriginal Rights" (1987) 66 Can Bar Rev 727.

Index of Cases

Index

Note: Page numbers followed by (f) refer to illustrations. For more information on cases, see the Index of Cases.

Printed and bound in Canada by Friesens
Text design: Will Brown
Set in Garamond by Artegraphica Design Co. Ltd.
Copy editor: Frank Chow
Indexer: Judy Dunlop
Cartographer: Eric Leinberger